BLOOD TIES AND FICTIVE TIES

BLOOD TIES AND FICTIVE TIES

ADOPTION AND FAMILY LIFE IN
EARLY MODERN FRANCE

Kristin Elizabeth Gager

PRINCETON UNIVERSITY PRESS   PRINCETON, NEW JERSEY

Copyright © 1996 by Princeton University Press
Published by Princeton University Press, 41 William Street,
Princeton, New Jersey 08540
In the United Kingdom: Princeton University Press,
Chichester, West Sussex
All Rights Reserved

Library of Congress Cataloging-in-Publication Data
Gager, Kristin Elizabeth.
Blood ties and fictive ties : adoption and family life
in early modern France / Kristin Elizabeth Gager.
p.   cm.
Includes bibliographical references and index.
ISBN 0-691-02984-9 (cl. : alk. paper)
1. Adoption—France—History.   2. Children, Adopted—
France—History.   3. Family—France—History.   I. Title.
HV875.58.F8G34   1996
362.7'34'0944—dc20   95-30462

This book has been composed in Galliard

Princeton University Press books are printed
on acid-free paper and meet the guidelines
for permanence and durability of the Committee
on Production Guidelines for Book Longevity
of the Council on Library Resources

Printed in the United States of America
by Princeton Academic Press

1   3   5   7   9   10   8   6   4   2

Contents

Acknowledgments

THE AUTHOR wishes to thank Natalie Zemon Davis, William C. Jordan, Anthony Grafton, Sarah Hanley, Moshe Sluhovsky, and Martha Hodes for guiding me through the initial dissertation phase of this project and for making helpful suggestions for revisions. My greatest thanks go to my adviser, Natalie Z. Davis, whose historical vision and untiring enthusiasm and support continue to provide me with an appreciation of the "possibilities of the past." Since the completion of the dissertation, I have also received helpful comments from Barbara B. Diefendorf, Peter Brown, Hendrik Hartog, and Rachel G. Fuchs. Additionally, I have gained extremely useful suggestions from the anonymous readers at Princeton University Press and from the history editor, Lauren Osborne.

I was aided in the process of writing and revising when portions of the project were presented at the Society for French Historical Studies and the Princeton Graduate Colloquium. I am also grateful to Mireille Corbier of the Centre National de la Recherche Scientifique in Paris for inviting me to present the work on adoption and family life at the colloquium entitled "Adoption and 'Fosterage' from Antiquity to the Present." Grants from the French government, the Princeton University history department and the University of New Hampshire history department have permitted research trips to France. Additionally, a postdoctoral fellowship awarded by the Princeton University history department that supported one semester's leave of absence proved indispensable for completing the revisions of the manuscript. The University of New Hampshire kindly allowed me to take a semester away from teaching in order to revise the manuscript. I would also like to thank my entire family and the many friends who have offered help and encouragement along the way. Special thanks go to my father, John G. Gager, who read many versions of the manuscript. Finally, to Gilles—*merci*.

Cambridge, Massachusetts
January 1995

Abbreviations

AN   Archives Nationales, Paris
AP   Archives de l'Assistance Publique, Paris
BN   Bibliothèque Nationale, Paris
Et.   Etude
MC   Minutier Central des Notaires Parisiens

BLOOD TIES AND FICTIVE TIES

Introduction

THE SEVENTEENTH-CENTURY jurist Denis Le Brun concluded in his comprehensive *Traité des successions* that "while adoption has always been practiced in most nations, we no longer practice it in France."[1] Le Brun did not stand alone in his pronouncement of the demise of adoption in early modern France; sixteenth- and seventeenth-century legal, literary, and religious texts abound with similar declarations. Legal commentary on adoption went beyond merely announcing its demise, however. Jurists such as Le Brun proposed that while adoption had been common in antiquity and even in the early Middle Ages, the institution was no longer commensurate with the structure and goals of the early modern family and consequently had fallen into disuse beginning in the sixteenth century. Many statements concerning the disappearance of adoption were coupled with assertions that adoption was "unnatural" and even "un-Christian." The eighteenth-century jurist Boutaric commented in this regard that "we have always held adoptions to be equally contrary to the laws of Nature and Christianity, which regard the rights of fathers over their children as sacred and, as such, inalienable; the duties of fathers toward their children must be envisioned as personal obligations which cannot be given over to strangers."[2] Although never explicitly prohibited in canon law, the Catholic Church had long discouraged adoption, fearing that it placed undue emphasis on temporal issues of heirship while eclipsing concerns for the soul's "inheritance" of salvation in the afterlife. On the Protestant side, reformers such as Theodore Beza in Geneva simply assumed that adoption had ceased to be practiced in that sixteenth-century community.[3] The stricter stance against extramarital sex embraced by both Protestant and Catholic reformers in the sixteenth century also influenced the fate of adoption. Because adoption had been employed historically as an avenue for fathers to bring their illegitimate sons surreptitiously into the legitimate family fold, the practice posed a threat to the reformers' insistence

---

[1] "Quoique les adoptions aient été de tout temps en usage chez la plupart des nations, la notre ne les a point conservées," in Denis Le Brun, *Traité des successions divisé en quatre livres*, 2 vols. (Paris, 1776 ed.), 1:37.

[2] Boutaric, *Les institutes de Justinien conférées avec le droit françois* (Toulouse, 1754), bk. 1, tit. 22, cited in Prost de Royer, *Dictionnaire de jurisprudence et des arrêts* (Lyon, 1783), 3:105.

[3] Theodore Beza, *Tractatio de repudiis et divortiis* (Geneva, 1573), p. 204, cited in Natalie Z. Davis, "Ghosts, Kin and Progeny: Some Features of Family Life in Early Modern France," *Daedalus* 106, no. 2 (spring 1977): 113n.56.

that marriage stand as the sole arena for sexual activity and as the sole avenue to the creation of a family.

To a certain extent popular practice followed suit; families of all social levels held multiple reasons of their own for hesitating to adopt. Although childlessness was a relatively common fate in early modern France as a result of high rates of infant mortality, many families nonetheless rejected adoption as a solution because the act invited public investigation of their barren state. Moreover, by choosing to adopt rather than quietly "accepting the will of God," adopting families risked being perceived as challenging the natural order of things.[4] The adoption of a child as an heir also served to disrupt the traditional pathways of succession in otherwise childless families; by the terms of Parisian customary law, the collateral heirs were poised to inherit the family property in the absence of biological children. Further, the introduction of an adopted child into a family raised the practical concern of placing additional burdens on the division of the patrimony if biological children were born in the future.

Many families also feared that adopting a non-natal child would compromise the purity and integrity of the family bloodline. A seventeenth-century legal dictionary argued in this regard that "we can act charitably toward strangers, but we cannot make them kin; only blood is capable of contracting kinship and alliance."[5] The work of Ellery Schalk, Arlette Jouanna, and André Devyer has proposed that biologically based notions of familial "stock" developed a particular significance for the upper classes in early modern France as pedigree came increasingly to define noble status.[6] Schalk suggests that noble status in the Middle Ages, while determined in part by biological lineage, was also achieved through a demonstrated prowess in military affairs, as well as in a broad range of other virtuous activities. Toward the end of the sixteenth century, however, medieval notions of noble status began to wane as pedigree displaced virtue as the central attribute of the nobility.[7] These new theories, emphasizing the cen-

---

[4] Sterility was often associated with witchcraft in the early modern period. On the stigma of infertility in this period, see Jacques Gélis, *History of Childbirth: Fertility, Pregnancy and Birth in Early Modern Europe*, trans. Rosemary Morris (Boston, 1991); Angus McClaren, *Reproductive Rituals: The Perception of Fertility in England from the Sixteenth Century to the Nineteenth Century* (London, 1984); Pierre Darmon, *Le mythe de la procréation à l'âge baroque* (Paris, 1976).

[5] *Nouveau dictionnaire civil et canonique* (Paris, 1697), p. 11.

[6] See Ellery Schalk, *From Valor to Pedigree: Ideas of Nobility in France in the Sixteenth and Seventeenth Centuries* (Princeton, N.J., 1986); Arlette Jouanna, *L'idée de race en France au XVIe et au début du XVIIe siècle* (Montpellier, 1981); André Devyer, *Le sang épuré: Les préjugés de race chez les gentilhommes français de l'ancien régime (1560–1720)* (Brussels, 1973).

[7] Both Schalk and Devyer explain this renewed focus on blood among the *noblesse de race* as a reaction to the rising *noblesse de la robe* and the vast numbers of offices and noble titles

trality of traits transmitted through the blood, became the basis for a revised hierarchical vision of society according to which access to the upper echelons of the nobility of the sword was possible (at least in theory), through birth alone. In such a cultural climate, childless noble families shunned the option of adopting a non-natal child as a substitute heir to the family line.[8]

Literary evidence suggests that the prejudice against adoption was further kindled by fears that the severing of ties between parents and their biological children through abandonment and adoption might lead to accidental incestuous unions between unsuspecting blood kin. Alluding to the cycle of abandonment and adoption found in the Oedipus myths, the seventeenth-century jurist Issali reiterated ancient warnings about the confusion over identity resulting from the rupturing of biological ties: "Sooner or later the memory of the alienated family fades away, and once the first mistake has occurred the crime of incest will never cease."[9] Late medieval and early modern literary tales frequently connect the cycle of child abandonment and subsequent adoption with future incestuous unions. Marie de France's lay of *Le Fresne* tells of a noblewoman who abandoned a daughter to be raised by others only to have her reappear years later to become engaged to the same woman's son. The girl was identified as her husband's sister just before the two were set to consummate the marriage. Marguerite de Navarre's *Heptameron* also includes a tale (story 30) in which the abandonment of a daughter to the care of others ultimately resulted in an incident of unwitting brother-sister incest.[10]

Although the practice of adoption was scorned and even feared, metaphors of adoption continued to be employed extensively in this period. Montaigne, for instance, chose to employ an adoption motif when he named his literary executor Mlle de Gournay his *fille d'alliance*.[11] In a similar vein, the seventeenth-century midwife, Louise Bourgeois, drew on

sold by the French Crown as a revenue-raising tactic in the sixteenth century. It should be noted that critics have faulted Schalk for overestimating the demise of the professional definition of the nobility of the sword, which, it seems, persisted through the reign of Louis XIV. On this point, see Mark Motley, *Becoming a French Aristocrat: The Education of the Court Nobility, 1580–1715* (Princeton, N.J., 1990). For a comparative look at notions of family "stock" among the English nobility, see Lawrence Stone and Jeanne Fawtier Stone, *An Open Elite? England, 1540–1880* (Oxford, 1986).

[8] For a discussion of the role of family "stock" for noble families in early modern France, see Davis, "Ghosts, Kin and Progeny."

[9] Issali, *Les plaidoyers et harangues de M. le Maistre* (Paris, 1657), pp. 150–51.

[10] For a comprehensive discussion of abandonment tales in late medieval Europe, see John Boswell, *The Kindness of Strangers: The Abandonment of Children in Western Europe from Late Antiquity to the Renaissance* (New York, 1988).

[11] See J. Morland, "Marie le Jars de Gournay, la 'fille d'alliance' de Montaigne," *Bibliothèque de la Société des Amis de Montaigne* 27 (1971): 45–54.

the language of adoption to underscore her position in a long line of historical midwives by designating herself the "adopted daughter" of the mother of Socrates, who was also a midwife.[12] Furthermore, while the Catholic Church had long discouraged adoption as a strategy of heirship, religious texts consistently invoke the metaphor of humans as "adopted children" of God to elucidate the notion of the "universal kinship" of humankind.[13] In a more secular vein, foreigners naturalized as French citizens were awarded letters of "naturalization and adoption."[14] Immigrants to early modern cities also considered themselves "adopted" residents; in a private letter to the sixteenth-century jurist Etienne Pasquier, Emeric Bigot, whose family was originally from Rouen, calls himself "a Parisian by adoption."[15] In addition, while noble families rejected infant adoption as incommensurate with the biological basis of noble lineage, in the absence of a male heir many appointed an adult kinsman such as a nephew to "adopt" the family name and coat of arms, though in these instances the kinsman was not awarded the status of legitimate heir, nor was the adoptive father awarded parental rights.

Despite the routine employment of metaphors of adoption to describe secondary alliances in a wide range of sources, early modern French civil law stopped short of embracing adoption as a legitimate avenue for creating primary ties of filiation. The most concrete manifestation of the legal prejudice against adoption appears in the multitude of regional customary law codes—newly compiled and edited in the sixteenth century—which explicitly denied adopted children the same inheritance rights accorded to legitimate, biological children. The jurist Jean Imbert put it quite succinctly when he commented that "in France, an adopted child cannot inherit."[16] More specifically, the revised Custom of Paris of 1580 prohibited adopted children from inheriting through intestate succession, or in the

---

[12] See Louise Bourgeois, *Observations diverses sur la stérilité, perte de fruict, foecondité, accouchements et maladies des femmes, & enfants nouveaux naiz*, ed. Françoise Olivier (1609; Paris, 1992), p. 174.

[13] Thus Paul's use of the metaphor of adoption in Romans 8:12–17b. On the language of adoption in the New Testament, see Francis Lyall, "Legal Metaphors in the Epistles," *Tyndale Bulletin* 32 (1981): 79–85. The *Dictionnaire de l'Académie française* (Paris, 1694) counts among the definitions of "adoption": "Jesus-Christ nous a fait enfans adoptifs de son Père," 1:152. On metaphors of abandonment and adoption in the early church, see Boswell, *The Kindness of Strangers*, esp. chap. 3, "Fathers of the Church and Parents of Children."

[14] The Code of Henry III contains a decision of Charles VI from 1406 on the process of naturalization that employs this language of adoption. The letters are termed "lettres de naturalité ou adoption, par laquelle ils sont adoptez et rendus Citoyens, comme s'ils estoient naiz, & habitans originaires du pays." See *Code du Roy Henri III, observations et annotations par L. Carondas le Caron* (Paris, 1615), p. 189a.

[15] *Estienne Pasquier, lettres familières* (Paris, 1974), p. 53.

[16] Jean Imbert, *Enchiridion ou recueil de droit écrit* (Paris, 1611), p. 103.

absence of a last will and testament. Considering that the standard channel for inheritance was precisely through intestate succession, subsequent jurists such as Denis Le Brun in the late seventeenth century contended that adoption was no longer a feasible act and had consequently ceased to be practiced.

The rejection of adoption by early modern civil law codes in France and in most other western European countries persisted until the twentieth century. To be sure, the French Revolution at first enthusiastically embraced adoption; revolutionary legislators envisioned a new class-free society partially ushered in by noble families adopting the children of peasants and peasant families adopting noble children. But the adoption laws ultimately promulgated in the Civil Code of 1804 (book. 1, tit. 8) retreated to more restrictive guidelines: only married couples over fifty years old with no biological children were permitted to adopt. Moreover, the adoption of minors under twenty-five years old was forbidden, an obstruction that did little to promote adoption as a charitable measure to aid orphaned and abandoned children.[17] It was not until after World War I and the law of 19 June 1923, that more flexible adoption laws were instituted, largely as an effort to find permanent homes for vast numbers of war orphans. [18] Even then, it was not until subsequent laws were promulgated in 1966 and 1976 that single parents and families with biological children were permitted to adopt.[19]

Given the existence of such formidable legal impediments to adoption

[17] The Civil Code instituted four different models of adoption. The first model was ordinary adoption permitted to those over fifty years old who were at least fifteen years older than the adoptee. In this model the adoptee had to have received care by the adoptive parents for at least six months during his or her minority. In addition, the adoptee's name was added to that of the adoptive parent and the adoptee did not formally become a member of the adoptive family except for the establishment of impediments to marriage. These adoptions were irrevocable contracts that were overseen by a justice of the peace. The three other models of adoption established by the code, it should be noted, were extremely rare: compensatory adoption, which awarded an individual who had saved the life of the adoptive parent (as in the first model, the adoptive parent had to be older than the adoptee); testamentary adoption; and a form of guardianship known as *tutelle officieuse*. On this point, see Pierre Mahillon, "Evolution historique de l'adoption depuis le droit romain," in *En Homage à Victor Gothot* (Liège, 1962), pp. 435–57.

[18] Like France, England did not institute comprehensive adoption laws until the Adoption Act of 1926. In the United States, although Massachusetts provided the first statute of adoption—the "Act to Provide for the Adoption of Children" in 1851—most states did not institute adoption laws until the early twentieth century. For a comparative look at contemporary adoption laws in western Europe and the United States, see R.A.C. Hoksbergen, ed., *Adoption in Worldwide Perspective: A Review of Programs, Policies and Legislation in Fourteen Countries* (Berwyn, Ill., 1986).

[19] For a discussion of the laws of 11 July 1966 and 22 December 1976 and for a lucid review of contemporary adoption laws in France more generally, see Pascale Salvage-Gerest, *L'adoption: Connaissance du droit* (Paris, 1992).

and the widespread cultural prejudice against adoption and nonbiological parenting, historians of the family have surmised that adoption was not practiced in early modern France. Histories of civil law propose that adoption began a steady decline throughout western Europe from the close of the Roman era, and, after gasping its last breath in the late Middle Ages, disappeared entirely from France and other western European countries in the sixteenth century. According to this scenario, adoption was not to be seen again until it was ushered back into popular practice by the revised law codes of the nineteenth and twentieth centuries.[20] This book departs, however, from the traditional trajectory that heralds the sixteenth century as the culmination of the steady demise of adoption since the Roman era. Contracts of adoption from the registers of assorted Parisian notaries bring to light customs of adoption by which childless couples and individuals from the artisan and merchant sectors of Parisian society adopted abandoned, orphaned, and other destitute children as their heirs throughout the sixteenth and seventeenth centuries. Although it would certainly surprise jurists such as Denis Le Brun who announced the end of adoption in seventeenth-century France, this book examines the role of adoption in shaping the nature of family life for certain sectors of Parisian society in the sixteenth and seventeenth centuries.

Despite all indications that research would yield little evidence of adoption practices, I suspected that adoption would retain an appeal for two sectors of Parisian society: first, for childless families who wanted to ensure that their family traditions, family name, and material goods would be reproduced into the next generation; and second, for the city's charity hospices, eager to integrate the children under their care into Parisian society. My inklings that adoption had not faded completely from social practice in early modern Paris were strengthened by the earlier work of Paul Gonnet and Jacqueline Roubert, who had analyzed the practice of adopting orphans and foundlings in early modern Lyon. The evidence from Lyon reveals that the desire for children among childless families, in combination with the growing numbers of destitute children cared for by the city's poor-relief system, served to sustain adoption practices well into the eighteenth century.[21] In fact, two forms of adoption were practiced in Lyon. The first model entailed the legal adoption of the orphans and

---

[20] In this regard, Jack Goody claims that adoption disappeared from western Europe from the eighth century to the nineteenth century. See Jack Goody, *The Development of the Family and Marriage in Europe* (Cambridge, 1983), pp. 39–45, 71–75. The place of adoption in the historiography of the family in early modern France is discussed more thoroughly in chapter 1 of this book.

[21] See Paul Gonnet, *L'adoption lyonnaise des orphelins légitimes (1536–1793)*, 2 vols. (Paris, 1935), and Jacqueline Roubert, "L'adoption des enfants par des particuliers à Lyon sous l'ancien régime," *Société française d'histoire des hôpitaux* 36–37 (1978): 3–30.

foundlings by the administrators of the city's Aumône générale, founded in 1534, and by the Lyonnais Hôtel-Dieu. In this form of institutional adoption, which lasted until 1793, the governors of the hospices were named, by royal decree, as the "adoptive parents" of the destitute children under their care. As Gonnet has shown, the administrators' obligations stemming from their role as the children's adoptive parents included raising and educating the children in addition to providing apprenticeships and marriage settlements for the girls and boys under their care.[22] In the second pattern of adoption, as both Gonnet and Roubert have demonstrated, many of the orphans and foundlings were formally adopted as heirs by artisan families who had no biological children of their own.[23]

Most legal and social histories of early modern France accredit the survival of adoption in Lyon to the legacy of Roman adoption laws in southern France. Although the heritage of Roman law played a significant role in facilitating adoption practices in Lyon, the legal climate would hold no significance if it were not for the desire of families to adopt non-natal children as their heirs. Thus, the findings of adoption in Lyon hold important implications for the history of adoption and family life in France by bringing to light a model of domestic life that was inclusive of adoptive ties of alliance. Additionally, from the standpoint of the history of poor relief, the Lyon evidence demonstrates the value of adoption to the charity hospices in allowing them to place many of the destitute children under their care in private homes throughout the city.

Although histories of the family present adoption in Lyon as an anomaly, my own case studies of adoption from the registers of numerous notaries in sixteenth- and seventeenth-century Paris suggest that Lyon was not an exception.[24] The notarized contracts of adoption from Paris reveal two

[22] See Gonnet, *L'adoption lyonnaise*, vol. 1, pt. 2, chap. 2.

[23] Paul Gonnet's examination of adoption by private families in sixteenth-century Lyon is based on forty-two cases of adoption between 1527 and 1584; Gonnet discovered only one act of formal adoption in the seventeenth century, in 1629, concluding that adoption by private families had faded away after the sixteenth century. See Gonnet, *L'adoption lyonnaise*. Jacqueline Roubert, however, unearthed forty-nine additional cases of adoption from the Hôtel-Dieu and the Charité (previously the Aumône générale) in Lyon by private families during the period 1629–1713 in the registers of the two hospices. See Roubert, "L'adoption des enfants."

[24] Paul Gonnet concludes his study by urging his readers "gardons fidèlement le souvenir de cette coutume d'adoption d'enfants, unique en son genre, et dont Lyon, la ville par excellence de la charité"; see *L'adoption lyonnaise*, 1:685. Jean-Pierre Gutton has recently published a useful historical survey of adoption in France from antiquity to the present day. While Gutton's book does not incorporate new archival findings, his general framework of analysis coincides with the perspective of the present study. For instance, Gutton notes that even while civil law rejected adoption after the classical age, adoption appears to have survived in practice during this period (roughly 800–1800). See Jean-Pierre Gutton, *Histoire de l'adoption en France* (Paris, 1993).

central ways in which children without families of their own were brought into new, adoptive homes in Paris beginning in the mid-sixteenth century. The first model involves the adoption of two categories of destitute children: abandoned children under the care of the foundling hospice in Paris, known as the Couche—or Cradle—of the Poor Foundlings (Couche des pauvres enfans trouvez), and orphans residing at the Parisian Hôtel-Dieu. The evidence of adoptions from the Couche surfaces in the registers of various notaries who worked closely with the foundling hospice in three separate phases of its institutional history: first, in the period from 1570 to 1638, when the Couche was run by the Chapter of Notre Dame and located at the Port St. Landry on the île-de-la-Cité; second, in the period after 1645, when the hospice was reorganized under the auspices of Vincent de Paul and moved to the faubourg St. Denis, where the daily work of caring for the foundlings was undertaken by the orders of the "Ladies and Sisters of Charity"; and, finally, in the period after 1670 when the hospice's administration was subsumed under the umbrella organization of the Hôpital général. The evidence of adoption from the city's charity hospices is supplemented by adoptions of orphans from the Hôtel-Dieu beginning in 1656, which were overseen by the "Ladies of Charity of the Hôtel-Dieu." Overall, I was able to unearth forty-five cases of formal adoption overseen by the foundling hospice and the Hôtel-Dieu between 1540 and 1677.

The second model consists of adoptions arranged privately between two sets of parents. In most of these instances some economic misfortune appears to have compelled the biological parents to give their children in adoption to willing neighbors, friends, and relatives, who often had no children of their own. The survey of these private adoptions proved more difficult inasmuch as the investigation into the notarial registers could not proceed from an institutional base such as the foundling hospice (although one notary, Mathieu Bontemps from the rue St. André-des-Arts, drew up both private adoptions and adoptions of foundlings from the Couche).[25] To locate the private adoptions, I undertook a sampling of twenty notaries who worked in various artisan and laboring neighborhoods of Paris for the period spanning 1550 to 1670. Ultimately, the search was narrowed to those notaries who had penned several adoption contracts, under the assumption, which proved generally correct, that these same notaries would be likely to draw up more adoption contracts in the future. The review of these private adoptions is based on adoption contracts from the period 1545–1690. (The earliest known case of a notarized "private" adoption in Paris is from 4 August 1484; this case seems to be an exception, however,

---

[25] For the contracts penned by Mathieu Bontemps, see AN, MC, Et. XXIII, 122 (6 July 1606); Et. LXXIII, 272 (1609); Et. LXXIII, 273 (1610).

as no other formal adoption cases have yet been found for the late fifteenth and early sixteenth centuries.)[26]

The information outlined in the notarized contracts allows us to reconstruct a preliminary portrait of adoption practices in sixteenth- and seventeenth-century Paris. Each contract records the names, residences, and professions of the adoptive parents. For the adopted children, the contracts reveal their sex, name, and age, and often explain how the child came to be placed in adoption. The contracts also describe the nature of the care to be given to the children in their new homes. The adoptive parents routinely promise to provide the children with a home, parental care and affection, an education, an apprenticeship, a dowry, and an inheritance. In return, the children promise to obey and "honor" their new parents. While the contracts offer a unique and unprecedented look into adoption practices in sixteenth- and seventeenth-century Paris, not surprisingly they also leave many questions unanswered.[27] The notarized contracts are rarely longer than two pages and, while many contracts detail the individual stories behind each case of adoption, by and large the contracts suffer from the formulaic language common to all notarial sources. Perhaps most problematic, these documents offer us only a static glance into an isolated moment of the lives of these adoptive families. In this regard, an analysis of the contracts threatens to offer an idealized portrait of the nature of adoption. Because of the difficulty in tracing such artisan families in the archives, we cannot in most cases know for certain if the terms of the adoption were ultimately carried out as initially outlined. Even given their drawbacks, however, these contracts prove invaluable in bringing to light the previously undocumented history of adoption practices in early modern Paris.

I wish to establish from the outset that this book does not propose to make claims about the frequency of adoption, nor does it presume to offer a statistical analysis of adoption practices. The central goal of *Blood Ties and Fictive Ties* is to offer a social and cultural portrait of adoption and family life in sixteenth- and seventeenth-century Paris. In recovering the history of adoption, the book seeks to broaden our portrait of the range of domestic configurations forged by the people of early modern Paris, often in defiance of reigning social, cultural, and legal norms. In this respect the notarial archives are not employed, as is often the case, as a repository for

---

[26] The case is cited in François Olivier-Martin, *Histoire de la coutume de la prévôté et vicomté de Paris*, (Paris, 1922), 1:151; the text of the document is also reproduced in Gonnet, *L'adoption lyonnaise*, 1:49n.13. This case is outlined in full in n. 3 to chapter 3 of this book.

[27] On the merits and drawbacks of notarial sources for social history, see *Problèmes et méthodes d'analyse historique de l'activité notariale (xve–xixe siècles): Actes du colloque de Toulouse (15–16 séptembre 1990)* (Toulouse, 1991).

quantitative history,[28] but serve instead as a cache of often surprising information regarding family life that has been overlooked by previous social histories of the family. As Arlette Farge has remarked of the judicial archives that form the basis of her portrait of the social life of eighteenth-century Paris, "the archives are always explosive, and their meaning is never grasped once and for all. . . . They are neither fanciful nor totally representative of [reality]; but they play their part in this reality, offering differences and alternatives to other possible statements."[29] Viewed in this light, the evidence of adoption supplied by the notarized contracts offers an alternative history of adoption to that outlined by the official law codes. The notarial registers reveal that the formal adoption of a child was a viable act in early modern Paris. The contracts also suggest that the range of options available to families as they forged kinship ties and attempted to pass on their patrimony to the next generation was greater than historians of the family have assumed.

Alongside the goal of reconstructing a portrait of adoption practices, the book is equally interested in exploring the cultural significance of the widespread prejudice against adoption apparent in these centuries. In this regard, the study considers the diverse social, cultural, and religious factors that influenced the rejection of formal adoption by customary law. From the standpoint of cultural history, the strong prejudice against adoption provides a unique perspective on how familial and extrafamilial alliances were constructed on a normative level. Taking a cue from anthropological studies, which routinely examine adoption practices to illuminate how a given society constructs its categories of kinship, *Blood Ties and Fictive Ties* offers a novel look at the nature of family life.[30] Because adoption involves the conscious choice of a particular child to become a family member, its practice reveals much about the composition of the domestic sphere. Who is considered an acceptable child and heir to the family property? Can girls fulfill this role as well as boys? Is the adopted child a member of the same kin group or is she or he a "stranger" to the lineage? The answers to such questions indicate the variety of ways in which families constructed kinship. Paralleling current debates in Europe and the United States over interracial and international adoptions, adoptions by single parents or gay couples, and open adoption,[31] commentary on the drawbacks and merits

[28] In the tradition, for example, of A. Daumard and F. Furet, "Méthodes de l'histoire sociale: Les Archives notariales et la Mécanographie," *Annales: E.S.C.* 14(1959): 676–93.

[29] Arlette Farge, *Fragile Lives: Violence, Power and Solidarity in Eighteenth-Century Paris*, trans. Carol Shelton (Cambridge, Mass., 1993), p. 5.

[30] For anthropological studies of adoption and kinship, see Ivan Brady, ed., *Transactions in Kinship: Adoption and Fosterage in Oceania* (Honolulu, 1976), and Vern Carroll, ed., *Adoption in Eastern Oceania* (Honolulu, 1970).

[31] On interracial adoption in the United States, see Rita J. Simon and Howard Altstein, eds., *Transracial Adoptees and Their Families: A Study of Identity and Commitment* (New

of adoption in early modern France bring to light a comparable "politics of the family." Moreover, just as recent medical techniques of reproduction ranging from in vitro fertilization to surrogate pregnancies serve increasingly to subvert attempts to draw connections between biology and juridical categories of parenthood, in a less dramatic vein these earlier debates over adoption explored the correlation between blood and kinship. The topic of adoption compelled an analysis of the relative roles of nurture and nature in the construction of familial bonds and even a reconsideration of the traditional definitions of categories such as "parent," "child," and "family."[32]

The historical relationship between governing cultural norms and popular practice forms a central theme woven into the following chapters. Guided by the assumption that popular practice almost invariably muddies the normative waters when it comes to the history of the law, the present examination of adoption combines an analysis of the written law codes with an exploration of how the law was interpreted and, more often than not, reinterpreted on the level of popular practice. The knowledge that adoption continued to be practiced in defiance of the obstacles placed in its way by the newly codified customary law suggests that the field of legal history must emphasize to a greater extent the manipulation of the law on the local level. The fact that the history of adoption has so far been studied nearly exclusively from the perspective of the written law codes and, consequently, has neglected to take into account the effects of the popular reception of the law, appears to stem in large part from the lack of dialogue between legal historians on the one hand and cultural and social historians on the other. Jacques Le Goff, for one, has attributed this impasse to long-standing "ingrained prejudices" and "mutual ignorance" that have separated the fields of legal and sociocultural history.[33] This is not to suggest that the field of legal history is devoid of models that offer more than an

---

York, 1987); J. Douglas Bates, *Gift Children: A Story of Race, Family, and Adoption in a Divided America* (New York, 1993). On the question of "open" adoption, see Elizabeth Bartholet, *Family Bonds: Adoption and the Politics of Parenting* (New York, 1993); Kathleen Silber, *Children of Open Adoption and Their Families* (San Antonio, Tex., 1990); Paul Sachdev, *Unlocking the Adoption Files* (Lexington, Mass., 1989); Ruth McRoy, *Openness in Adoption: New Practices, New Issues* (New York, 1988); Erica Haimes and Noel Timms, *Adoption, Identity and Social Policy: The Search for Distant Relatives* (Brookfield, Vt., 1985).

[32] For an intriguing historical account of the evolution of the term "family" in western Europe, see David Herlihy, "Family," *American Historical Review* 96, no. 1 (1991): 1–16. See also the sociological analysis of the term "family" in Martine Segalen, *Historical Anthropology of the Family*, trans. J. C. Whitehouse and Sarah Matthews (Cambridge, 1986).

[33] Jacques Le Goff, "Histoire médiévale et histoire du droit: Un dialogue difficile," in *Storia sociale e dimensione giuridica* (Atti dell'incontro di studio, Florence, 26–27 April 1985) (Milan, 1986), pp. 23–63. On the relationship between legal and social history, see also Paul Ourliac, "Histoire nouvelle et histoire du droit," *Revue historique de droit français et étranger* 3 (1992): 363–71.

analysis of changing written law codes. Cynthia B. Herrup's study of the operation of the criminal legal system in early modern England, to cite one prominent example, provides an approach to the history of the law that successfully unites social, cultural and legal history.[34] Herrup's work is particularly instructive in underscoring the centrality of the local, communal context as it shaped the reception of the criminal law in early modern England. If we extend Herrup's framework to the study of civil law in early modern France, we can view the law not as a static entity imposed from above, but rather as a process of continual negotiation between the lawmakers on the one hand and the families and notaries who interacted with the law on the other hand.[35] Along these lines, the approach to the history of adoption outlined in the succeeding chapters has been influenced by Roger Chartier's vision of cultural history. Although Chartier's own work has not focused on legal texts, his emphasis on the notion of appropriation has proved instrumental in a study of the reception of law codes on the local level. Chartier suggests that "We can reformulate the notion of appropriation and place it at the center of a cultural historical approach that focuses on differentiated practices and contrasted uses."[36] Indeed, the history of adoption practices in early modern France presents a striking case of local notaries and individual families strategically interpreting certain aspects of the newly codified customary law codes to suit their own needs.

With this perspective on the history of the law in mind, we may now return to the assertion cited at the outset by the jurist Denis Le Brun, who claimed that adoption was no longer practiced in the seventeenth century. From the perspective of written law, there is no doubt about the veracity of Le Brun's statement. The termination of complete inheritance rights for adopted children in the sixteenth-century customary law codes signaled a rejection of earlier models of adoption—in particular the Roman model—

[34] Cynthia B. Herrup, *The Common Peace: Participation and the Criminal Law in Seventeenth-Century England* (Cambridge, 1987).

[35] Gregory Hanlon and Elsbeth Carruthers demonstrate a similar disjuncture between local customary laws on marriage and actual family practices as seen in testaments in "Wills, Inheritance and the Moral Order in the 17th-Century Agenais," *Journal of Family History* 15, no. 2 (1990): 149–61. The collection of articles in Robert Wheaton and Tamara K. Hareven, eds., *Family and Sexuality in French History* (Philadelphia, 1980), offers a similar approach to the history of the family in early modern France, which explores the interaction of structure and culture.

[36] Roger Chartier, *Cultural History between Practices and Representations,* trans. Lydia G. Cochrane (Cambridge, 1988), p. 13. My approach also heeds the methodological advice offered by Pierre Bourdieu, whose critique of the structuralist approach to the study of civil law calls for greater attention to individual families manipulating the official laws to suit their own needs. Bourdieu notes that "The interesting thing is not the 'structures,' which do not really help us understand the complexity of a local society, but the way in which the norms of conduct evolve and can be adapted to individual needs." Pierre Bourdieu, *Outline of a Theory of Practice*, trans. Richard Nice (New York, 1977), p. 10.

which created legal ties of filiation and which granted adopted children inheritance privileges equal to those enjoyed by biological children. But when we turn from the world of the written law to the world of popular practice, Le Brun's statement misleads. While the rejection of adoption in the revised customary law codes of the sixteenth century led most jurists to pronounce its demise, we will see in the following chapters that this same process of legal codification inspired individual Parisian families and local notaries to improvise and to develop legal strategies aimed to circumvent the law and ensure the continued viability of adoption as a means of reproducing the family into the next generation. The actions of these adoptive families ultimately served to question the law's insistence that ties of flesh and blood alone created ties of filiation; through notarized adoption agreements these households established "fictive" (i.e., invented) ties of affiliation that carried the same duties, obligations, and emotional bonds accompanying biological kinship ties.

CHAPTER ONE

The Many Families of Early Modern Paris

BEFORE PROCEEDING to explore the role of adoption practices in shaping the nature of family life, we must first address the various meanings assigned to the term "the family" in sixteenth- and seventeenth-century France. A standard definition of the family from the modern period, offered by the *Grand Larousse* of 1878, characterizes it as "the assemblage of persons living under the same roof who are united by blood—especially the father, the mother and the children."[1] In the earlier centuries, however, research has shown that the family was understood in a twofold sense, referring both to the household community (composed of kin and non-kin), as well as to extended kin networks. Jean-Louis Flandrin explains that "in former times, the word 'family' . . . referred to a set of kinsfolk who did not live together, while it also designated an assemblage of co-residents who were not necessarily linked by ties of blood and marriage."[2] On the one hand, then, the construction of the family derived from co-residence encompassing all of the individuals, both kin and non-kin such as servants and apprentices, living in a single household. The primary definition of the family found in dictionaries of the ancien régime, in fact, characterized it as a locus of co-residence.[3] Thus the *Dictionnaire de l'Académie française* of 1694 defines the family as "all of the persons who live in the same house, under the same head."[4] By these terms, the family group included not only parents and their birth children, but additionally servants and others living in the same household. In early modern

---

[1] *Grand Larousse de la langue française* (Paris, 1878), vol. 3.

[2] Jean-Louis Flandrin, *Families in Former Times: Kinship, Household and Sexuality*, trans. Richard Southern (Cambridge, 1979), p. 4. The word *famiglia* held the same twofold meaning in Renaissance Italy. See Francis William Kent, *Household and Lineage in Renaissance Florence* (Princeton, N.J., 1977).

[3] The French word *ménage* was used to designate the household as a familial domain of co-residence, while the word *maison* referred not to the domestic group but, for the nobility, to the lineage.

[4] "Toutes les personnes qui vivent dans une même maison, sous un même chef," in *Dictionnaire de l'Académie françoise* (Paris, 1694), 1:436. André Burguière concurs that the early modern family corresponds "Tout juste à une résidence et jusqu'à un certain point à une activité économique commune; mais elle ne constitue ni une communauté biologique ni une communauté affective." Cited in *Familles et sociétés domestiques*, Recherches économiques et sociales, n.s., 2 (Paris, 1982), p. 15.

France the family was also understood to represent the extended lineage, including those individuals bound by marriage as well as those descended from a common biological ancestor. Hence the secondary definition of the family found in the *Dictionnaire de l'Académie* speaks of "all those who descend from one and the same stock and who are, consequently, of the same blood."[5] The image of the genealogical family tree (arbor consanguinitatis) was the most popular way of representing the extended lineage in the early modern period.

Histories of the family have proposed that beginning in the late sixteenth and early seventeenth centuries the idea as well as the structure of the family slowly evolved into a more privatized and streamlined domestic unit, which excluded individuals such as servants from the ranks of family members, while at the same time pruning the branches of the family tree, thereby weakening ties with the extended kin. By the late eighteenth and nineteenth centuries this process of domestic streamlining culminated in an understanding of the family offered at the outset by the *Grand Larousse*, whereby blood ties and co-residence have collapsed in upon each other to produce a domestic group based exclusively on bonds of blood and marriage. In order to contextualize these changes in the domestic sphere, historians have looked in part to the effects of the process of state building in early modern France. Whereas in the Middle Ages, powerful noble families came close to ruling the provinces of France as minikingdoms, by the end of the sixteenth century the French Crown had succeeded in imposing a degree of central royal control. The state benefited from the waning of large, lineage-based family factions and, accordingly, encouraged the streamlined, tightly controlled domestic group. In political treatises of the day, the authority of the French monarch was coupled with calls for fathers to fashion themselves as domestic monarchs, ruling wives and children with an iron hand. The sixteenth-century jurist and political theorist Jean Bodin, for one, referred to families as "seminaries" of the state, envisioning a "natural" link between the familial and political realms.[6] As one of the first theorists of absolute monarchy, Bodin argued that, to construct a sound and strong republic, it was necessary to "return to the fathers the power of life and death, a law that God and Nature gave to them."[7]

Lawrence Stone and others have emphasized changes in the religious sphere as key to understanding modifications of the family group in England in this period. Stone suggests that Puritanism succeeded in displacing competing forms of socialization (such as confraternities, parish solidarities, and festivals), in the process creating a new, sentimental, and

---

[5] *Dictionnaire de l'Académie*, 1:436.
[6] Jean Bodin, *Les six livres de la république* (Paris, 1583), p. 10.
[7] Ibid., p. 32.

inward-looking domestic group. The Puritans' stress on individual access to biblical texts, moreover, positioned the household as the center of the individual's spiritual life and the father as its "domestic priest."[8] Jean-Louis Flandrin, among others, points not so much to the Protestants as to the Catholic Counter-Reformation as the primary initiator of changes within the familial sphere in France. Flandrin's examination of sixteenth- and seventeenth-century confession manuals, reveals an ever increasing interest on the part of the church in domestic affairs.[9] Much like the Protestants, the Counter-Reformation church privileged the family as a locus of religious indoctrination. The Milanese archbishop Charles Borromeo, for example, proposed that fathers of families convene monthly with parish curés to collaborate on the proper running of the domestic sphere.[10]

Alongside the political and religious changes affecting the domestic realm, Natalie Zemon Davis has stressed the role that families themselves played in shaping historical developments. While external institutions, such as church and state, had an undeniable stake in fostering the development of particular domestic configurations, families had their own reasons for acting in certain ways. Davis sees as characteristic of most families above the level of the indigent a heightened sense of "family planning" for future generations:

> What we see here, however, is historical change flowing from the decisions of myriad small groups, some rich and powerful, but many of only middling affluence in provincial towns and smaller rural centers. Their push toward planning, toward manipulation of property and persons for private goals, and their blending of beliefs in virtue with beliefs in stock were assisted by the growth of the state and of commercial capitalism and the professions, but were also in defiance of some of the forces of their time, both demographic and social.[11]

Davis cites two overriding factors guiding the trend toward a more concentrated and focused family planning in this period. The waning influence of collateral kin in certain matters of inheritance allowed the family more

---

[8] For this approach, see Lawrence Stone, *The Family, Sex and Marriage in England, 1500–1800* (London, 1977; New York, 1979), and John Demos, *A Little Commonwealth: Family Life in Plymouth Colony* (New York, 1970).

[9] On this point see also Jules Basdevant, *Des rapports de l'église et de l'état dans la législation de mariage du Concile de Trente au Code civil* (Paris, 1900).

[10] John Bossy makes the important point, however, that extrafamilial associations did not lose all of their vitality in the early modern period. See Bossy, *Christianity in the West, 1400–1700* (Oxford, 1985).

[11] Natalie Z. Davis, "Ghosts, Kin and Progeny: Some Features of Family Life in Early Modern France," *Daedalus* 106, no. 2 (1977): 108.

freedom in deciding the fate of the patrimony. Second, changes in the urban economy resulted in a greater overall mobility among the population and in expanded possibilities regarding such critical family matters as career paths and marriage for the children.[12] Davis proposes that one result of this new emphasis on family planning was a redrawing of boundaries around the immediate domestic group of parents and children. This privatization of the domestic group[13] grew hand in hand with a renewed emphasis on notions of familial "stock," or, we might say, on the lineage now restricted to the nuclear core. Manifested in the growing popularity of family journals (*livres de raison*), which harbored each family's story and fostered its sense of uniqueness,[14] as well as by the appearance in literary and legal texts of a new accent on the physical resemblance of parents and children, notions of family "stock" brought biology to the fore in the domestic realm, causing a redrawing of its boundaries.

What role, if any, were adoptive ties assigned in the shifting definitions of "the family"? When we consider the history of the family from the perspective of official dictionaries and law codes, it becomes clear that beginning in the sixteenth century "fictive" family ties, such as those forged through adoption, were steadily excluded from definitions of the family. In other words, as the notion of the family became increasingly based on the dual criteria of blood and marriage, the adopted child— tied to the family through a legal fiction rather than through biological ties—threatened to violate the sanctioned ordering of the domestic sphere.

Histories of the family have, for the most part, interpreted the rejection of adoptive ties from official definitions of the family as correlating with the actual demise of adoption practices. The historian Marcel Garaud suggests that "the institution of adoption, seldom practiced though still in force in the both customary and written law regions of France in the fourteenth century, declined rapidly and finally disappeared in all areas in fifteenth and sixteenth centuries."[15] The legal historian P. C. Timbal, in his comparative study of Roman and French law, attributes the disappearance of adoption in sixteenth-century France to "the triumph of a familial structure which had always only begrudgingly accepted the intrusion of

---

[12] Ibid., p. 90.

[13] For a discussion of the privatization of the family sphere in this period, see Phillipe Ariès and Georges Duby, eds., *Histoire de la vie privée*, vol. 2, *De l'Europe féodale à la Renaissance* (Paris, 1985).

[14] For an intriguing look at the role of such journals in familial "mythmaking" in Renaissance Italy, see Christiane Klapisch-Zuber, *La maison et le nom: Stratégies et rituels dans l'Italie de la Renaissance* (Paris, 1990).

[15] See Marcel Garaud and Romauld Szramkiewicz, *La Révolution française et la famille* (Paris, 1978), p. 93.

foreign elements."[16] Along similar lines, in his study of medieval adoptions in the Roman law region of Provence, the legal historian René Aubenas attributes the waning of adoptions in southern France beginning in the sixteenth century to "the individualist spirit engendered by the era of the Renaissance and Reformation." Aubenas concludes that, after the mid-sixteenth century, "we no longer find any trace of the communitarian practices that had been so common in the Middle Ages."[17]

THE TALE OF YOUNG JACQUES

An exploration of the contours of daily household life in early modern Paris reveals that even in a cultural context where blood and marriage represented the cornerstones of the domestic sphere, family life continued, particularly for the laboring and artisan sectors of society, to be shaped by myriad "fictive" ties of affiliation. An intriguing court case involving an adopted child from 1654 serves as an introduction to popular attitudes regarding blood ties and fictive ties. This compelling case of abandonment and adoption is described by a lawyer involved in the case as a story of "a mother, to whom they want to give a child who is not hers; a father, from whom they want to take away a child who is his, and a child whose true identity is suspended between the artifice of lies and the truth of his birth."[18] Although the story did not unfold in Paris, but in the town of Vernon,[19] the case was frequently cited and discussed by Parisian jurists, who used it to develop arguments in support of adoption or to muster material underscoring its inadequacies. The tale centers on a young boy named Jacques who was

[16] P. C. Timbal, *Droit romain et ancien droit français* (Paris, 1960), p. 103.

[17] René Aubenas, "L'adoption en Provence au Moyen âge (XIVe–XVIe siècles)," *Revue historique de droit français et étranger* 13 (1934): 711. The legal historian Jean Brissaud connects the demise of adoption with changes in the family in the early modern period, noting that "adoption appeared to our old jurisconsults as a Roman institution which had been rejected by customary law"; see *A History of French Private Law*, trans. Rapelje Howell (Boston, 1912), p. 218. Similarly, Gilles Bollenot proposes that "adoption could find no place . . . in a society in which the definition of the family rested uniquely on blood and marriage"; see "L'adoption au XIXe siècle: 'La Fortune de Gaspard' de la comtesse de Ségur," *Revue historique* 271 (1984): 313.

[18] "Une mère, à qui on veut donner un enfant qui n'est pas à elle; un père, à qui on veut arracher un enfant qui luy appartient; un enfant, dont la condition est suspendue entre l'artifice du mensonge et la vérité de sa naissance," in Bignon, *Divers plaidoyers touchant la cause des gueux de Vernon* (Paris, 1665), p. 217. The case is also discussed in Catherine Holmès, *L'éloquence judiciaire de 1620 à 1660, reflet des problèmes sociaux, religieux, et politiques de l'époque* (Paris, 1967).

[19] There are four Vernons listed in the French postal directory. This Vernon is most likely in the department of the Eure, near Evreux. The other three are found in the Vienne, near Poitiers, in the Ardèche, and in the Loiret.

abandoned in infancy by his mother at the Hôtel-Dieu in Vernon and subsequently "adopted" by an itinerant beggar named Monrousseau. Years later, this same Monrousseau and Jacques passed through the town of Vernon, seeking alms. The judges of Vernon, sparked by statements of villagers who took the young boy to be the son of a local widow named Jeanne Vacherot, initiated an inquiry into the child's identity. Monrousseau was charged with the crime of abduction and was placed in prison to await the court's decision. A lawyer was appointed to plead the case of each individual involved, and witnesses from Vernon, who had known the young boy in his infancy, were called to testify. The inquiry was complicated by the fact that Vacherot denied that Jacques was her son, while Monrousseau claimed not to have abducted the boy from his natal mother, as the royal prosecutor claimed, but to have adopted him from the hospice where his mother had abandoned him in his infancy.[20] Jacques, then only eight years old, appeared as confused as everyone else about his familial status.

In an attempt to resolve the question of Jacques's parentage, the judicial pleadings draw on both ancient and contemporary discussions of the relative merits of biological and fictive family ties. The central issue in this case turned around whether Monrousseau and Jacques constituted a family, given that they held no biological ties to one another. The royal prosecutor pleading the case for the lieutenant general of Vernon argued that adoptive ties possessed no legal validity, claiming instead that only blood ties could create a family. In his pleading the prosecutor accredits lineal blood with supernatural powers, possessing the ability to unite (or, in this case, divide) individuals according to membership in the same biological family group. According to the prosecutor, the fact that Monrousseau was in jail, and thus separated from Jacques, reflected the illegitimacy of the bond that linked them:

> St. John Chrysostom remarks that the love based on blood resembles a fire, which always separates bodies of different sorts and brings together those who are of the same substance. If, Messieurs, Jean Monrousseau and this child were of the same blood line, *love would have brought them together;* they must be of different bloodlines because they are now separated.[21]

The prosecutor contends, then, that familial love could only emanate from ties of blood.

The lawyer for Jeanne Vacherot, de Montauban, also held blood capable of determining true lines of filiation. Vacherot's disavowal of the boy must

---

[20] The tale was complicated by the fact that Vacherot had "lost" two sons of her own a few years earlier. Yet, Vacherot substantiated her claim that Jacques was not her true son by reporting that one of her two lost sons had returned and reported that his brother had died. See Bignon, *Divers plaidoyers*, p. 187.

[21] Ibid., p. 305; emphasis added.

be taken as truth, he concludes, as a mother would be compelled "by nature" to recognize her son if the same blood ran through their veins:

> My party does not recognize these marks (of Nature); she remains silent as the mother of Ulysses. If this were her child, she surely would have spoken as the common blood running through their veins would have compelled her to recognize him as her son.[22]

Popular tales indicate that the belief in the mystical powers of lineal blood had strong roots in early modern French culture. Studies of late medieval narratives have shown that in cases of loss or abandonment, even if a child spends considerable time in the care of others, in most instances the ties of blood ultimately triumph, almost supernaturally reuniting separated kin. The tale of Tristan, reprinted often in sixteenth-century France, depicts Tristan and King Mark as drawn to each other immediately upon Tristan's arrival at court; only later does it emerge that Tristan is Mark's nephew.[23] Similarly, Barbara Estrin has shown that in Renaissance English foundling tales, even when abandoned children undergo a positive "adoptive interlude" with foster parents, they are almost always reunited with their natal kin in the end.[24]

The Vernon case reveals, however, that even in a culture that placed biology as the cornerstone of the family, the kinship categories of "parent" and "child" could also be defined by the criteria of nurturing and mutual affection.[25] In this regard the lawyer for Monrousseau, Du Fourcroy, situated "nurture" above "nature" in determining lines of filiation:

[22] Ibid., p. 201.

[23] See Clair Haydn Bell, "The Call of the Blood in Medieval German Epic," *Modern Language Notes* 37, no. 1 (1922):17–26. On tales of Tristan, see E. Loseth, *Le roman de Tristan, le roman de Palamede, et la compilation de Rusticien de Pise* (Paris, 1891). See also John Boswell's discussion of medieval tales of abandonment and adoption in *The Kindness of Strangers: The Abandonment of Children in Western Europe from Late Antiquity to the Renaissance* (New York, 1988), and Charles Dunn, *The Foundling and the Werewolf: A Literary-Historical Study of Guillaume de Palerne*, University of Toronto Studies and Texts, 8 (Toronto, 1960).

[24] Barbara L. Estrin, *The Raven and the Lark: Lost Children in Literature of the English Renaissance* (London, 1985). Estrin notes that although "nature" might triumph over "nurture," the adoptive interludes present foster parenting in a positive light. Speaking of foundling tales from Moses in the Hebrew Bible to Spenser and Shakespeare, the author remarks (pp. 14–15): "The good of art appears in the adoptive sections where the supremacy of inheritance is superseded by the idealization of the replacement. Thus the aristocratic court is supplanted by the simple country, the proud king by a modest peasant. During the 'diaspora,' the lost child absorbs values that his biological parents could never teach him. . . . a stranger can sustain the child as well as his parents can."

[25] It is here that the debates over the definition of the family in this seventeenth-century case approximate modern-day debates among anthropologists over the relative importance of biology or sociology in determining kinship relations. Claude Lévi-Strauss, for one, argues

The jurists are of this inclination, when speaking about the ownership of a plant, not to consider who planted it, but instead to consider to whom the ground belongs on which it was nourished and preserved. . . . in the end, between all the causes of filiation, there has never been a stronger argument to justify filiation than that which derives from education, nurturing, and preservation. . . . this is exactly why nurturing forms a second birth.[26]

Pleading for his client, Du Fourcroy employs the criterion of nurturing (a process that he terms a "second birth") to substantiate Monrousseau's claim to be Jacques's father; although Monrousseau was not Jacques's biological father, his claim to be Jacques's father was valid as it was he, and not the natal parents, who nourished and raised Jacques from infancy. Du Fourcroy offers as additional proof of the bonds linking the two the fact that when the young Jacques was asked whether he preferred to stay with Monrousseau, he answered that "he very well should do so, considering that he was his father and that he did not wish to renounce his father."[27]

Du Fourcroy did not stand alone in emphasizing the merits of "fictive" ties in early modern France. For the essayist Michel de Montaigne, friendship competed with ties of blood, often superseding them in endurance and sincerity.[28] In his essay, "On the Affection of Fathers for Their Children," Montaigne appears characteristically skeptical about the existence of a natural basis for affection between blood kin: "It seems from experience that this natural affection, on which we place such a great deal of weight, in reality has very weak roots."[29] Montaigne continues:

> Let us consider this simple proposition that we love our children simply because we engendered them. . . . it seems to me that some of our other "products" merit just as much, if not greater, attention: I speak of that which we engender from the soul, give birth to from our spirit and our courage, all of which emanate from a more noble part of ourselves than the corporal, and, in the end, form more a part of ourselves.[30]

---

that "it is the social relationship more than the biological tie implied by the terms 'father,' 'mother,' 'son,' 'daughter,' 'brother,' and 'sister,' that acts as the determinant"; see *The Elementary Structures of Kinship*, trans. James Harle Bell (Boston, 1969), p. 30.

[26] Bignon, *Divers plaidoyers*, pp. 256–57.

[27] Ibid., p. 260.

[28] Montaigne, "De l'amitié," in *Essais* (Paris, 1979), 1: no. XXVIII.

[29] Montaigne, "De l'affection des pères aux enfants," in *Essais*, 2: no. VIII, p. 70.

[30] Ibid., p. 71. Adoptive ties formed an integral part of Montaigne's own family life, as evidenced by his relationship with his "fille d'alliance" and literary executor, Marie le Jars de Gournay. See Mario L. Schiff, *La fille d'alliance de Montaigne, Marie de Gournay* (Paris, 1910; reprint Geneva, 1978), and J. Morland, "Marie le Jars de Gournay, la 'fille d'alliance' de Montaigne," *Bibliothèque de la Société des Amis de Montaigne* 27 (1971): 45–54. In a similar vein, Thomas More in his *Utopia* envisioned a system of child care in which children

Many of the lawyers sitting in the courtroom of Vernon, however, did not concur with the judgment of the "weak roots" of biological ties binding parents and children advanced by humanists such as Montaigne. If biological ties were not considered paramount, worried the lawyer Bignon, children risked becoming a kind of communal property rather than belonging clearly to a single set of parents. Refuting the analogy made by Du Fourcroy between the rearing of children and the care of a plant, Bignon argues that:

> We cannot speak of the same type of ownership and possession when it comes to children as we do for other products of nature, which are used in common by all men without any right of ownership. . . . these goods can change master because, by natural law, they belong no more to one than to another; yet this same natural law renders children a different sort of property which cannot be exchanged.[31]

What does this unique court case from Vernon reveal about the nature of family life? For one, the case indicates the existence of lively debates over the composition of the domestic sphere; while some of the lawyers insisted that biological ties alone defined family ties, others argued that bonds of nurture also constituted family ties. Jacques's tale also brings to light the belief that adoptive ties served to upset the accepted ordering of both family and society. Jacques's adoption by Monrousseau entailed a dramatic shift in his social status, the movement from the household of a relatively well-off and settled member of the community into the care of an itinerant beggar (at one point, Jacques's fate is blamed on a "miserable adoption"[32]). Fears that adopted children might unduly blur social boundaries are also voiced from the other side in this case; Jeanne Vacherot made it clear that she did not want to "adopt" and bring into her household the child of a beggar. Her lawyer, de Montauban, claims that his client would never consider bringing Jacques into her household, "because she did not want to dishonor her family by such a base and shameful adoption."[33] If Jeanne Vacherot was forced to recognize a beggar's son as a legitimate member of her family, the line of reasoning went, the family "honor" and "lineage" would be irreparably tainted.

The connection between adoption and socially disruptive ruses of children of "base stock" making false claims to the name, honor, and property of upper-class families surfaces in other early modern court cases. One

---

were not bound to remain with their biological parents, but could chose to move to a new household to be educated and apprenticed in a new trade with another set of parents.

[31] Bignon, *Divers plaidoyers*, pp. 12–13.

[32] Ibid., p. 22.

[33] Ibid., p. 253.

such case from the seventeenth century tells of a "miserable young wood-working apprentice" from Paris, who, "suddenly forgetting his appointed lot in the workshop and the baseness of his condition, insolently proceeded to take a place in the carriage of a noblewoman unknown to him."[34] The impostor theme also appears in popular folktales treating the theme of changelings and other strangers who enter into a family (usually through deceitful means, as did Arnauld du Tihl in the story of Martin Guerre),[35] making claims to its property, upsetting its natural balance, and threatening its continued existence.[36] The jurist Bignon, in fact, remarked on the similarities between the Vernon case and popular tales of abandonment and mistaken identity, commenting that:

> The subject of this case has much in common with tales invented for pleasure; both with those fables that antiquity has left us, as well as those that poetry offers us now . . . the surprise of novelty, the intrigue, the juxtaposition of personae, the vicissitudes of grand passions, and, finally, the incertitude of events.[37]

FICTIVE FAMILY TIES AND PARISIAN NEIGHBORHOOD LIFE

Moving from the courtroom of Vernon to the world of the neighborhoods of sixteenth- and seventeenth-century Paris, we find that the same type of "fictive" ties that bound Monrousseau and Jacques in a familial relationship played an important role in shaping the nature of daily family life. Indeed, we find that an extended network of ties of affiliation established a family culture in which a spectrum of "secondary parents" participated in the upbringing of children. David Garrioch's study of artisan family life in

[34] Benigne Lordelot, *Plaidoyé contre un enfant supposé et déclaré un imposteur* (Paris, 1686), pp. 43–44.

[35] See Natalie Z. Davis, *The Return of Martin Guerre* (Cambridge, Mass., 1983).

[36] For additional cases involving impostors and pseudo-adoptions see J. C. de la Ville, *Causes célèbres et intéressantes avec les jugemens qui les ont décidées*, vol. 1 (Paris, 1769). The theme of impostors was closely tied to that of the "supposition d'enfant." A case involving such a "faked" pregnancy appears in a pleading of Le Maistre who compares the crime with that of falsifying money. See Issali, *Les plaidoyez et harangues de M. le Maistre* (Paris, 1657), p. 123. The same metaphor of counterfeit money is employed in the Vernon case, where it is compared to the crime of disavowing a child by the natal parents. See Bignon, *Divers plaidoyers*, p. 354. In both instances, then, "cheating" nature parallels "cheating" the king. For folktales involving "changelings" and suppositious children, see Stith Thompson, *Motif Index of Folk-Literature*, 6 vols. (Bloomington, Ind., 1955–58), types F32.1, F451.5.2.3, K184.7, K192.2. For one rendition of a changeling tale, see "The False Child" (L'enfant supposé), in *French Folktales from the Collection of Henri Pourrat*, trans. Royall Tyler (New York, 1989), pp. 14–17.

[37] Bignon, *Divers plaidoyers*, p. 1.

eighteenth-century Paris serves as a valuable model for our exploration of the role of blood ties and fictive ties in family life in the earlier centuries.[38] Garrioch's study highlights the interdependence of household and neighborhood in shaping the nature of family life, an interdependence that stemmed in part from the absence of the modern distinction between the public world of the street and the neighborhood and the private sphere of family and household.[39] Garrioch suggests that the proximity of apartments to workshops and courtyards inevitably intertwined the lives of different artisan families. Daniel Roche concurs that among the popular classes "there was no division between house and street, into which the whole neighborhood overflowed from nearby houses, workshops, shops and taverns."[40]

The public nature of family life in the laboring and artisan neighborhoods shaped customs of child-rearing. Unlike upper-class families, which tended to keep their children sheltered from the public world of the neighborhood, laboring and artisan families often could not afford to hire live-in servants or to send their children to boarding schools. Thus, working-class children grew up very much in the public eye, with neighbors participating in almost every stage of their upbringing.[41] Although Garrioch's study does not investigate fostering agreements between neighbors, it is easy to see how secondary parenting arrangements formed an extension of this culture of urban sociability in which domestic and neighborhood boundaries overlapped (in subsequent chapters we shall

[38] David Garrioch, *Neighbourhood and Community in Paris, 1740–1790* (Cambridge, 1986). For a masterful overview of the outlay of the city of Paris and its social and economic contours in the sixteenth century, see the opening chapters of Barbara B. Diefendorf's *Beneath the Cross: Catholics and Huguenots in Sixteenth-Century Paris* (Oxford, 1991). For a social geography of sixteenth-century Paris, see also Robert Descimon, "Paris on the Eve of Saint Bartholomew: Taxation, Privilege, and Social Geography," in Phillip Benedict, ed., *Cities and Social Change in Early Modern France* (New York, 1989), pp. 69–104.

[39] James Farr's study of artisans in sixteenth- and seventeenth-century Dijon also underscores the importance of the daily experience of the neighborhood in the lives and cultural identity of the artisan class. See James R. Farr, *Hands of Honor: Artisans and Their World in Dijon, 1550–1650* (Ithaca, N.Y., 1988).

[40] Daniel Roche, *The People of Paris: An Essay in Popular Culture in the 18th Century*, trans. Marie Evans (New York, 1987), p. 246; see also pt. 2, chap. 4, "Housing and Accommodation." Arlette Farge offers a similar portrait of the interdependence of family life and neighborhood life in *Fragile Lives: Violence, Power and Solidarity in Eighteenth-Century Paris*, trans. Carol Shelton (Cambridge, Mass., 1993), esp. chap. 1: "Space and Ways of Life."

[41] Garrioch, in *Neighbourhood and Community*, p. 60, notes that "among working people . . . family and neighborhood complemented each other in bringing up children. Parents undoubtedly had the primary responsibility, but neighbors often helped, and in socialization they played a vital role."

see, for instance, that neighbors were often the ones to step in and formally adopt a child of a destitute or gravely ill neighbor who was no longer
able to fulfill his or her parenting role).

Servants and Masters

The presence of non-kin within a household who were considered affiliated family members might seem incommensurate with modern notions
of the family. Yet, in the late medieval and early modern periods many
families sent their children, often beginning as early as age nine or ten, to
reside and work in the household of a friend, neighbor, or relative. The
terms of such servant contracts varied, and the length of the child's stay in
the new household could range from two years to as many as ten or
more.[42] This practice of sending out one's children to serve in another
household was practiced by families across the social spectrum.[43] The
historian François Le Brun notes that "at all levels of society, families exchanged their children so they might gain a 'savoir-faire' and a 'savoir-
vivre': the *coqs du village*, artisans, merchants, nobility of the robe, and the
nobility of the sword."[44] While wealthy families would routinely hire a
team of male and female servants, modest artisan families often took a
single female servant to help the woman of the house with the cooking
and other domestic chores, or to assist in her trade.[45]

Because children were frequently sent away from home at a very young
age to serve in other households, much of their early youth and adolescence was spent in the care of adults other than their biological parents.
The long duration of many servant contracts helps to explain why the
relationship between master and servant was often characterized as mirror-
ing that of the parent-child relationship. Although labor lay at the heart of
the master-servant association, the master and his wife were still expected

[42] On the social history of children and the cycle of servanthood in the early modern
period, see André Burguière, ed., *Histoire de la famille*, 2 vols. (Paris, 1986); Grant Mc-
Cracken, "The Exchange of Children in Tudor England: An Anthropological Phenomenon
in Historical Context," *Journal of Family History* 8 (winter 1983): 303–13.

[43] Cissie Fairchilds notes of servants in lower-class households: "Among the lower classes
servants were most likely to be found in the households of artisans and textile
workers . . . and in the food, lodging, and transport sectors." She adds that servants were
not needed in households of wage laborers. See Fairchilds, *Domestic Enemies: Servants and
Their Masters in Old Régime France* (Baltimore, 1984), p. 8. See also the study of servant-
master relations by Sarah Maza, *Servants and Masters in Eighteenth-Century France: The Uses
of Loyalty* (Princeton, N.J., 1983).

[44] "A tous échelons de la société, les familles s'échangeaient leurs enfants pour apprendre
un savoir-faire et le savoir-vivre: chez les 'coqs du village,' les artisans, les négociants, les gens
de robe, comme dans la noblesse d'épée," in *Histoire de la famille*, 2:43.

[45] See Garrioch, *Neighbourhood and Community*, chap. 3: "Work."

to treat the servant in a humane manner, offering him or her basic care and often the rudiments of a religious education. The child was expected to serve the master and mistress of the new household and, in return, the surrogate parents were expected to provide the child with the moral education otherwise provided by the biological parents.[46] In many respects, then, the servant profession established a system of nonbiological parenting (although servants were often poor kin relations),[47] by which children were effectively raised by a family other than their own. Although the assumption was that enduring affective bonds would be forged only between masters and servants in upper-class households (which Garrioch has termed the "loyalty-affection" model),[48] it appears that emotional ties between servants and masters also developed in artisan and laboring households. In some instances such servants were provided with a dowry or some portion of the family wealth. In 1608, for example, Magdeleyne Le Prebstre included a donation of twenty-six livres in the codicil to her last will and testament for a young servant girl whom she and her husband had brought into their Parisian home one year before, at the age of six, to live with and serve them until she was eighteen. In her will Magdeleyne described the young girl, Geneviefve Petit, as "a poor little girl living in her house" and asked that the money be used to teach her a trade and to provide for her other necessities.[49]

Some domestic manuals even went so far as to describe servants as "adopted family members whom parents must care for like children of their own."[50] Along similar lines, notarial contracts often employed the language of adoption to fashion the act of taking a child into the household as a servant. In 1604 Ester Jobier, herself a domestic servant in Paris, gave her fifteen-year-old orphaned niece, Francoyse Jobier, to Marie Leschasseur, "in service and adoption" for the period of five years.[51] Similarly,

[46] The expectation of a "cultural apprenticeship" was particularly strong for noble families. Cissie Fairchilds, in *Domestic Enemies,* p. 4, notes that, among the nobility, the sending of a son to serve in another household was a means to achieve "courteous" behavior as well as the protection and patronage of the Lord.

[47] Cissie Fairchilds notes that poor relations were often taken in as servants, to labor in the family business and to perform housework in return for room and board (ibid., p. 5).

[48] Garrioch notes that "the loyalty-affection" model of the servant-employer relationship was not relevant to the material conditions of most working people" (*Neighbourhood and Community,* p. 135).

[49] The original contract for the terms of Geneviefve's stay in her new household can be found in AN, MC, Et. XXIX, 159 (7 August 1607); Magdeleyne's original last will and testament in Et. XXIII, 161 (7 December 1604), and the codicil in Et. XXIII, 117 (25 December 1608).

[50] From Audiger, *La maison réglée d'un grand seigneur et autres, tant à la ville qu'à la campagne, et le devoir de tous les officiers et autres domestiques en général* (Paris, 1692), cited in Fairchilds, *Domestic Enemies,* p. 5.

[51] AN, MC, Et. XXIX, 156 (5 March 1604).

in 1610 Blaise Billanet, a day worker, and his wife, Nicolle Marne, both from Paris, placed their ten-year-old daughter, Fleury, "in adoption and service" of François de la Roche, a merchant, and his wife Marguerite Bonart, also from Paris, for a period of six years.[52] The use of the word "adoption" in these service contracts, while employed in a different manner from the formal adoption contracts to be examined in later chapters, was intended to underscore the temporary transfer of parental duties and rights that accompanied the placement of a child as a servant in a new household. In the Vernon case, it is significant that one of the most important witnesses called to resolve the identity of the young Jacques was a female domestic servant who had resided in the home of Jeanne Vacherot and had helped to raise the children. "Who could better identify the boy than this girl?" asked the lawyer; "if nature formed this child in the mother's womb, he was raised in the arms of this servant girl."[53]

Apprenticeship

Households in early modern Paris opened their doors to other outsiders at various points in the domestic life cycle such as apprentices, who, like servants, became affiliated family members of sorts. Highlighting the degree of integration of an apprentice in his new household, the historian François Le Brun comments that "the young man lived in the home of the master and his wife. He ate at their table, slept under their roof, and owed them the same obedience and the same respect that he would toward his own father and mother."[54] (The comparison of the servant-master or apprentice-master relationship with that of parent and child was intended normatively; of course, like children with cruel parents, many apprentices and servants fared miserably under the harsh rule of their masters.)[55] Le Brun suggests further that the terms of an apprenticeship involved a temporary transfer from the father to the master of the rights of paternal authority (*puissance paternelle*) over the apprentice.[56] An apprenticeship contract from 1624 highlights the surrogate-parenting role taken over by Nicholas Tavet, a Parisian merchant, and his wife Marye Lescripvain, who took Anne Forelle into their service for four years as a servant and appren-

---

[52] AN, MC, Et. XXIX, 162 (24 August 1610).

[53] Bignon, *Divers plaidoyers*, p. 316.

[54] "Le jeune garçon vit désormais au foyer du maître et de son épouse. Il mange à leur table, dort sous leur toit, leur doit la même obéissance et le même respect que vis-à-vis ses père et mère" (*Histoire de la famille*, 2:153).

[55] On the harsh treatment of servants in the ancien régime, in addition to the studies of Cissie Fairchilds and Sarah Maza, see Wendy Gibson, *Women in Seventeenth-Century France* (Basingstoke, 1989), "Women at Work, II."

[56] *Histoire de la famille*, 2:153.

tice. In addition to a vocational apprenticeship, the couple promised to "furnish her with all things necessary in their household . . . and to treat and honor her as their child," indicating that during Anne's term as servant and apprentice in the Tavet household Nicholas and Marye assumed a parental role.[57] Not only was the couple expected to provide her with the basic necessities and to educate her in a trade, but, more important, they were expected to raise her temporarily as their child.[58] In some instances parents arranged to exchange the care given to another family's child for the securing of an apprenticeship for their own child. Thus, in 1550 Jean de Clery, a mason's helper from Paris, sent his son Jacques for a term of apprenticeship with Jacques Desmoulins, a journeyman tailor in Paris at the Port St. Landry. In return de Clery and his wife promised to take in Desmoulins's two-year-old daughter Jehanne for one year.[59]

Godparents and Godchildren

In addition to sending children to be raised as servants in other households, families also forged "fictive" kinship ties with members of the surrounding community through the rite of baptism, participation in which united individuals in bonds of spiritual kinship. While godparents were often chosen from within the web of blood kin,[60] it was also common for families to name non-kin as spiritual guardians (families often selected four or more godparents for a single infant before the Council of Trent restricted the numbers to one of each sex). Thus the rite of baptism presented a family with an opportunity to forge alliances with non-kin as well as to strengthen those with kin. In his study of spiritual kinship in the early Middle Ages, Joseph Lynch suggested that "in both the popular and the official view, baptism was the occasion for the creation of a web of kinship, a family that was the mirror image of the natural family."[61]

[57] AN, MC, Et. CV, 529 (3 April 1624).

[58] Françoise Michaud-Frejaville in her study of apprenticeships in the Middle Ages remarks on the fluid lines between apprenticeship and guardianship, noting that in some cases apprentices received some form of inheritance from their master's household. See "Contrats d'apprentissage en Orléanais: Les enfants au travail (1380–1450)," in *L'enfant au moyen-âge: Litterature et civilisation* (Paris, 1980), pp. 61–72

[59] AN, MC, Et. XXXIII, 35 (June 1550).

[60] See the discussion of the godparents chosen from the cognatic and affinal kin by the family of Jean Verosis, a lawyer in sixteenth-century Paris, in Flandrin, *Families in Former Times: Kinship, Household, and Sexuality*, p. 30. Flandrin demonstrates that the Verosis family institutionalized and reinforced existing kinship bonds by selecting kin as godparents to their children.

[61] Joseph Lynch, *Godparents and Kinship in Early Medieval Europe* (Princeton, N.J., 1986), p. 275.

As with biological kinship, ties of spiritual kinship entailed a spectrum of parenting duties. Sixteenth-century confession manuals and legal commentators inform us that godparents were partially responsible for the religious education and the general "moral" upbringing of their god-children.[62] Ties of spiritual kinship formed enduring bonds, which often culminated in donations of family property later in life, gifts that were inspired by gratitude and emotional attachment. In one such case, Jehan Briçonnet, president of the Royal Chambre des Comptes, made a donation to his godson, an orphan he had taken in from the Hôtel-Dieu fifteen years before whom he had baptized and given his name of Jehan Briçonnet. The notarized document of 1549 tells us that due to the "love [*bonne amour*] that the president has for the aforementioned Jehan Briçonnet," he made an irrevocable donation of 320 arpents of land outside of Paris to his godson.[63]

Wet Nurses

Alongside spiritual kinship there were many other settings in which individuals entered into secondary parent-child relationships. While the godparents entered into a child's life in its first weeks at the moment of baptism, in many families it was often a wet nurse, not the biological mother, who nourished the child during its first years.[64] Families turned to wet-nursing for a variety of reasons. Some parents sent their children to

[62] The Catholic Church maintained that godparents were the guarantors of the *castitas, justitia*, and *caritas* of their godchildren. See Christiane Klapisch-Zuber, "Parrains et Filleuls," *Medieval Prosopography* 6, no. 2 (1985): p. 60. On godparent's responsibilities regarding the religious education of their godchildren, see Lynch *Godparents and Kinship.*

[63] AN, MC, Et. XLIX, 90 (28 August 1549). The contract does not state whether the orphan Briçonnet resided in the president's household. For an analysis of spiritual kinship as an institution that formed ties between the nobility and commoners in sixteenth-century Jura, see Abbé Berthet, "Un réactif social: Le parrainage du XVIe siècle à la Révolution," *Annales: E.S.C.* 1 (1946): 43–50. Berthet views the linking of disparate social classes through the rite of baptism as particular to the sixteenth and early seventeenth centuries: "La société d'alors admet ces relations de copaternité avec des gens de classes forts différentes"(p. 47).

[64] For a comparative look at wet-nursing outside of France, see Christiane Klapisch-Zuber, "Parents de sang, parents de lait: La mise en nourrice à Florence (1300–1530)" *Annales de démographie historique*, special issue, "Mères et nourrissons" (1983): 33–64; Valerie Fildes, *Wet Nursing: A History from Antiquity to the Present* (Oxford, 1988); Fiona Newall, "Wet Nursing and Child Care in Aldenham, Hertfordshire, 1595–1726: Some Evidence on the Circumstances and Effects of Seventeenth-Century Child-Rearing Practices," in Valerie Fildes, ed., *Women as Mothers in Pre-Industrial England* (London, 1990), pp. 122–39; Elizabeth W. Marvick, "Nature versus Nurture: Patterns and Trends in Seventeenth-Century French Child-Rearing," in Lloyd de Mause, ed., *The History of Childhood* (New York, 1974), pp. 259–301.

wet nurses due to the economic necessity of freeing the mother to continue working. Other families believed that the qualities of the wet nurse's milk would benefit the child more than the biological mother's breast milk.[65] In either case, the choice of a wet nurse entailed just as much planning and forethought as did the choice of godparents, given that early modern theories concerning the influence of bodily humors and fluids held that traits of a wet nurse would be passed on to the nursing infant through her breast milk. Accordingly, parents were urged to find a wet nurse whose physical and moral characteristics were suitable to expectations for their child. The sixteenth-century physician Ambroise Paré counseled parents to choose a wet nurse with upstanding moral traits considering that "after the father and the mother, a child receives the most 'natural' traits from the wet nurse."[66] This transmission of traits occurred, Paré explains, because breast milk constituted "whitened blood," linking the wet nurse and the infant: "We can tell if the breast milk is good by looking at its color, because this milk is nothing other than whitened blood [*sang blanchi*]."[67] The seventeenth-century midwife to the queen, Louise Bourgeois, also counseled mothers to be vigilant when choosing a wet nurse, whom she considered "second mothers":

> There is good reason for women, who cannot or do not wish to nurse their children, and who desire to give them a second mother from whom they will receive just as many, if not more, good or bad habits as from themselves, to choose [one with] a disposition [*une humeur*] that they wish their children to follow.[68]

Bourgeois further suggests that the ideal wet nurse have an agreeable disposition, good teeth, and brown or light-brown hair, come from a healthy "stock," not be too fat, and, above all, be of a loving nature.[69]

The bond formed between the wet nurse and the infant in her care might last well into the child's adulthood and could lead to continued contact and to exchanges of gifts between the two. In a case from 1545

[65] On various interpretations of the history of wet-nursing, see the work of Edward Shorter, *The Making of the Modern Family* (New York, 1975), who argues that wet-nursing betrayed a lack of maternal sentiment, and the revised interpretation offered by George Sussman, *Selling Mother's Milk: The Wet-nursing Business in France* (Urbana, Ill., 1982).

[66] "L'enfant ne tire tant du naturel à personne, après le père et la mère, que de sa nourrice à raison du laict qu'il tete"; Ambroise Paré, *Ouevres complètes* (Paris, 1840), 2:683.

[67] "On peut juger le laict pareillement estre bon par sa couleur, par-ce que ledit laict n'est autre chose qu'un *sang blanchi*"; Paré, *Oeuvres complètes*, 2:688. The physiological basis for this claim, as Paré explains, was that it was the mother's blood which "fed" the breast milk, or the "sang blanchi" (2:683).

[68] Louise Bourgeois, *Observations diverses sur la stérilité, perte de fruict, foecondité, accouchements et maladies des femmes, & enfants nouveaux naiz* (Rouen, 1626), p. 163.

[69] Bourgeois, *Observations diverses*, pp. 164–65.

involving a manual worker and his wife, Macé Larmeurier and Guillemette Godette donated a house to Jean Vorse, a lawyer at the Paris Châtelet, whom Guillemette had wet-nursed years before. The donation was undertaken due to the "good love which they hold toward the said Vorse, whom the said woman had breast-fed." By the terms of such a *donation*, the couple most likely continued to live in the house and even received care in their old age from Vorse, who acted in this respect as a son.[70] As we shall see in a later chapter, the emotional attachment between a wet nurse and her nursing infant could be strong enough to lead her family to adopt an infant orphan or foundling under her care.

Guardianship of Legitimate and Illegitimate Children

Guardianship, or *tutelle*, of children orphaned of one or both parents provided another avenue through which new "family members" were introduced into a child's life. When one parent died, a committee of kin was meant to gather in order to select the proper guardian for the child or children. This process of selection was carefully monitored as property concerns were paramount. Guardians also made decisions regarding apprenticeship, marriage, and inheritance arrangements for the minor children under their supervision. While the surviving parent was often chosen to fulfill this task, it was also possible that an extended kin or a nonfamily member would be chosen as a guardian.[71]

Alternative family structures were also forged outside of the institution of marriage when the unmarried parents of illegitimate children drew up formal child-care arrangements before a notary. As is well known, a child born out of wedlock, although considered "natural" blood kin, nonetheless maintained incomplete legal ties to the family and larger kinship group.[72] Most significantly, illegitimate children were cut off from the succession rights accorded to biological children born in legal marriage. Unless legitimated by subsequent marriage of the parents or by letters of the king or pope, civil law mandated that children born outside of legal marriage, like adopted children, could not stand as full heirs to the family patrimony or to the family name.[73] The notarial records introduce us to many unmarried and pregnant women who, on realizing that the marriage

[70] "pour la bonne amour qu'ilz ont audict Vorse, que ladite femme a nourry de mamelle." This case is found in Registre des Insinuations, no. 1577 (15 January 1545).

[71] On the institution of guardianship, see François Olivier-Martin, *Histoire de la coutume de la prévôté et vicomté de Paris*, 2 vols. (Paris, 1922), 1:185–99.

[72] The jurist René Choppin noted in this regard that "la condition de la naissance illégitime n'est point purgée par la qualité de fils," in *Oeuvres complètes* (Paris, 1662), 1:363.

[73] See Renée Barbarin, *La condition juridique du bâtard d'après la jurisprudence du Parlement de Paris* (Mayenne, 1960).

promise made by the biological father of their child would never be ful-filled, compelled the natural father to accept his paternal obligation to raise the child.[74] Many of these accords show the biological father con-senting to "adopt" the child, even while forgoing marriage to the child's mother. In a case from 1610, Marie Saussier, a twenty-five-year-old *fille à marier* from the parish of St. Germain des Prés, succeeded in obtaining promises from the father of her future child, the master ropemaker Fran-çois Dumont, to pay her "reparations, expenses, and damages" due to the "carnal company that the said Dumont had with her and because of which she is pregnant with child." François promised to "take the child with which she is pregnant into his guard and charge and to instruct it in the commandments of God and the Church and to raise and care for him from then and forever."[75] In a similar agreement from 1608 Jacques Alliot, a sergeant for the king who worked at the Abbey of St. Germain des Prés, promised Catherine Faibe to raise her newborn child "for the honor of God" despite the fact that he maintained that the child was not his. Whether or not we choose to believe that the child Jacques Alliot agreed to "adopt" was not his own biological child, this case, and the others like it, reveal the variety of domestic arrangements forged by individual parents outside of the context of legal marriage as they calculated the best means of survival for themselves and their offspring in early modern Paris.[76]

CONCLUSIONS

Returning to the Vernon case, the collected courtroom speeches leave the ultimate fate of the young Jacques unclear for the historical record. In his summary pleading, the lawyer Bignon chastised Jeanne Vacherot for hav-ing abandoned "her son," and, yet, concluded by asking the court to re-lease Monrousseau from prison and to place Jacques, "whom he shall recognize as his son," into his care.[77] The facts presented in this case leave us wondering about Jacques's precise familial identity much as they did the lawyers of the day who were equally unable to sift out artifice from reality. Bignon warned the panel of judges on this point:

[74] For more on these proceedings, see ibid., chap. 1.

[75] AN, MC, Et. II, 71 (21 December 1610).

[76] AN, MC, Et. XXIII, 160 (26 December 1608). In a case from 1602, Jehanne Marchant, living in the parish of St. Eustache demanded compensation from the father of her five-month-old child, claiming that he had promised her marriage during the time that they were together. The father, Michel Roget, a master beltmaker, also from the parish of St. Eustache, agreed to take in and raise his son in the Catholic faith. AN, MC, Et. XXXIX, 12 (13 February 1602). In a case from 1628, the natural father promised to take in his natural son and raise him "comme son propre enffan." AN, MC, Et. XXXIX, 60 (23 May 1628).

[77] Bignon, *Divers plaidoyers*, p. 50.

> What is most difficult is that you must overcome the eloquence of several jurists whom we have heard here, all of whom are capable through their flowery speech of rendering a lie equally as agreeable and appealing as the truth itself.[78]

Even though the identity of the young Jacques remains a mystery, however, the pleadings of the lawyers in this case offer us a unique glimpse into debates over the nature of parent-child bonds and the structuring of the domestic sphere in early modern France. The pleadings, which continually juxtapose the blood ties that bound Jacques to his natal mother, Vacherot, to the "fictive" ties that bound him to his adoptive father, Monrousseau, bring to light intriguing discussions regarding the ordering of the family. As we have seen, while many of the lawyers followed the paradigm of the family upheld by civil law and insisted that only ties of blood and legal marriage formed a family, other lawyers put forth a model of the family based on ties of nurturing and affiliation.

Shifting focus from the courtroom of Vernon to the households of early modern Paris, we have seen that bonds of alliance similar to those which linked Monrousseau and Jacques played a formative role in the daily life of many Parisian families. While studies of family life have shown that upper-class families moved increasingly to sever ties with the surrounding community, the domestic life of laboring and artisan households remained intertwined with the life of the neighborhood. In this context, family ties were forged with neighbors, co-workers, godparents, wet nurses, and others who participated in the upbringing of children. From the perspective of the history of the family, the movement of children between households as servants and apprentices highlights the flexible nature of household boundaries in early modern Paris. Evidence of family life from the archives reveals that the task of raising children was, in fact, rarely confined to the biological parents; particularly in laboring and artisan families many children spent a good portion of their adolescence being trained, educated and raised in other households under the care of a second set of "parents." This is not to say that concerns of lineage were entirely absent from the working classes. Indeed, James Farr's work on early modern Dijon has shown that over the course of the sixteenth and seventeenth centuries concerns of lineage rose in importance for the master-artisans of Dijon as these families closed ranks with the aim of protecting their economic and social status. In his review of inheritance provisions in marriage contracts from 1551 to 1650, Farr found that property became increasingly earmarked for members of the lineage in the event that a couple produced no heir. He concludes that the "artisans of seventeenth-century Dijon emphasized family solidarity defined by blood

[78] Ibid., p. 332.

more than their sixteenth-century forbears had."[79] Yet, as we will see in subsequent chapters, many Parisian families from the laboring and artisan classes placed concerns about lineage aside and opted to secure the continuity of their family line into the next generation by adopting a child from outside of the lineage group. Offering an alternative model of family life from the biologically based one articulated by the majority of the jurists involved in the Vernon trial, many families in early modern Paris were successful in achieving a relatively peaceful balance between blood ties and fictive ties in the domestic realm.

[79] Farr, *Hands of Honor*, p. 145; on artisan concepts of lineage, see Chap. 3, "Hierarchy and Solidarity."

CHAPTER TWO

Adoption Laws from Antiquity to the Early Modern Period

> We do not recognize in this kingdom any other
> form of filiation, kinship, or civil alliance than
> that which derives from blood and Nature.
> (Les institutions du droit français, *1753*)[1]

WE HAVE SEEN that sixteenth-century French customary law codes rejected adoption as a means of creating legitimate ties of filiation. Adoption had figured prominently, however, in law codes throughout antiquity and the early Middle Ages. Provisions for adoption appear in Babylonian and Egyptian[2] law codes, and the Hebrew Bible offers two oft-cited examples of adoption, that of the foundling Moses by the Pharaoh's daughter (Exodus 2:10) and of the orphaned Esther by her father's nephew, Mordechai (Esther 2:7).[3] Adoption was more widespread in ancient Greece where it served primarily religious ends, ensuring the survival of the domestic cult and the care of childless individuals in their old age.[4] In Rome adoption was even more prevalent than in Greece, also serving, at least initially, to guard against the extinction of the domestic cult. Soon, however, adoption began to realize broader social and political ends, as these arrangements were employed to solidify patron-client networks and even to ensure succession to the throne in imperial Rome.[5] Paul Veyne proposes

---

[1] Claude Serres, *Les institutions du droit françois suivant l'ordre de celles de Justinien* (Paris, 1753), s.v. "adoption."

[2] David Martin, *Die adoption im altbabylonischen recht* (Leipzig, 1927). E. Révillout, "Contrats de mariage et d'adoption dans l'Egypte et dans la Chaldée," *Proceedings of the Society of Biblical Archeology* 9 (1887): 167ff.

[3] Jack Goody notes, however, that adoption was fairly rare in ancient Israel due to the availability of alternative strategies, such as the levirate marriage, for producing legitimate heirs. See Jack Goody, *The Oriental, the Ancient and the Primitive* (Cambridge, 1990), pp. 352–53.

[4] In Attic law only men could adopt and only in the absence of natural children, although the adopted child might be a girl. See Mahillon, "Evolution historique de l'adoption depuis le droit romain," in *En hommage à Victor Gothot* (Liège, 1962), p. 437; Fausto Brindesi, *La famiglia attica: Il matrimonio e l'adozione* (Florence, 1961); Lene Rubenstein, *Adoption in Fourth-Century Athens* (Copenhagen, 1993).

[5] The emperors were able to employ adoption in this way due to the absence of strict laws

that Roman adoption provided an avenue of social mobility akin to marriage.[6] Through adoption one could acquire a child outside of legal marriage, prevent a family line from dying out, acquire the status of *pater familias* required for certain honors and public offices, as well as lay claim to the fortune of an adopted son-in-law.[7] Mireille Corbier has shown that while Romans did adopt non-kin, the most common model was to adopt an adult male from within the extended kin group.[8] Two forms of adoption existed in Roman law: adrogation, by which a person emancipated from paternal authority (usually a male adult) is adopted by another "father of a family," and adoption proper, by which a child still under the *potestas* of the biological father is adopted by another head of the household.[9] By the terms of classical Roman law, an adopted child entered the new family as a full and legitimate member, which signified, most importantly, that the child was accorded the same inheritance privileges as a biological child.

In order to explain the popularity of adoption in Rome, historians have pointed to the structure of the Roman family; while biological ties certainly played a critical role in designating kinship ties, family ties could also be constructed through legal "fictions" such as adoption. Mireille Corbier comments that "there was a profound rupture between classical Rome and later ages. Unlike their European successors, on whom the church imposed strict rules of filiation and alliance, Romans enjoyed a large degree

---

of devolution, which are characteristic of modern monarchies. Hence, Julius adopted Augustus, Augustus adopted Tiberius, and Claudius adopted Nero. See Mahillon, "Evolution historique," p. 439. On adoption in Rome in general, see Beryl Rawson, ed., *The Family in Ancient Rome: New Perspectives* (London, 1986); Marek Kurylowicz, *Die adoptio im klassichen romischen recht*, Studia Antiqua (Warsaw, 1981); D. I. Kertzer and R. P. Saller, eds., *The Family in Italy from Antiquity to the Present* (New Haven, Conn., 1991).

[6] Paul Veyne notes that "apparently one gave a child for adoption as one might give a daughter in marriage, particularly a 'good marriage.'" See "The Roman Empire," in Paul Veyne, ed., *A History of Private Life*, vol. 1, *From Pagan Rome to Byzantium*, trans. Arthur Goldhammer (Cambridge, 1987), p. 17.

[7] Veyne, *A History of Private Life*, 1:17.

[8] See Mireille Corbier, "Divorce and Adoption as Roman Familial Strategies," in Beryl Rawson, ed., *Marriage, Divorce, and Children in Ancient Rome* (Oxford, 1991), pp. 47–78, and Mireille Corbier, "Constructing Kinship in Rome: Marriage and Divorce, Filiation and Adoption," in David I. Kertzer and Richard P. Saller, *The Family in Italy from Antiquity to the Present* (New Haven, 1991), pp. 127–46.

[9] With adrogation all ties to the natal family and domestic cult were severed and the adopted adult (and *his* dependents) switched their loyalty to new family. For this reason, Roman society insisted that such transfers of familial status had to be approved by public officials. Women could be adopted, but not adrogated. On this point, see Mahillon, "Evolution historique," pp. 437–38.

of liberty to create their kinship groups and also, through the use of testaments, to choose their heirs."[10] The wide range of ways in which Romans were able to "construct kinship" ties has led some historians to claim that children born into a family were not automatically, or "naturally," counted among its members.[11] This Roman concept of "voluntary fatherhood" meant that Roman law, at least in its early manifestations, knew no distinct category of the "illegitimate" child.[12] Thus, a father could adopt the child of his concubine.[13] Although biological and affective ties certainly played important roles, for the purposes of comparison with the early modern period it is important to note that the Roman family was defined less as an organic, or biological, entity than as a civil or juridical group deriving its legitimacy from the head of the household.[14] Paul Veyne proposes in this regard that "the frequency of adoption is yet another proof that nature played little part in the Roman conception of the family."[15]

Traditions of adoption were weakened somewhat by Justinian's legal reforms in the sixth century, which altered the law of adoption so that it no longer represented a total break with the natal family and did not confer *patria potestas* on the adoptive father.[16] It seems that Justinian's revisions of adoption laws reflected the new Christian perspective on the family which placed marriage and biological ties as the cornerstones of the domestic sphere. Thus, the family was no longer the "social" or legal group it

[10] Mireille Corbier, "Constructing Kinship in Rome: Marriage and Divorce, Filiation and Adoption," in Kertzer and Saller, eds., *The Family in Italy*, p. 128.

[11] On the question of the acceptance of offspring into the family, see Veyne, "The Roman Empire." Suzanne Dixon speaks of the "pragmatism" of the Roman family where child-care and child custody arrangements were concerned. See her *The Roman Family* (Baltimore, 1992). Richard Saller notes, however, that from a legal standpoint biological ties were paramount in determining membership in the family. See Saller, "Roman Heirship Strategies in Principle and in Practice," in Kertzer and Saller, *The Family in Italy*, pp. 26–47. For a more general discussion of *patria potestas*, see Jean Gaudemet, *Droit privé romain* (Paris, 1974).

[12] On this point and on Roman conceptions of paternity and the family, see Jean Delumeau and Daniel Roche, *Histoire des pères et de la paternité* (Paris, 1990).

[13] Gaudemet, *Droit privé romain*, p. 13. See also W. K. Lacey, "Patria Potestas," in Rawson, *The Family in Ancient Rome*, pp. 121–44. The most common means of rejecting a child was to abandon it, although children could also be sold into slavery.

[14] The father's absolute will extended to matters of inheritance, enabling him to name whom he wished as universal heir. Some protection against disinheritance of children existed under the empire, by which one-quarter of the family wealth was reserved for the children.

[15] Veyne, *A History of Private Life*, 1:17. Pierre Mahillon makes a similar connection: "Comme la famille romaine se fondait sur des conceptions plus juridiques que biologiques, il se comprend que l'adoption soit entrée aussi aisément dans les moeurs," in "Evolution historique," p. 438.

[16] See the *Institutes*, tit. 11, *de adoptionibus*. This modified form of adoption was termed *adoptio minus plena*.

had been under classical Roman law.[17] Even under the reformed adoption laws, however, an adopted child retained the right to inherit *ab intestat* from the adoptive parents. In addition, the *Institutes* held that "adoptio naturam imitatur" (tit. 11, 4), which meant that those not "naturally" able to engender children, such as eunuchs, could not adopt. Justinian did, however, accord childless widows the right to adopt inasmuch as the revised model of adoption *minus plena* no longer conferred *patria potestas* on the adoptive parent.

MEDIEVAL ADOPTION LAWS

Histories of civil law in western Europe underscore the waning, and ultimate demise, of adoption in the postclassical era.[18] Jack Goody notes that, "given its dominant position in Roman law, its disappearance was remarkably abrupt,"[19] and F. Schultz concludes that the law of adoption was "drastically reformed in the post-classical period."[20] To evaluate the strength of these claims, we want to examine briefly the place of adoption in the three legal traditions that preceded and influenced early modern French customary law: Germanic law, canon law, and later medieval feudal law.

Several compilations of Germanic law contain references to an institution known as *affatomia*, which, though technically a transfer of property, appears in many respects to be tantamount to adoption.[21] In these instances the "adopted" individual (most likely an adult male) received a gift of property from an adoptive parent who retained usufruct of the property during his lifetime. The property transfers that formed the basis of such "adoptions" led the legal historian André Perraud to conclude that *affatomia* essentially comprised an *inter vivos* donation by which future rights to an inheritance were promised in exchange for filial care during the lifetime of the donor.[22] Various ceremonies accompanied this form of

[17] Justinian's reforms also reflected the Christian rejection of adoption as a means to ensure the continuity of the domestic cult.

[18] Adoption continued to be practiced in many non-Western societies such as China and Japan. On adoption in early modern China see Ann Waltner, *Getting an Heir: Adoption and the Construction of Kinship in Late Imperial China* (Honolulu, 1990).

[19] Jack Goody, *The Development of the Family and Marriage in Europe* (Cambridge, 1983), p. 72.

[20] F. Schultz, *Classical Roman Law* (Oxford, 1951), p. 148.

[21] Gabriel Lepointe suggests that adoption survived in Germanic law due a combination of the legacy of imperial Roman traditions and to their own customary law traditions. See *Droit romain et ancien droit français* (Paris, 1958), no. 312. The same author discusses the relationship between adoption and *affatomia* in *La famille dans l'ancien droit* (Paris, 1947).

[22] See André Perraud, *Etude sur le testament d'après la coutume de Bretagne* (Rennes,

adoption. If private, an act of *affatomia* would be carried out *per festucam* (with a wand), and if to guarantee dynastic succession, *per hastam* (with a lance).[23] The institution of *affatomia* appears in the Frankish Salic law code (tit. 46 from the earliest sixth-century redaction), as well as in the law code of the Ripuarian Franks from the seventh century (tit. 50).[24] The institution of *affatomia* also appears in Lombard legal codes of the seventh century.[25] In addition to the endurance of adoption practices through the institution of *affatomia*, we find more evidence of the survival of adoption in several medieval law codes, including the capitularies of Dagobert (d. 639) and later in the ninth-century capitularies of Louis-le-Debonaire and Charles the Bald.[26]

If Germanic law knew a modified version of the Roman adoption practices, legal histories routinely cite the medieval church as playing the decisive role in precipitating the disappearance of adoption in western Europe. Although it is important to note that canon law never explicitly banned adoption,[27] the new Christian view of the family deemed biological repro-

---

1921), p. 42. The employment of an *inter vivos* donation should not cause surprise in an era when wills were not yet common practice. See Lepointe, *Droit romain et ancien droit français*, p. 177.

[23] The adoption in 661–62 of Childebert (II) by his uncle Gontran, the king of Orléans and Bourgogne, was marked in this way, although André Perraud claims that this dynastic adoption was carried out *per festucam*. See Perraud, *Etude sur le testament*, p. 42n.4. On this particular adoption and on Merovingian adoptions in general, see K. A. Eckhardt, *Studia Merovingica*, Bibliotheca Rerum Historicarum, 11 (Aalen, 1975). In addition to such rituals involved in political adoptions, private adoptions were marked by passing the child *per pallium et indusium* (under the shirt and cloak), symbolizing rebirth, a pagan rite carried over to Christian practices. See Paul Viollet, *Histoire du droit civil français*, 3rd ed. (Aalen, 1966), p. 526. Pierre Mahillon outlines yet another Germanic ceremonial accompanying an adoption by which the adoptive father cut the hair or beard of his adopted son. Mahillon doubts, however, that this represented a legal act. See Mahillon, "Evolution historique," p. 440.

[24] The Ripuarian code required that the adoptive parents have no children at the time of the adoption, rendering it an adoption *in hereditate*. For a discussion of Frankish laws of adoption, see the *Laws of the Salian and Ripuarian Franks*, trans. Theodore John Rivers (New York, 1986). For the Salic law of *acfatmire*, see tit. 46, p. 92, and for the Ripuarian institution of *adfatimire* see tit. 50, nos. 48, 49, p. 190. In addition, see Joseph Lynch, *Godparents and Kinship in Early Medieval Europe* (Princeton, N.J., 1986), esp. pp. 179–81, Mahillon, "Evolution historique," and Lepointe, *Droit romain et ancien droit français*, chap. 5.

[25] Mahillon, "Evolution historique," p. 440. According to Mahillon, the Lombard code, like the Ripuarian, required that the adopting parents be childless.

[26] Henri Beaune notes that these capitularies were directly inspired by Roman law sources such as Justinian's *Novellas*. See *Introduction à l'étude historique du droit coutumier français* (Lyon, 1880), pp. 222–23. For additional examples of medieval adoption cases, see those referred to in John Boswell, *The Kindness of Strangers: The Abandonment of Children in Western Europe from Late Antiquity to the Renaissance* (New York, 1988), p. 224n.155.

[27] Pierre Mahillon notes that canon law never even formally forbade priests from adopting children. See his "Evolution historique," p. 442n.3. The sixteenth-century jurist Jean Coras discusses the issue of priests and the "adoption" of their illegitimate children in *Résolution de*

duction within marriage as the sole avenue to paternity. By the later Middle Ages this notion of the family would not only restrict reproduction to marriage, but insist further that procreation become a duty of the conjugal couple (the notion of the "conjugal debt").[28] Interestingly, however, the church's rejection of adoption as a strategy of heirship developed in a religious culture replete with adoption motifs. With the social context of Roman adoption clearly in mind,[29] early Christian authors such as Paul relied on the language of adoption to articulate a theology of salvation, which, through baptism, resulted in a divine "adoption"—thus Christians are described as "adopted children of God" (Galatians 4:5–7 and Romans 8:12–17).[30] Reflecting the common use of adoption in Roman society as a avenue of "upward social mobility," Paul's use of adoptive language reflects a hope for "adoption" by the highest patron of all—God.

Reinterpreting the language of adoption found in many early Christian texts, later Christian writers condemned the practice of adoption as a strategy of heirship. Representative of this shift is the fifth-century priest from Marseille, Salvian, who condemned adoption as unduly placing earthly concerns about heirship above devotion to the entire "family" of the church: "In this way some very wretched and most unholy people, who are not bound by the bonds of children, nevertheless provide themselves with chains to bind the unfortunate necks of their own souls."[31] An important factor behind the church's rejection of adoption derived from its pagan roots as a means of perpetuating the domestic cult. Furthermore, adoption, while helpful in articulating a theology of conversion, proved problematic when applied to Christ's own lineage. The various permuta-

---

droict contenans cent questions notables de matières bénéficiales, civiles & criminelles (Paris, 1610), pp. 324–27.

[28] The insistence that legal marriage stand as the sole determinant of paternity gave rise to the form of legitimation through subsequent marriage in canon law. On canon law and paternity, see Delumeau and Roche, *Histoire des pères et de la paternité.* On marriage philosophies in the Middle Ages, see Georges Duby, *Medieval Marriage: Two Models from Twelfth-Century France,* trans. Elborg Forster (Baltimore, 1978); idem, *The Knight, the Lady, and the Priest: The Making of Modern Marriage in Medieval France,* trans. Barbara Bray (Chicago, 1983).

[29] On the social context of Roman adoption, see Francis Lyall, "Legal Metaphors in the Epistles," *Tyndale Bulletin* 32 (1981): 79–95, where the author argues that, given Paul's own citizenship and the community of the addressees, the Roman legal system was the most influential model for the epistles. On the issue of adoption in the New Testament see also William H. Rossell, "New Testament Adoption: Graeco-Roman or Semitic?" *Journal of Biblical Literature* 71, no. 4 (1952): 233–34.

[30] Paul also mentions adoption in an eschatological context when he remarks that "We ourselves groan with ourselves waiting for the adoption, to wit, the redemption of our body," Romans 8:23.

[31] Salvian, *Ad ecclesiam,* 3.4, cited in Goody, *The Development of the Family and Marriage,* p. 101.

tions of the "adoptionist heresy," as the debates came to be known, attempted to resolve the issue of Christ's two natures by claiming that one or the other had been "adopted" by God.[32] In the early Christian centuries proponents of adoptionism held that Christ became divine only at the moment of his baptism when he was adopted by God. Adoptionism subsequently resurfaced in eighth- and ninth-century Spain when Elipandus, bishop of Toledo, and Felix of Urgel were branded heretics by their foremost opponent on this issue, Alcuin, for espousing "the false doctrine . . . that there was an adoption of the Son of God."[33] In the medieval version it was the human nature of Christ that was adopted by God. Felix of Urgel wrote:

> For if in his flesh, which he took upon himself at his very conception from the womb of the Virgin, our Redeemer is not the adoptive [Son] of the father but is the true and proper Son, then how can you avoid saying that this flesh of his was not created and made from the mass of the human race nor from the flesh of his mother, but was begotten from the essence of his Father, just as his divinity was?[34]

Without attempting to unravel the theological complexities of the adoptionist controversy, it is clear that the nature of Christ's lineage stood at the center of these debates. Who exactly was Christ's father and for which part of his two natures? Although adoptionist theology offered a creative solution to this issue, it offended the orthodox in that an act of adoption appeared to render incomplete the bond linking Christ to his divine "father."[35]

The anthropologist Jack Goody in his monumental *Development of the Family and Marriage in Europe* has proposed a broad overall framework for analyzing the rejection of adoption as a strategy of heirship by the church. Goody proposes that beginning in the fourth century, the church mounted a concerted effort to increase its fortune by capitalizing on the donations and bequests of childless families. The property-building aims

[32] On the adoptionist christologies, see Jaroslav Pelikan, *The Christian Tradition: A History of the Development of Doctrine*, vol. 1, *The Emergence of the Catholic Tradition (100–600)* (Chicago, 1971), pp. 175ff., and vol. 3, *The Growth of Medieval Theology* (Chicago, 1978), pp. 52–58. For the medieval variant, see John C. Cavadini, *The Last Christology of the West: Adoptionism in Spain and Gaul, 785–820* (Philadelphia, 1993).

[33] Cited in Pelikan, *Growth,* 3:52.

[34] Cited in ibid., 3:53.

[35] An interesting note on problems connected with Christ's lineage (and the growing importance of the physical resemblance of children to parents) from the seventeenth century is Philippe Ariès's observation that "people thought that St. Joseph resembled his adopted son, thus stressing the importance of the family bond." Philippe Ariès, *Centuries of Childhood: A Social History of Family Life,* trans. Robert Baldick (New York, 1962), p. 364.

of the church, Goody contends, led it encourage heirlessness by discouraging practices common in the Greco-Roman world, such as adoption, which created fictional heirs.[36] In discouraging practices such as adoption, Goody argues, the church articulated a notion of the family based exclusively on ties of consanguinity, a framework he claims was to hold sway and eclipse adoption well into the twentieth century. Goody notes that "if wealth was to be passed on between kin, then it should be kept within the restricted, elementary family. Fictional heirs, heirs who were not 'of the body,' 'natural' kin of the parents, were not admitted."[37] From the church's perspective, adoption conceived as a strategy of heirship focused too much attention on private, familial succession, thereby overshadowing the act of a "divine adoption" and "inherited salvation" through baptism (in addition to denying potential bequests of property to the church). Goody contends that to avoid such problems the church assimilated adoption into the realm of the spiritual, thereby divorcing it from its original function of altering property relations. Goody proposes further that godparenthood, a spiritualized form of adoptive kinship based on the rite of baptism and not on a transfer of property, replaced secular adoption: "Just as Christian baptism was held to replace the Jewish circumcision . . . so too the later institution of godparenthood replaced the Roman adoption which had been rejected in many Christian circles."[38]

The disapproving attitude toward adoption articulated by the church in late antiquity and the early Middle Ages held a long legacy in western Europe.[39] In sixteenth-century France, for instance, we find jurists and churchmen echoing the words of Salvian, depicting legal fictions such as adoption as marks of human folly and pride. The sixteenth-century jurist Charles Dumoulin viewed the creation of an heir as a manifestation of human artifice that disrupted the "natural" scheme of things, claiming that "those who wish that their name live forever after them rise up against God himself as well as against the vicissitudes of Nature, trying to imitate

---

[36] Goody, *The Development of the Family and Marriage*, p. 100.

[37] Ibid., p. 101.

[38] Ibid., pp. 74–75. Lynch, in *Godparents and Kinship*, p. 181, suggests that baptismal sponsorship eventually replaced other forms of alliance, such as *affatomia*, in Frankish society: "In the Frankish realm, sponsorship became the preferred way to integrate outsiders into the kin group or to reinforce other personal bonds."

[39] As Evelyene Patlagean has shown, the Eastern church incorporated and expanded the Roman law of adoption into its own traditions, rather than discouraging its practice as did the Western church. In the sixth century, for example, Leo VI extended the principle of adoption as an "imitation of nature" to eunuchs and "all those who have the misfortune to be without offspring." Patlagean shows further that adoption in Byzantium persisted through the Middle Ages, citing in particular a thirteenth-century Cypriot formula that spells out the rules of succession for adopted children. See Patlagean, "Christianisation et parentés rituelles: Le domaine de Byzance," *Annales: E.S.C.* 33 (1978): 625–36.

the giants."[40] Similarly the sixteenth-century jurist, Claude Henrys, in one of his courtroom pleadings, condemned parents who, having no children, wished to adopt those of others:

> Adoptions were abolished a long time ago, not only by our own traditions and customary law, but by the general law of Christianity, as St. Justin Martyr and Tertullian remarked in their Apologies. This is because adoptions run not only against the demands of nature, but also against the precept of the Gospel, which obliges fathers and mothers to oversee the education of their children and which connects the work of their salvation to this obligation, according to the word of the apostle.[41]

The fact that metaphors of adoption figured prominently in Christian theology, while the practice of secular adoption was discouraged by the church, struck many in the early modern period as puzzling, however. The eighteenth-century jurist and administrator of the Aumône générale in Lyon, which itself "adopted" legitimate orphans throughout the ancien régime, commented that the prejudice against adoption by the laity "is even more bizarre on the part of the clergy, among whom we find the tradition, image, and the effects in the cloisters themselves of affiliation and adoption . . . acts by which the clergy, after having spurned all knots of nature, create a new family."[42]

In evaluating Goody's account of the "spiritualization" of adoption in the Christian West, we must ask whether the church's articulation of a metaphorical understanding of adoption through spiritual kinship served to replace both the desire for and the practice of adoption on the level of popular practice. Goody argues that "metaphor takes over the core meaning; 'symbol' becomes the dominant reality."[43] Yet, can we not envision the coexistence of a spiritual and a secular understanding of adoption, with the spiritual serving as a model for lay people interested in adopting children? Certainly such a symbiotic relationship existed with other familial-based metaphors employed in the Christian tradition. The marriage metaphor, for instance, was grounded in social reality (particularly as conjugality grew to become the defining element of family life), which, in turn, served to strengthen its legitimizing function on the metaphorical level (Christ as the bridegroom of the church; nuns as "married" to

---

[40] "Ceux qui veulent que leur nom vive toujours après eux, s'élèvent contre Dieu mesme, et contre les changemens de la Nature, à imitation des géants." Cited in Issali, *Les plaidoyez et harangues de M. le Maistre* (Paris, 1657), p. 273.

[41] *Les oeuvres de M. Claude Henrys* (Paris, 1708), 1:978.

[42] Prost de Royer, *Dictionnaire de jurisprudence et des arrêts* (Lyon, 1783), 3:95.

[43] Goody, *The Development of the Family and Marriage*, p. 196. Goody ties this shift to the leitmotif of his study, namely the church's desire to gain more property by encouraging heirlessness.

Christ). Viewed from this perspective it is hard to imagine that adoption motifs would have sustained a role in Christian theology through the ages if their grounding in social reality had eroded entirely. Indeed, Evelyene Patlagean has shown for Byzantium that a spiritual understanding of "adoption through baptism" grew out of and continued to coexist with practices of secular adoption, both construed as instances of "voluntary kinship."[44]

What, then, may we conclude regarding Goody's contention that in the Christian West adoption was supplanted by godparenthood? For one, although godparenthood might have replaced adoption to the extent that it served as a form of alliance akin to patronage, it could never fully replace adoption as a strategy of heirship for families without children of their own (especially considering that the church discouraged other Greco-Roman methods of procuring an heir, such as divorce, the levirate marriage, and concubinage). In the end, Goody's thesis on the fate of adoption in western Europe fails to take into account the possibility that the church, even while attempting to monopolize various forms of extrafamilial alliances, ultimately constructed models on which lay people could draw according to their own needs.[45] Rather than assuming that metaphor served to replace reality, one might speculate that lay people viewed Christian adoption motifs, such as those connected with the rite of baptism, as models for their own family life. Early modern texts and liturgical ceremonies frequently employed the language of adoption and the notion of a heavenly "inheritance" to describe the effects of the rite of baptism: "The sacred water of baptism extinguishes the original sin, and ushers us into a life of grace, conferring upon us the justice, the sanctity, the adoption, the inheritance, and the fraternity of Jesus Christ."[46] How could the adoption of a child be "un-Christian," lay people might have queried, if, through baptism, we are all "adopted children of God" and "heirs" to the heavenly kingdom?

In addition to its connection with godparenthood, further evidence of

[44] See Patlagean, "Christianisation et parentés rituelles," pp. 625–36.

[45] Critics have faulted Goody for the overdetermined nature of his distinction between "family" and "church." Natalie Z. Davis points out that family and church can not be viewed as mutually exclusive entities, as most families had kin within the church. Davis's critique would seem to support the possibility that adoption could have served as a link between these two worlds, even though employed in different manners. See Davis's review of Goody's book in the *American Ethnologist* 12, no. 1 (1985): 149–51.

[46] "C'est elle qui dans l'eau sacrée du baptesme esteignant le péché originel, nous donne la vie de la grâce, et nous confère la justice, la saincteté, l'adoption, l'héritage, la fraternité de Jésus-Christ." Cited in *Les oeuvres de M. Simon d'Olive* (Lyon, 1640), p. 142. Similarly, the 1694 edition of the dictionary of the Académie française defines the adjective *adoptif/ive* as, "Qui est adopté: enfans adoptifs, fils adoptif, fille adoptive. Jésus-Christ nous a fait enfans adoptifs de son Père"; see *Dictionnaire de l'Académie françoise*, vol. 1, (Paris, 1694).

the survival of adoption in the Middle Ages appears in the discussions of medieval and early modern canon lawyers regarding impediments to marriage. Gratian, for example, discusses adoption in his account of the impediments to marriage created by spiritual kinship,[47] and later thirteenth-century decretals mention adoption as creating impediments to marriage between adopted brothers and sisters.[48] Similarly, the 1557 Synod of Paris qualified adoption as a form of legal kinship that created impediments to marriage.[49] More evidence for a tacit acceptance of adoption on the part of the church derives from the papal approval given to dynastic adoptions as late as the fourteenth century. In 1380 Jeanne I, queen of Naples, adopted Louis d'Anjou, which was confirmed by papal letters of Clement VII from Avignon. Subsequently, in 1421 and 1434, Jeanne II adopted first Alphonse V of Aragon and, after he was disinherited, Louis III d'Anjou and then René d'Anjou.[50]

ADOPTION IN FEUDAL LAW

While the prejudicial stance on adoption espoused by the church and canon lawyers contributed to the weakening of adoption traditions in western Europe, legal histories cite the system of landholding and property transferal characteristic of feudal Europe as wielding the fatal blow. The broad rights over inheritance matters accorded to local lords severely curtailed an individual's right to dispense freely of his or her property. Further, feudal law from the eleventh century on stated quite explicitly that an adopted child was barred from inheriting a fief: *adoptivus filius in*

[47] Gratian, *Decretum*, secs. 1 and 5, cap. 3, qu. 3: "A godchild could not be less closely related to its godfather than an adopted child to its adoptive father. The act of the godfather was likened to an act of adoption before God." Cited in Goody, *The Development of the Family and Marriage*, p. 75. Canon law followed Roman law on the issue of adoption as an impediment to marriage. See Justinian, *Digest*, 1.23, tit. 2, lex. 17. On the sixth-century origins of sexual impediments between spiritual kin see Lynch, *Godparents and Kinship*, esp. chap. 9.

[48] See Mahillon, "Evolution historique," p. 442.

[49] See Laurent Bouchel, *Decretorum ecclesiae gallicanae*, 8 vols. (Paris, 1621), 5: chap. 73, p. 425.

[50] See Mahillon, "Evolution historique," p. 441, and Emile G. Léonard, *Les Angevins de Naples* (Paris, 1954). On the adoption of Louis III D'Anjou, see the royal decree of 1530 in *Ordonnances des rois de France: Régne de François Ier*, 9 vols. (Paris, 1902–89), vol. 6, pt. 1, p. 66, which recognizes the "adoption et institucion d'héritier facite par Jehanne seconde . . . au prouffit de Loys d'Anjou." Finally, John Boswell's work on the history of child abandonment has revealed that traditions of adoption were kept alive within the institutions of the church itself through oblation, the practice of abandoning infants to be "adopted" by monasteries. See Boswell, *The Kindness of Strangers*.

feudum non succedit[51] (the common gloss on this law concluded that only a blood relative was capable of inheriting a fief).[52] Thus, in her review of adoption laws in western Europe, Mary Benet views feudal laws of succession as decisive in extinguishing adoption practices, remarking that in medieval society "there was no place for adoption in this strict system, where only the chief had enough freedom of action to decide on the disposition of property."[53] Paul Gonnet, however, has rejected the thesis that feudalism marked the inevitable disappearance of adoption. Gonnet notes that although adoption would stand in the way of feudal *retrait* and the escheat of *main-morte*, there would be no reason to prohibit it altogether.[54] Jacek Kochanowicz's study of peasant inheritance patterns in early modern Poland adds support to Gonnet's assessment by bringing to light many case studies of peasants who managed to adopt heirs within a feudal landholding system. Kochanowicz concludes that his evidence of adoption demonstrates that "the demographic characteristics of the family were not determined solely by the lord."[55]

How can we account for the endurance of adoption practices in the seemingly hostile legal and cultural climate of medieval Europe? The legacy of Roman law traditions, particularly influential in the southern regions of France, offers one explanation for the survival of adoption in the Middle Ages. René Aubenas, for instance, points to this legacy to explain a series of notarized contracts of adoption from the thirteenth to the sixteenth centuries from Provence.[56] Paul Gonnet also accredits the vitality

[51] *Feudorum*, bk. 2, tit. 26. For a sixteenth-century commentary on this, see André Tiraqueau, *De nobilitate et iure primigeniorum* (Paris, 1549), p. 418v.

[52] See Paul Gonnet, *L'adoption lyonnaise des orphelins légitimes (1536–1793)* (Paris, 1935), 1:16.

[53] Mary Benet, *The Politics of Adoption* (Boston, 1976), p. 39.

[54] Gonnet, *L'adoption lyonnaise,* 1:16.

[55] "The Peasant Family as an Economic Unit in the Polish Feudal Economy of the Eighteenth Century," in Richard Wall and Peter Laslett, eds., *Family Forms in Historic Europe* (Cambridge, 1983), p. 163.

[56] R. Aubenas, "L'adoption en Provence au moyen âge (XVIe–XVIe siècles)," *Revue historique de droit français et étranger* 13 (1934): 700–726. Aubenas contends, however, that adoption did begin to wane in the sixteenth century: "Si l'adoption disparaît, à la fin du XVIe siècle, comme l'ont constaté déjà d'anciens jurisconsultes, elle n'en a pas moins été une institution très vivante et pratiquée couramment pendant les siècles précédents" (p. 700). Aubenas notes that adoptions in Provence should not cause surprise as adoption was practiced in medieval Spain and Italy. For Spain see *Siete partidas* (quarta partida, tit. 16, ley. 9) and Du Fresne, *Glossarium* . . . s.v. "adoptio", who cites an Aragonese case from 1247. For Italy, see Pertile, *Storia del diritto italiano* (1894), 3:396, and Salvioli, *Manuale di storia des diritto italiano* (1899), par. 205, which outlines several thirteenth-century municipal statutes regulating adoption (for instance in Bologna), as well as several notarial formularies that contain model adoption contracts.

of adoption practices in early modern Lyon to the legacy of Roman law.[57] Medievalists have also suggested that other factors may lie behind the endurance of adoption in the post-Roman era. Andrée Courtemanche, for instance, argues that a series of notarized contracts of adoption in the town of Manosque in Haute-Provence in the fifteenth century,[58] rather than representing the last traces of Roman law traditions, depict instead a revival of adoptive traditions encouraged by the post–Black Death demographic conditions of western Europe. With fecundity on the decrease and infant mortality and migration on the rise, elderly individuals employed the *donation entre vifs* to adopt children, thereby exchanging their patrimony for security in their old age.[59]

In medieval Europe evidence of adoption can also be located in the northern regions of the country that abided by regimes of local customary law. Brittany appears as the locale of an oft-cited case of adoption in the ninth century, whereby Roiantdreh, a widow with two daughters, adopted (*adoptare* is the word used in the charter) Salomon, the duke of Brittany.[60] In eleventh-century Brittany the vicomte Eude, who, unlike Roiantdreh, had no children, adopted Count Geoffroy.[61] In 1428, again in Brittany,

---

[57] Gonnet, *L'adoption lyonnaise,* vol. 1, pt. 1. On adoption in Lyon, see also the study by Jacqueline Roubert, "L'adoption des enfants par des particuliers à Lyon sous l'ancien régime," *Société française d'histoire des hôpitaux* 36–37 (1978): 3–30.

[58] Andrée Courtemanche, "Lutter contre la solitude: Adoption et affiliation à Manosque au XVe siècle," *Médiévales* 19 (fall 1990): 37–42.

[59] On the other side of the Channel, Cicely Howell found adoptions taking place in medieval England in conjunction with *ad opus* transfers of land. Howell notes such adoptions were often undertaken by elderly couples with no heir to maintain the family land or to aid them in their old age: "It is difficult not to conceive of the phrase *ad opus*, with its overtones of guardianship, trust conveyance of land by legal arrangement rather than by hereditary right, as the most appropriate phrase *to adopt* in the abbreviated entries of the court rolls"; see Howell, *Land, Family and Inheritance in Transition: Kinsworth Harcourt, 1280–1700* (Cambridge, 1983), p. 247. Similar to Andrée Courtemanche's thesis for adoptions in Provence in these same centuries, Howell attributes the adoptive nature of these land transfers in England to post–Black Death demographic conditions. Regarding adoption in England, which, like France, did not promulgate comprehensive adoption laws until the twentieth century, F. W. Maitland notes that medieval English law recognized adoption de facto. See the early fourteenth-century case of "adoption" in *Year Books of Edward II*, ed. F. W. Maitland (London, 1904), 1:186–87.

[60] *Cart. Redon,* n. 109 (29 November 869) This case is cited by Lobineau, *Histoire de Bretagne* (Paris, 1707; repr., Paris, 1973), 1:63. and analyzed by the twentieth-century legal scholar Marcel Planiol in his *Histoire des institutions de la Bretagne* (Mayenne, 1981), 2:181–82. While Planiol notes that the charter in question reveals that adoption was still practiced in this period, he also warns of the ambiguity of the language employed: "On ne sait donc pas si on a affaire à une véritable adoption ou à une simple institution d'héritier" (p. 181).

[61] *Cart. S. Georges de Rennes,* n. 10 (ca. 1034), cited in Perraud, *Etude sur le testament,* p. 42n.6. Perraud maintains that both cases entailed a mixture of adoption and the institution

Artus of Brittany adopted Pierre, the eldest son of his brother, the duke of Brittany, an adoption that was confirmed by royal letters of Charles VII on 24 October of that same year.[62] In his fourteenth-century treatise, *La somme rurale*, Jean Bouteillier claimed that adoptions, although rare, were practiced in the north of France as well as in the southern, Roman-law regions of the country in his time.[63] And the legal historian François Olivier-Martin uncovered several notarized contracts of adoption from the Paris region dating from the fifteenth and early sixteenth centuries.[64]

Our brief review of the place of adoption in Germanic, canon, and feudal law demonstrates the difficulty of reaching any definite conclusion on the status of adoption in medieval Europe. Even so, contrary to the statements found in many histories of civil law, there is enough evidence to question the contention that adoption disappeared from the Western legal tradition in the postclassical age. As we have seen, the survival of adoption can be attributed in large part to the legacy of Roman law traditions of adoption, which during the thirteenth century most likely migrated north with the importation of the notarial regime in customary law regions.[65] The evidence has also suggested the presence of adoption in customary law regions of France in the late Middle Ages and early modern period. Perhaps further research, particularly into local notarial archives, can uncover more private adoptions, which would permit more definitive conclusions about the history of adoption laws and popular practice preceding the sixteenth century.[66]

---

of an heir: "les deux choses sont inséparables, l'institution d'héritier étant le but même de l'adoption" (p. 42). Perraud cites a passage from the same charter that highlights the relationship between the two institutions: "non habens liberos . . . in loco filii adoptavit . . . et sue hereditatis successorem reliquit" (p. 42n.7). Another charter indicates that illegitimate children could not be named as heirs: "bastardum autem habebat, sed eum heredem non posse facere"; *Cart. S. Georges de Rennes*, n. 28 (1032), in Perraud, p. 42.

[62] Under a "title of adoption," Artus gave his nephew and adopted son lands given to him in appanage by his brother, the duke. The royal letters of adoption are from 24 October 1428. On this case, see Denis Le Brun, *Traité des successions divisé en quatre livres* (Paris, 1776), 1:40.

[63] Jean Bouteillier, *La somme rurale ou le grand coustumier général de pratique civil et canon* (Paris, 1603). Bouteillier was a lieutenant of the bailliage of Tournai. According to the legal historian, Alphonse Tardif, Bouteillier's treatise drew heavily on Roman law and was even hostile to French customary law. On this point, see Tardif, *Histoire des sources de droit français, origines romaines* (Paris, 1890), p. 450.

[64] F. Olivier-Martin, *Histoire de la coutume de la prévôté et vicomté de Paris* (Paris, 1922), 1:151n.1.

[65] See René Aubenas, *Etude sur le notariat provençal au moyen âge* (Aix, 1931).

[66] René Aubenas notes that "Les actes de la pratique et, particulièrement, les registres notariaux du moyen-âge . . . constituent . . . une source à tous égards capitale pour l'étude de l'ancien droit privé depuis le XIIIe siècle," in "L'adoption en Provence," p. 701. It is

ADOPTION IN SIXTEENTH-CENTURY FRENCH
CUSTOMARY LAW

The fate of adoption in French civil law was closely bound up with the editing of the regional customary law codes that began in the sixteenth century. The campaign of legal codification was initiated by a 1454 royal ordinance of Montilz-les-Tours (art. 125), which called for the redaction in writing of all the regional customary law traditions, although the actual work of editing did not get under way until the first decades of the sixteenth century. The Custom of Paris was first edited in 1510 and was revised and expanded in 1580 through the addition of numerous parliamentary edicts.[67] Although the history of adoption in medieval law remains somewhat elusive, sixteenth-century French jurists herald their period as the critical turning point marking the "disappearance" of adoption in French law.[68] Indeed, the majority of regional custumals severely

---

certain, for example, that traditions of fostering continued through the Middle Ages, another indication that an overreliance on written law codes may not offer a complete history of adoption practices. On medieval fostering, see the discussions in Boswell, *The Kindness of Strangers*, and Lynch, *Godparents and Kinship*. Ester N. Goody's study, *Contexts of Kinship: An Essay in the Family Sociology of the Gonja of Northern Ghana* (Cambridge, 1973), offers some suggestions for differentiating between fostering (which she defines as involving no change in legal or social identity) and formal adoption.

[67] For the most important studies of customary law in France, see Jean Yver, *Egalité des héritiers et exclusion des enfants dotés: Essai de géographie coutumière* (Paris, 1966); E. Le Roy Ladurie, "Family Structures and Inheritance Customs in Sixteenth-Century France," in Jack Goody, Joan Thirsk, and E. P. Thompson, eds., *Family and Inheritance: Rural Society in Western Europe, 1200–1800* (Cambridge, 1976), pp. 37–70; Beaune, *Introduction à l'étude historique;* Henri Klimrath, "Etudes sur les coutumes," in M. L. A. Warnkoenig, ed., *Travaux sur l'histoire de droit français* 2 vols. (Paris 1843); Pierre Paillot, *La représentation successorale dans les coutumes du nord de la France: Contribution à l'étude du droit familial* (Paris, 1935); Tardif, *Histoire des sources.* For the Custom of Paris in particular, see the exhaustive study of Olivier-Martin, *Histoire de la coutume.*

[68] Highlighting the dramatic changes in adoption law over the centuries, some early modern jurists claimed that adoption had earlier been employed for succession to the French Crown, following the Salic law prescription that only males could ascend to the throne. See P. J. Brillon, *Dictionnaire des arrests ou jurisprudence universelle des parlements de France,* vol. I. (Paris, 1711), s.v. "adoption." The only reference to a continuation of adoption practice in the early modern period is a claim by the jurist Claude de Ferrière that adoption by "letters of the king" (which did not confer paternal rights or make the child a "natural heir," but simply a recipient of the family property) was still technically possible in seventeenth-century France, see de Ferrière, *Dictionnaire de droit,* s.v. "adoption." In the Saintonge, Nivernais, Bourbonnais, Berry, and the duchy of Bourgogne, a form of adoption, known as *affiliation,* was contracted by commoners through marriage and through which inheritance rights were accorded to the affiliated son and/or daughter-in-law. The custumal of Saint Jean d'Angely, for example, accorded affiliates through marriage succession to the movables

restricted the inheritance rights of adopted children, which were now extended beyond the incapacity to inherit a fief to a denial of all rights of succession. Echoing the contention of Masuer, whose fifteenth-century *Pratique judiciare* declared for the first time that "only natural children, and not adopted children, have rights of inheritance,"[69] virtually all sixteenth-century regional compilations of French customary law upheld the denial of inheritance rights to adopted children.[70]

Several custumals went so far as to proscribe adoption outright.[71] In regions where it was not expressly prohibited, customary law prevented adopted children from sharing in the normal privileges enjoyed by biological children and extended kin. Adopted children could not hold the right of the *retrait lignager*, a privilege awarded to kin by which they held the first rights to buy (or buy back) the lineage property (the *propres*),[72] or claim the *légitime*, a safeguard ensuring children a portion of the patrimony against excessive lifetime gifts and testamentary bequests by par-

---

and the immovable acquisitions (and to some of the *propres* if a special arrangement was made), even in the presence of natal children. In other regions (e.g., Bourbonnois, art. 265, and Nivernois, tit. *des gens mariés*, art. 25), however, the affiliate held no rights to the lineage property. The jurist Auroux des Pommiers explains the "marriage by exchange" as regulated by the custumal of Bourbonnois (art. 265): "Si personnes marient leurs enfans les uns avec les autres, les enfans ainsi mariez (que l'on appelle par échange) ont droit tant en meubles, héritages que conquêts, tels qu'avoient ceux au lieu desquels ils sont subrogez & en demeurent saisis & vetus & succèdent aux père, mère & ascendens en directe ligne . . . comme s'ils étoient enfans légitimes & naturels"; see *Coutumes générales et locales du pais duché de Bourbonnois* (Paris, 1732), p. 421. Also see Denis Le Brun, *Traité des successions*, vol. 1, bk. 3, chap. 3, *des adoptions et affiliations*, who considers affiliation the only surviving form of adoption in early modern France.

[69] Masuer, *La pratique judiciare* (Paris, 1606), p. 242.

[70] The sole *coutumier* that did contain regulations regarding adoptions is from Bueil in the maritime Alps. See Charles Antoine Bourdot de Richebourg, *Nouveau coutumier général*, 4 vol. (Paris, 1724), vol. 2, *Statuts et anciennes coutumes de le comté et baronnie de Bueil* (1580), chap. 9, where it is written that: "A celle fin que par cy-après les adoptions & émancipations des enfants se seront dans les terres de nostre Jurisdiction soient faictes avec la considération que se convient, & que sur icelles soit suivie la volonté de ceux qui les feront & observée la disposition de la Loy & et droict commun. Nous ordonnons que telles adoptions & émancipations seront d'oresenavant faictes & passées devant nostre Juge-Majeur d'appellation, et non ailleurs" (p. 1237). Paul Gonnet notes that before the late fifteenth century, it was never claimed by French jurists that adoption had been *abolished*. Gonnet, *L'adoption lyonnaise*, 1:20.

[71] Proscriptions: Coutume de la chatellenie de Lille, tit. vxi, art. 4; Coutume d'Audenarde, rubrique 20, art. 3.

[72] "Fils adoptif n'est reçu au retrait lignager," in Jean Imbert, *Echiridion ou recueil de droit écrit* (Paris, 1611), s.v. "fils adoptif" and Tiraqueau, *De retrait*, in *Opera Omnia du Andreae Tiraquelli*, 7 vols. (Frankfurt-am-Main, 1597), par. 1, glos. 8, n. 16. In addition, the New Custom of Paris (1580) states that "Qui n'est habile à succéder comme un bastard ne vient à retrait" (tit. 158). For a general study of the *retrait* in early modern law, see Louis Falletti, *Le retrait lignager en droit coutumier français* (Paris, 1923).

ents.[73] Unlike the birth of a biological child an adoption would not revoke any previous donations.[74] The adoptive parent would now exercise no official parental authority (*puissance paternelle*) over the child, nor would the child (if a son) hold rights of primogeniture.[75] In legal terms, then, an adopted child was rendered an incomplete member of its new family and extended kin group. The inability of adopted children to inherit through intestate succession was the most significant obstacle to adoption in the custumals.[76] The prohibition was an especially troubling one in customary law regions of France, such as Paris, where, unlike the south, the testament was not the normal means of passing on the patrimony.[77] The reformed Custom of Paris of 1580 contains no specific article on adoption; instead, the disposition of customary law appears in glosses on articles relating to other aspects of inheritance. The section of the custom that establishes the rules of the devolution of property to descendants contains the most important legal commentary on adoption in the Paris region. Thus, the leading sixteenth-century commentator on the Custom of Paris, Charles Dumoulin, excluded adopted children from the rubric "descendants" as in-

---

[73] The New Custom of Paris (1580), art. 298, defines the *légitime* as "La moitié de telle part et portion que chacun enfan eut eu en la succession desdits père, mère ou autres ascendans n'eussent disposé par donation entre vifs ou de dernière volonté, sur le tout déduits les dettes et frais funéraux."

[74] See the treatise by Etienne Papon, *Commentaire sur la loy si unquam C. de revocand. donat.* (Lyon, 1616), where he maintains that: "Ces mots s'il a enfans, doivent estre comme ils sont communément entendus d'enfans vray, naturels, & legitimes, non pas ceux qui sont legitimes seulement, comme adoptifs, spirituels ou autrement feincts, ou naturels seulement, comme tous tiennent en ceste loy si unquam" (p. 53).

[75] On *puissance paternelle*, see Gonnet, *L'adoption lyonnaise*, 1:14. On primogeniture, see Charles du Moulin, *Commentarii in consuetudines parisienses* (Paris, 1576), tit. 1, par. 8, s.v. "fils aisné," and André Tiraqueau, *De nobilitate et iure primigeniorum*, (Paris, 1549) pt. 2, quest. 84, pp. 417–19.

[76] Although I have found no supporting evidence in early modern sources, Paul Viollet maintains that adopted children were meant to inherit from their natural parents in early modern France. See Viollet, *Histoire du droit civil*, p. 530. Prohibitions on *ab intestat* succession appear in Masuer, *La pratique judiciare, tit. de probat.*, 16, num. 38; Jean Benedicti., *La somme des péchez et les remèdes d'iceux ad cap. Raynut.*, in s.v. "Et uxorem," 5, nos. 196, 197; André Tiraqueau, *Tractatus cessante causa cessat effectus. Le mort saisit le vif . . .* (Lyon, 1559), "le mort saisit le vif," pt. 2, 14, no. 2; Jean Papon, *Recueil d'arrests notables des cours souveraines de France* (Lyon, 1556), not. 1, liv. 7, tit. "de la nullité des testamens"; Imbert, *Enchiridion*, s.v. "fils adoptif," p. 103: "Fils adoptif en France ne succède point." Evidence from the Midi in the fifteenth century regarding an adopted child's right to inherit *ab intestat* from the adoptive family appears in Joh. Berberii, *Viatorium juris utriusque*, tertia pars. *de successionibus ab intestato.* Cited in Viollet, *Histoire du droit civil*, p. 530n.2.

[77] Barbara Diefendorf notes that in the Paris region the testament was employed primarily to outline funeral rites and for charitable bequests. See *Paris City Councillors in the Sixteenth Century: The Politics of Patrimony* (Princeton, N.J., 1983), p. 267. See also Perraud, *Etude sur le testament* and Jean Engelmann, *Les testaments coutumiers au XVe siècle* (reprint, Geneva, 1975).

tended in title 1, paragraph 2 of the 1580 custumal: "Nec potest legitimus tantum (= adoptivus) quicquam habere vi successionis . . . sed solum vi donationis aut contractus."[78]

It is worth pausing for a moment to inquire why sixteenth-century French customary law rejected a model of adoption that accorded inheritance rights to adopted children? One answer is that the customary law characteristic of northwestern France rejected an individual's ability to designate an heir and insisted instead on a system of intestate succession (often referred to as "forced inheritance"), by which the collateral kin inherited in the absence of biological children. Already in the thirteenth century the earliest regional custumals had fixed the principle for the devolution of property within the web of kinship: "Le mort saisit le vif, son plus prochain hoir habil à lui succéder."[79] While Parisian customary law in many ways favored the "nuclear" family unit over the extended kin (unlike the western custumals where, in the absence of children, the *propres* would ascend back to their line of origin according to the rules of *materna maternis, paterna paternis*), it insisted nonetheless that family property was not "private property" to be disposed of at will. In this context, heirs could not be named by the donor; they were named, in essence, by the structures of the lineage. Accordingly, the 1580 Custom of Paris maintains that the institution, or selection, of an heir "does not exist, that is to say that it is not necessary for the validity of a will."[80] The sixteenth-century jurist Simon Marion offered the following gloss on the maxim:

> The institution of an heir has been abolished because families are constrained by a strong line binding them to their kin, for which reason our custumals have abolished completely adoption and the institution of an heir, the princi-

---

[78] Charles Dumoulin, *Opera Omnia*, 4 vols. (Paris, 1657), vol. 1, *Coutume de Paris*, tit. 1, par. 2 and 3, 05 s.v. "descendans," No. 10, p. 248. The reading of *legitimus tantum* as "adopted child" is that of Gonnet, *L'adoption lyonnaise*, 1:19n.12. Gonnet's interpretation is supported by the fact that early modern jurists refer to adopted children as "solely legitimate," as opposed to birth children who were "natural and legitimate," or illegitimate children who were "solely natural."

[79] On the development of rules of devolution, see Paillot, *La représentation successorale*.

[80] New Custom of Paris, tit. ccxcix. Laws regarding the "institution of an heir," which, in Roman law was necessary for the validity of a will, suffered the same fate as adoption in the postclassical era. The naming of an heir was first rejected by Ranulf de Glanville in the twelfth century: "Solus Deus heredem facere potest, non homo." (*De legibus et consuetudinibus regni Angliae*, ed. George E. Woodbing [New Haven, 1932], VII, I, par. 6), and then repeated by jurists after this, including Antoine Loysel in his sixteenth-century *Institutes coutumières*, (Paris, 1846) who remarks that "institution d'héritier n'a point de lieu." The legal scholar Paul Ourliac proposes that the institution of an heir, because it attempted to "repair Nature" represented an intermediary stage between an adoption and the drawing up of a last will and testament; see Paul Ourliac and J. de Malafosse, *Histoire du droit privé* (Paris, 1968), 3:511.

ple columns of liberty in Roman law. For, in which way could civil law be more prodigal than to allow a citizen to feign a child during his lifetime and an heir after his death?[81]

In rejecting the "liberty" of the individual in matters of inheritance characteristic of Roman law, early modern jurists upheld the inheritance claims of natal children and collateral heirs, thereby defining "the family" as extending beyond the conjugal couple and its children (as Marion maintained, "families are constrained by a strong line binding them to their kin"). The oft-repeated gloss that appears in conjunction with legal commentaries on adoption explains that "Our custumals have abolished adoption and the institution of an heir in order to ensure that collateral heirs are justly favored, as our law is always concerned to pass on property to biological kin rather than to strangers."[82]

In addition to the threat it posed to the inheritance claims of collateral heirs, the Roman legal roots of adoption served ultimately to undermine its viability in the eyes of many early modern jurists. While French humanists lauded many aspects of Roman society, an evolving sense of historical distance simultaneously called into question the applicability of Roman law for their own society.[83] For instance, the sixteenth-century jurist Etienne Pasquier concluded that adoption was practiced frequently in Rome because Roman society did not abide "so strictly" by the same "law of consanguinity . . . that we follow today."[84] The sixteenth-century jurist and humanist François Hotman remarked along similar lines in his *Antitribonian* that "the nature of the Roman Republic is vastly different from the French state."[85] For Hotman, as for many of his contemporaries, Roman laws of adoption epitomized the gap separating ancient and "mod-

---

[81] "Que les particuliers sont astreints d'un lien ferme à la reconnoissance de leur parenté dont nos Coutumes ont du tout aboli l'adoption et l'institution, colonnes principales de l'effrénée liberté du Droit Romain. Car en quoi pouvoit être la loi plus prodigue qu'en donnant puissance à son citoyen de se feindre un enfant durant sa vie, & un héritier après sa mort?" Simon Marion, *Plaidoyez . . . avec les arrests donnez sur iceux* (Paris, 1594), p. 237.

[82] See François Jamet de la Guessière, *Journal des principales audiences du Parlement (1657–1666)*, (Paris, 1678), 2:905.

[83] On the battle between French customary law and Roman law in these centuries, see Vincenzo Piano Mortari, *Diritto romano e diritto nazionale in Francia nel secolo XVI* (Milan, 1962); René Filhol, *Le premier Président Christofle de Thou et la réformation des coutumes* (Paris, 1937). On the relationship between law and the evolution of historical thinking in the Renaissance, see Donald R. Kelley, *Foundations of Historical Scholarship: Language, Law and History in the French Renaissance* (New York, 1970).

[84] Etienne Pasquier, *Des recherches de la France* (Paris, 1581), p. 189v.

[85] "L'estat de la République romaine est fort différent de celuy de France," in François Hotman, *Antitribonian ou discours d'un grand et renommé jurisconsulte de nostre temps sur l'estude des loix* (Paris, 1603), reprinted in *Images et témoins de l'âge classique*, vol. 9 (Paris, 1980), p. 12.

ern" social and familial values. Hotman pointed out that the frequency of adoption in Rome grew out of the unmitigated power of fathers over the fate of their children (who could be killed at birth, sold into slavery, or given away in adoption). Hotman also connected the frequency of adoption practices in antiquity with the granting to those who "detested the state of marriage" the right to name heirs nonetheless.[86] In the context of a mounting Gallicanism in legal theory, then, adoption was rejected by many jurists as an alien Roman method of constructing a family, which was more concerned with legal or "fictive" ties than with blood ties.

ADOPTION IN THE COURTS: TWO CASES BEFORE THE PARLEMENT OF PARIS

The customary law restrictions on the inheritance capabilities of adopted children were upheld in two cases cited regularly in sixteenth- and seventeenth-century juridical commentaries. The first case, brought before the Parlement of Paris in 1582, involves the "adoption" of an orphaned nephew as a son and universal heir by the marquis d'Allègre.[87] The second case entails a dispute over the succession of a son adopted by a naturalized French subject in Touraine. Let us begin with d'Allegre. In 1576 Yves III, the marquis d'Allègre, having no children of his own and finding himself (after one of the religious wars) a captive of the duke of Casimir in Lorraine, named his nephew and ward, Yves, as his universal heir.[88] Ailing and concerned about the effects of captivity on his health, the marquis arranged for his nephew and newly named universal heir to take his place in captivity. The duke of Casimir was not content, however, to accept a universal heir as a hostage and demanded instead a "real son." The marquis hoped to solve his own predicament and appease the duke at

---

[86] Hotman, *Antitribonian* p. 26. Those jurists who supported a revival of adoption laws in early modern France, such as Jean Bodin, supported them in the context of a return to the broad powers of "life and death" inherent in the *patria potestas* wielded by Roman heads of households. See *Les six livres de la république* (Paris, 1583), bk. 1, chap. 4, "De la puissance paternelle, & s'il est bon d'en user comme les anciens Rommains".

[87] The modern spelling of the family name is Alègre. Yves IV was the orphaned son of Yves III's brother, Antoine d'Allègre, sieur de Meilhard.

[88] The inheritance included six thousand livres de rente in addition to a château and land in Normandy. The relevant section of the text reads as follows: "En considération du périlleux voyage qu'il est près de faire au pays d'Allemagne, il institue son héritier universel en tous ses biens meubles et immeubles, M. de Meilhaud, son nepvue." From the courtroom pleading of M. Simon Marion, lawyer at the Parlement of Paris, of 26 June 1582 in favor of Yves IV d'Allègre, in the *Les plaidoyers de M. Simon Marion* (Paris, 1609), p. 378. Yves III was also tutor to his niece, Isabelle, to whom he donated one thousand livres.

the same time by formally adopting his nephew. The adoption was carried out in 1576 and the following notarized document sent to the duke as reassurance:

> We, Yves, the marquis d'Allègre, viscount of Maisy, baron of Blainville, and royal chevalier . . . at the present time, as commanded by the king, a hostage of the duke Jean Casimir, the count Palantine of the Rhine and duke of Bavaria . . . hereby substitute Yves d'Allègre, my adopted son and my heir.[89]

The adoption might have satisfied the duke of Casimir,[90] but it did not sit well with other members of the d'Allègre family, notably with the brother, Christophe, seigneur of St. Just, who was hoping to inherit from the otherwise childless marquis d'Allègre. The plot thickened when, in 1577, just after Yves had gone to Germany to take the place of his captive uncle and adoptive father, the latter was murdered in France and Yves fell under the guardianship of the same seigneur of St. Just. In 1581, when the king of France finally sent the ransom money to Germany, the young Millaut was freed and came back to Normandy to claim his inheritance of the d'Allègre title and estate due to his status as adopted son. Yves IV returned only to find that his uncle had claimed the inheritance and assumed the title of marquis. An additional twist in the story was added in 1580 after Christophe had died on a trip to Rome, which he allegedly took to receive a papal pardon for his heretical ways.[91] A court battle thus ensued between Yves IV and the widow of Christophe over the issue of Yves's status as adopted son of his uncle. Our account of the trial comes from the pleading of the lawyer at the Parlement of Paris, Simon Marion, who defended Yves's claims to the patrimony against the rival claims of Christophe's widow and children.[92]

Not surprisingly, considering the disposition of customary law toward adoption, Marion opted to defend Yves IV's claim to his uncle's inheritance through the institution of guardianship (*tutelle*), which his uncle

---

[89] "Nous, Yves, Marquis d'Allègre, vicomte de Maisy, baron de Blainville, chevalier de l'ordre du Roy . . . estant, de présent, par le commandement du Roy, pour ostage auprès de M. le Duc Jean-Casimir, compte palatin du Rhin, duc de Bavière, selon le traité faict . . . laissant et substituant Yves d'Allègre, *mon fils adoptif et héritier*." BN, Ms. fr. 15.904, fol. 92, cited in Pierre de Vaissière, *Une famille les d'Alègre* (Paris, 1914), p. 123.

[90] Many sixteenth-century French jurists, while claiming that France no longer knew the law of adoption, maintained that it was still practiced "in the Roman style" in Lorraine. See, for example, Nicolle de Lescut, *Commentaire des Institutes de Justinien* (Paris, 1543), tit. 11 *de adoptionibus*.

[91] Christophe had been a Protestant at the beginning of the religious wars, but then seems to have reconverted to Catholicism by 1563, only to change sides again in 1576. These religious differences were surely influential in Yves III's decision to name his nephew rather than his brother his universal heir. See Vaissière, *Une famille*, pp. 160–61.

[92] The pleading of the lawyer for the widow of Christophe de St. Just was unavailable.

exercised over him, rather than on the basis of the adoption.[93] Marion concluded, in fact, that Yves III had abused his status of guardian of Yves IV by adopting him in order to free himself from captivity. The final decision in the case, related by the seventeenth-century jurist Denis Le Brun, was that the Grand Council allowed the marquis d'Allègre [Yves IV] to maintain the title of marquis, and to keep the property that his uncle could have given to him through a lifetime gift.[94] Le Brun relates that the court announced that "in customary law areas [of France] adoption has no other legal power than a *donation entre vifs*, and therefore remains subject to any local restrictions on donations."[95] The court maintained, then, that adoption did not constitute a distinct legal transaction that created ties of filiation and conferred inheritance rights. What this meant most importantly was that Yves IV's claims to any of Yves III's estate had to follow the regional customary law prescriptions for *inter vivos* donations.[96]

The second case, also before the Parlement of Paris, involves the adoption of Augustin Drouet by a naturalized Frenchman, Augustin de Champagnon,[97] from Touraine. In order to avoid having his property escheat to the Crown, as would be the case if he did not have children born in France (*enfants regnicoles*),[98] de Champagnon adopted Drouet with the charge of

[93] Marion noted that the transaction could not be considered an adoption "parce qu'il n'en a la solemnité; joinct que par nos moeurs elle n'est receüe"; see *Les Plaidoyez de M. Simon Marion*, p. 388. In addition, the lawyer for widow of Christophe, Sr. de St. Just, pointed out that Yves IV had received donations at the same time that he was the presumptive heir, a double status forbidden not only in the custom of Normandy but in almost all of the sixteenth-century custumals. On this point, see Vaissière, *Une famille*, p. 200.

[94] In Normandy only one-third of the immovable property could be alienated to a stranger or to the presumptive heir.

[95] "Se contenta de maintenir le sieur marquis d'Allègre dans le marquisat d'Allègre, & les autres biens dont le sieur marquis d'Allègre oncle avoit pu disposer entre vifs, & jugea par là que l'adoption en pays coutumier, n'a force que de donation entre vifs; & qu'elle demeure sujette aux réserves coutumières." Le Brun, *Traité des successions*, 1:43.

[96] For a review of the restrictions in customary law on alienating immovable property through the *inter vivos* donation, see Jean Brissaud, *A History of French Private Law*, trans. Rapelje Howell (Boston, 1912), pp. 426–49, 703–15.

[97] The spelling alternates in the printed legal sources between de Champagnon and de Champagne.

[98] See Jean Papon, *Recueil d'arrests notables* (Lyon, 1616), bk. 5, tit. 2, art. 4, who maintains that "Le Roy a droit de se faire saisir & mettre en sa main biens vacans, et la succession d'un estranger n'ayant lettres de naturalité et celles des bastards qui sont morts sans enfans" (p. 241). Papon also notes that "Toutesfois quant aux bastards, ils peuvent tester," while non-naturalized foreigners had to dispose of their goods though "donation ou contract entre vifs . . . pourveu que ce ne soit en fraude du Fisque" (p. 242). Jean Bacquet also comments on this law of escheat to the king: "Le Roy succédant à l'estranger naturalisé, qui n'a laissé aucuns héritiers Regnicoles, ne pourra débattre cette donation, ou legs universel, non plus le Seigneur haut-Justicier ne la pourroit impugner succédant à un Francois, à titre de biens vagrans. Parce que la coustume prohibant ou restraignant la disposition des

taking his name and inheriting his property, including some land in the bailiwick of Touraine. De Champagnon died in 1542, followed not long after by Drouet, and a good while later a royal attorney seized the goods of the deceased Drouet from his widow. The attorney justified the seizure by declaring the donation invalid according to article 233 of the reformed custumal of Touraine, which restricts the amount of a donation to one-third of the lineage property (the *propres*), which could be given "only for life" whereas the movables could be donated in perpetuity.[99] The case was heard before the Parlement of Paris in appeal against the actions of the royal attorney.[100]

The final sentence of the court (of 8 June 1576) adjudged the donation to the widow of Drouet, including "the movables and the immovable acquisitions."[101] Similar to the court's decision in the d'Allègre case, however, Drouet (or by this time his widow) did not receive the property due to the status of adopted son. The jurist Bacquet, paraphrasing the Parlement's decision, noted that "the adoption undertaken by Champagne was in no way taken into account: in customary law regions of France, we do not accept the institution of adoption, and adopted children cannot inherit. For this reason donations or testamentary provisions must be used [in order to pass on property to them], as Champagne did."[102] In both cases, then, the Parlement of Paris maintained that adoption held no distinct legal validity in the eyes of the law. Just as in the d'Allègre case, the court's ruling upheld the customary law insistence that adoption did not confer legal ties of filiation complete with inheritance rights.

---

héritages propres, ou aquests . . . afin de conserver les héritages anciens de famille & qui de nouvel ont esté acquis y demeurent: non pas en faveur d'un héritier étranger anormal & irregulier . . . et ainsi a esté jugée pour les biens d'Augustin de Champagne, estranger naturalisé." See Jean Bacquet, *Les oeuvres* (Paris, 1688), p. 709.

99 Ibid.

100 It seems that royal attorneys made a habit of seizing illegally the property of naturalized subjects, who did indeed have children born in France. See the three sixteenth-century court cases brought against the agents of the Crown in Papon, *Recueil d'arrests notables*, bk. 5, tit. 2, art. 4, p. 242.

101 Bacquet, *Les oeuvres*, p. 709. Brillon's commentary reads "Un étranger ayant obtenu lettres de naturalité, pourvu qu'il eut enfans regnicoles, adopta un de son nom, à qui la succession fut déferré par Arrêt du Parlement de Paris de 8 juin 1576 contre le Procureur du Roy" (*Dictionnaire*, 1:56). Jean Papon's summary of the case reads: "Un estranger nommé Champagnon ayant obtenu lettres de naturalité, pourveu qu'il eust enfans regnicoles. Il advient qu'il adopta un de son nom lequel voulant succéder, il est empesché par le Procureur du Roy par arrest le 8 juin 1576. La succession a esté adjugée aud. adoptif." See *Recueil d'arrests notables*, bk. 5, tit. 2, art. 4, p. 243.

102 "L'adoption faite par de Champagne n'estoit aucunement considérable: parce qu'au Pays Coutumier de France les adoptions ne sont receües, et les enfants adoptez ne succedént point. Tellement qu'il est besoin leur faire donations ou legs testamentaires, comme avoit fait ledit Champagne." Bacquet, *Les oeuvres*, p. 709.

What demands further explanation in both the d'Allègre and de Champagnon cases is not so much that childless individuals continued to turn to adoption in order to gain an heir (as we will see much more of this in subsequent chapters), but that the notaries in both cases consented to drawing up contracts of adoption in the face of decisions of customary law and of the higher courts to deny natural rights of succession to adopted children. There are two ways to begin unraveling this enigma. On the one hand, recent studies of notarial practice in early modern France have shown that notaries were quite capable of consciously ignoring the prescriptions of the revised customary law codes.[103] In the Parisian case, however, although incapacitated, adoption was never expressly prohibited by the customary law. Viewed in this light, we can conclude that the notaries were not transgressing Parisian customary law on adoption, but rather following its dictate that, while adopted children could not inherit through intestate succession, they could receive property through alternative means. The cases of d'Allègre and Champagnon also indicate that adoption was not considered to have disappeared completely from popular practice at the end of the sixteenth century. It is significant in this regard that in the d'Allègre case the Parlement did not reject Yves's claim to his uncle's inheritance by citing the fact that adoption "no longer existed." The court's pronouncement upheld the rejection of a specific model of adoption that accorded "natural" inheritance rights to an adopted child (and here I think we must understand the phrase regarding the law of adoption not being received in *customary* law regions as referring specifically to the *Roman* model of adoption). In other words, the Parlement did not maintain that there were no adopted children in its jurisdiction, but that, if there were, they would not be accorded full rights of inheritance. Although it is certainly true that the judges might have assumed that adoption had ceased to be practiced due to the limitations placed on adoption by customary law, both court cases reveal that from the vantage point of popular practice adoption continued to be employed as a means to transmit property to an adopted heir.[104]

[103] On this point, see, for example, Jean Hillaire, "Coutumes redigées et gens du champs (Angoumois, Aunis, Saintonge)," *Revue historique de droit français et étranger* 4 (1987): 545–73. The major study on notaries in ancien régime France is Jean-Paul Poisson, *Notaires et société: Travaux d'histoire et de sociologie notariales*, vol. 1 (Paris, 1985); vol. 2 (Paris, 1990). See also B. Vogler, ed., *Les actes notariés, sources de l'histoire sociale XVIe–XIXe siècles* (Strasbourg, 1979); Jean Gaston, *La communauté des notaires de Bourdeaux (1520–1791)* (Toulouse, 1990); *Notaires, notariat et société sous l'ancien régime: Etudes réunies et présentées par Jean L. Lafont* (Toulouse, 1990). A helpful guide to the notarial archives in Paris is presented in *Le Gnommon: Revue internationale d'histoire du notariat*, special issue, "Archives Notariales et Minutier Central Parisien," 18 (May 1980).

[104] From the standpoint of popular practice, it is significant that, despite the decision of the court not to judge the case on the basis of adoption, first in Allègre's 1576 letter to the duke Casimir and later in a copy of the Allègre family tree from the seventeenth century, Yves

For the most part, however, histories of adoption have not discriminated between a study of adoption laws and a history of adoption practices; rather, the literature has assumed that the law's denial of inheritance rights to adopted children dictated the end of adoption practices in early modern France. Yet, as we have seen in the court cases outlined here, the Parlement of Paris itself suggested a means of solving the inheritance problem by associating adoption with *inter vivos* donations and testamentary legacies.[105] Sixteenth-century jurists took the same twofold approach to the issue of adoption, upholding the customary law restrictions on inheritance in their legal commentaries, while maintaining at the same time that property could be legitimately passed on to adopted children through donations and testamentary legacies. Following this principle, the sixteenth-century jurist Charles Dumoulin maintained that "adopted children have no rights of succession, and therefore can only receive property through donations made in a contract."[106] Similarly, the jurist Pierre Guénois commented that "adoption holds no validity in France, unless there is an explicit and legal contract."[107] Later seventeenth-century jurists continued to interpret the decisions of the Parlement of Paris regarding adoption as sanctioning the use of donations and testamentary legacies to transmit property to adopted children. The seventeenth-century jurist Brillon, in his review of Roman laws of adoption, concluded that "we do not accept the [Roman] law of adoption in France, and adopted children cannot inherit; thus the only way to favor them is through testamentary legacies."[108] In Brillon's statement, as in all of the juridical commentaries on

---

is named as the marquis's "fils adoptif." See Titres Généalogiques, dossier II, "Allègre (d')" from Auvergne, n.d. (most likely late seventeenth century), AN, M260.

[105] The Custom of Paris, compared to many other custumals, allowed a great deal of freedom regarding *inter vivos* donations. Commenting on tit. 13, art. 272 of the custom, the jurist Fortin notes that "Il est loisible à toute personne âgée de vingt-cinq ans accomplis & saine d'entendement, donner & disposer par donation & disposition entre-vifs, de tous les meubles & héritages, propres, acquests & conquests, à personne capable"; see M. G. Fortin, *La coustume de Paris conférée avec les autres coustumes de France* (Paris, 1666), p. 320. It should be noted that the irrevocability of lifetime gifts did not apply in cases of ingratitude or the subsequent birth of children. If the donor had children, the amount of the donations was restricted even further by the *légitime*, which guaranteed the lawful heirs a certain amount of the lineage property. On the development of laws governing lifetime gifts, see Jean Brissaud, *A History of French Private Law*, pp. 703–15.

[106] "Nec potest legitimus tantem (=adoptivus) quicquam habere vi successionis, *sed solum vi donationis aut contractus,*" Dumoulin, *Opera Omnia* vol. 1, Custom of Paris, tit. 1, par. 2 and 3.

[107] "Adoption n'a point de lieu en France *s'il n'y a contrat exprès et permis.*" Jean Bacquet, *Conférence des coustumes de France* (Paris, 1596), 1:9v.

[108] "En France le droit d'adoption n'est pas reçu, et les enfans adoptez ne succèdent point; en sorte que tout l'avantage qu'on leur peut faire, doit être, *per modum legati.*" Brillon, *Dictionnaire,* (Paris, 1711), 1:56, s.v. "adoption".

adoption, a very specific aspect of the "law of adoption" is rejected: the right of adopted children to inherit *ab intestat* under the same terms as biological children. In conformity with the stance of the Custom of Paris and the judgments of the Parlement of Paris, sixteenth- and seventeenth-century jurists never state that Parisian customary law prohibited the act of adopting a child itself (independent, that is, of the issue of heirship).

In the end, it seems most fruitful to follow the lead of the early modern jurists themselves and to approach the study of laws of adoption by taking into account two avenues of historical development: one line of inquiry taking into account the contraction of liberal laws of adoption since the classical Roman era, culminating in the denial of "full and natural" inheritance rights for adoptees in the newly codified sixteenth-century customary law codes, and the other line of inquiry investigating the flexibility of the law, which, as we have seen, accepted the transmission of property to adopted children through donations and testaments. In this regard we must entertain the possibility that early modern civil law could simultaneously assert two seemingly contradictory positions on adoption: "French law does not know adoption," and "adopted children can receive property through donations and testaments." Once it is understood that these two positions are not, in fact, contradictory, evidence of continued adoption *practices* in early modern France, albeit within restricted legal parameters, becomes less of a mystery. Adopted children could not inherit *ab intestat* as "natural" heirs, but they could, and did, continue to receive property through other channels, such as the *donation entre vifs*.

ADOPTION AND FAMILY LAW IN SIXTEENTH-CENTURY FRANCE

It is worthwhile pausing to ask what broader message about family life was being conveyed through the customary law prohibitions against adopted children standing as full heirs? In early modern France, inheritance rules, although often circumvented on the level of practice, formed one of the principle means by which individuals understood and affirmed their identity within the household community and within the broader kinship group.[109] The moment of inheritance, whether through a dowry, intestate succession, a testament, or lifetime gifts, represented an affirmation of fa-

---

[109] The anthropologist Jack Goody emphasizes that in any society the rules of the devolution of property are related to the "social and cultural patterns, to the institutions and *mentalités*, to the formal and informal structures of the people who practise (or are forced to practise) particular ways of passing down rights over material objects"; see Jack Goody, Joan Thirsk, and E. P. Thompson, eds., *Family and Inheritance: Rural Society in Western Europe, 1200–1800* (Cambridge, 1976), p. 1.

milial relationships as well as a time of potential conflict. Should rules of primogeniture be followed?[110] How should younger sons and daughters partake in the patrimony? What claims did collateral heirs have? What were the inheritance rights of illegitimate children? These issues were answered in two ways: on the one hand, by a body of civil and criminal law (comprising customary law, royal edicts, and parliamentary decisions) regulating matters of inheritance, and, on the other hand, by the needs and desires of individual families, whose decisions in these matters often challenged the official legal guidelines.[111] Whatever solution was achieved, inheritance decisions determined more than the nature and size of an individual's share of the family wealth; they determined to a large extent an individual's status in society.

To be fully comprehended, the legal posture toward adoption and inheritance must be considered in the broader context of developments in other areas of "family law." Sixteenth-century family law was altered in many respects, affecting such domestic matters as reproduction, marriage, and inheritance. Due in part to demands from families themselves, and in part to the desires of the Crown, changes in civil law kept pace with, and at the same time promoted, the construction of a more streamlined and "well-ordered" family group. A common feature of the family law in this period was a concern to ensure that reproduction remain confined to the context of legal marriage. For instance, the edict "Against clandestine pregnancy and birth," issued in 1556 under Henri II, attempted to curb illegitimate births by bringing the workings of childbirth under the watchful eye of the public authorities. Reflecting a general movement in the sixteenth century to regulate sexual conduct more closely, the edict charged that many stillborn births were, in fact, disguised cases of infanticide undertaken by women in order to protect "their honor" from the shame of giving birth to an illegitimate child. Evidencing a concern that the "secretive" circumstances of childbirth served to encourage infanticide under the guise of stillbirth, the edict held that:

> Any woman who hides or covers up her pregnancy or the act of giving birth, and who does not declare them or have witnesses to testify the state of the child at the time of birth, will be found to have murdered her child and will be punished with death.[112]

[110] On the issue of primogeniture, see Joan Thirsk, "The European Debate on Customs of Inheritance, 1500–1700," in Jack Goody et al., *Family and Inheritance*, pp. 177–91.

[111] See Gregory Hanlon and Elsbeth Carruthers, "Wills, Inheritance and the Moral Order in 17th-Century Agenais," *Journal of Family History* 15, no. 2 (1990): 149–61, which discusses discrepancies between popular practice and customary law.

[112] For the full text of the edict, see Isambert, *Recueil général des anciennes lois depuis l'an 420 jusqu'à la Révolution de 1789*, 29 vols. (Paris, 1821–33), 13:471–73.

In an attempt to enforce the mandates of the edict, pregnant women were required to make public declarations (the *déclarations de la grossesse*) of their pregnant state at local civil registries or with their mistresses. This same edict also condemned the practice of "faking" a birth in order to bring a child secretly into the family fold (a crime known as the *supposition d'enfant*), which, like illegitimate births, in essence provided an alternative route to reproduction outside of marriage.[113]

In terms of safeguarding the inheritance claims of biological kin, a 1560 edict "On second marriages" curtailed a widow's management of her property with the aim of preventing her from "ruining her children's future" through lavish donations of property to a second husband.[114] The edict hoped to avoid the "desolation of good families [that] consequently, diminish the strength of the public estate," by prohibiting widows from donating any of the *propres*, the movable property or the acquisitions to their second husbands.[115] The safeguarding of biological heirs was also central to the royal ordinance of 1539, which revised the rules regarding donations from the patrimony. This edict required that donations be contracted in front of a notary (with both parties present), and mandated that such transactions be registered within four months in the royal courts.[116] This act of registration (*insinuation*), which French law inherited from Roman law, served to produce a public record of property transactions that offered the heirs a means of keeping track of the family property. François Oliver-Martin concludes that "without a doubt this ordinance [of 1539] had a financial end in mind, but it also served to restrict donations of the immovable property, thereby safeguarding the rights of the natural heirs."[117] It was not until the sixteenth century, in fact, that a comprehensive philosophy of donations from the property emerged in Parisian customary law. Whereas medieval law codes and the old Custom of Paris contained only a few articles regulating donations from the patrimony,[118]

---

[113] On this edict and the declarations, see Sarah Hanley, "Engendering the State: Family Formation and State Building in Early Modern France," *French Historical Studies* 16, no. 1 (1989): 11, and M. C. Phan, "Les déclarations de la grossesse en France (XVIe–XVIIIe): Essai institutionel," *Revue d'histoire moderne et contemporaine* 22 (1975):61–88.

[114] For the full text of the edict, see Isambert, *Recueil général des anciennes lois françaises*, 14:36–37. The edict made explicit that the "infirmity" of the female sex necessitated such regulation.

[115] Barbara Diefendorf notes that the amount of donation to a second husband was meant to be no larger than the smallest amount given to any of the widow's children or grandchildren. See her "Widowhood and Remarriage in Sixteenth-Century Paris," *Journal of Family History* 7 (winter 1982): 379–95.

[116] For the full text of the *Ordonnance sur le fait de la justice* of 1539, see Isambert, *Recueil général des anciennes lois*, 12:600–640.

[117] Olivier-Martin, *Histoire de la coutume*, 1:215; 2: chap. 8: "Donations et Testaments."

[118] Olivier-Martin, (ibid., 2:479–85) suggests that early juridical theories of donations

the reformed Parisian custumal of 1580 included a section devoted exclusively to regulating gifts from the patrimony.[119]

Although we cannot point to a particular royal edict or parliamentary decision, the process of legitimation of children born out of wedlock was changing as it, too, aimed to restrict full membership in the family unit (including inheritance rights) to those born in legal marriage. Whereas inheritance claims of illegitimate children had been tolerated in ancient and early medieval law codes, these rights were progressively eroded in the early modern period.[120] As we have seen, in classical Roman society a child's place in the family group was determined less by the criterion of birth to legally married parents than by an act of recognition on the part of the head of the household.[121] Despite repeated admonitions from the Catholic Church, adoption continued through the Middle Ages to serve as a means for fathers to legitimate their illegitimate offspring. A case from 1372 demonstrates this process of legitimation through an adoption of sorts:

> On Saturday 19 June 1372, Jehans le Sauvage from Wanebrecies, a resident of Lille, presented himself in the chambers of the echevins along with three of his illegitimate children [enfans bastars]. The eldest, whom he had with Marie Bonduelle, named Jehan le Sauvage is nineteen years old or thereabouts. Jehans le Sauvage, as a bourgeois of Lille, adopts [avoa] these three children and takes them for his children. On the day that they were born they [the parents] were not bound by any tie or by marriage . . . and these three children will pass from today as children of a bourgeois.[122]

By the sixteenth century the process of legitimation had severed its ties to adoption and had evolved into a separate act carried out under greater public scrutiny. Rather than being able to bring illegitimate children into the family fold discreetly through adoption, as Jehans le Sauvage had done, fathers were now compelled either to marry the children's mother (the traditional means of legitimation in canon law), or to request royal letters of legitimation, a process that had begun to replace papal legitima-

---

grew out of a need to ensure that foreigners, barred from drawing up wills, had a means to dispense of their property.

[119] New Custom of Paris (1580), tit. "De donations et don mutuel."

[120] See Robert Génestal, *Histoire de la légitimation des enfants naturels en droit canonique* (Paris, 1905).

[121] See Ourliac and Malafosse, *Histoire du droit privé*, vol. 3.

[122] Case cited in full in "Documents inédits . . . des usages et des moeurs aux Xive et Xve siècles," *Annuaire bulletin de la société de l'histoire de la France* 2 (1864): 80–115 (case appears on p. 91). A. Lefebvre-Teillard found a similar model of "adoption" of illegitimate children through notarized contracts by kin in late medieval France. See "L'enfant naturel dans l'ancien droit français," *Recueils de la société Jean Bodin* 36, no. 2 (Brussels, 1976): 265n.5.

tions in the fourteenth century.[123] Legitimation by letters of the king or by subsequent marriage pleased not only lay and ecclesiastical officials, for whom the legally sanctioned family group assured the foundation of a well-ordered society, but the "legitimate" heirs as well, who now felt more secure against the threat of displacement by clandestinely legitimated rivals. In many respects, then, the formalization of the process of legitimation replaced one of the traditional functions served by adoption in earlier centuries.[124]

What connections can be established between the changes in sixteenth-century family law regarding matters of reproduction, marriage, and inheritance and the law's rejection of adoption? On a broad interpretive level we can propose a correlation between the changes in various areas of family law, including adoption, and new notions regarding the ordering of the domestic sphere based on the dual criteria of blood and marriage. In this regard, because adoption entailed the transfer of children between different sets of parents, the practice was perceived as a threat to the belief in the inviolability of the blood ties linking parents and children. The seventeenth-century jurist Simon d'Olive, for one, feared that the rupturing of the biological bonds linking parents and children would undermine the harmony and integrity of the entire "body social":

> Children are the communal products of conjugal love, the common concern of a marriage, and the common hope of the household: through the act of birth Nature attaches them to their parents, just as limbs are attached to the body.[125]

Thus, to many in the sixteenth and seventeenth centuries the adoption of a non-natal child into the family group was equally as "unnatural" as the crimes of infanticide and the *supposition d'enfant* (both condemned in the edict of 1556), inasmuch as the act entailed the rupturing of the ties of flesh and blood binding parents and children.[126] Moreover, like the crime

---

[123] On the origin of royal legitimation see Olivier-Martin, *Histoire de la coutume*, 2:396. Only a royal legitimation, and not subsequent marriage, could legitimate incestuous and adulterine children. There was a third means of legitimation through papal letters, but the parlements and customary law held that the pope could not legitimate individuals in France, but only had the power to dispense letters that allowed them entry into the orders and gave them rights to benefices. Thus papal legitimation held no power where "family law" was concerned. See Renée Barbarin, *La condition juridique du bâtard d'après la jurisprudence du Parlement de Paris* (Mayenne, 1960), p. 56n.1.

[124] Pierre Mahillon makes precisely this point in "Evolution historique," p. 446n.3.

[125] *Les oeuvres de M. Simon d'Olive*, 1:147.

[126] The literary historian of the Renaissance Marc Shell notes that "bastards and changelings indicate the indeterminability of biological parenthood; they suggest its fictional aspects." We could easily add adopted children to his list inasmuch as they also challenged the notion that marital and biological ties were the sole avenues to the creation of a family. See

of faking a birth and conceiving out of wedlock, adoption threatened the position of legal marriage as the cornerstone of the family unit by offering an alternative method of "reproduction."

The judgment that adoption undermines the ordering of the domestic sphere is, of course, not an inevitable one. If the civil law mandates a transfer of identity and property claims from the natal family to the adoptive family (as was the case in classical Roman law or in many twentieth-century societies), adoption serves to ratify the traditional structures of the nuclear family unit. Alternately, if a society accepts the existence of multiple sets of parents, as do the cultures of present-day Oceania and West Africa, among many others, the movement of children between different sets of parents does not pose a threat to the integrity of domestic boundaries. As we have seen, however, early modern French law refused to categorize the ties binding adoptive parents and children as forming complete and legitimate bonds of filiation. Furthermore, the ties binding parents to their biological children were held to be inviolable (even though in practice, as we have seen, children were frequently raised by several sets of surrogate parents). In such a cultural context, adoption represented an institution that compromised the structure of the domestic realm.

The perception of adoption as a potentially destabalizing factor for the family unit is better understood when we recall that adoption was employed most frequently in metaphorical terms to represent nonhierarchical communities, most often religious communities, shaped by the ideal of "universal siblinghood" and the egalitarian vision of all Christians as "adopted children of God." As is well known, the model of a hierarchical and patriarchal family became an increasingly popular metaphor for the social order in the sixteenth and seventeenth centuries (with the power of the father paralleling the power of the king). A royal decree of 1639 exemplifies the connection frequently made between the nature of the ties binding children to their parents with those binding subjects to their king: "The natural reverence that children hold for their parents represents the link to the legitimate obedience that subjects should maintain toward their sovereign." For the sixteenth-century Catholic theologian, Jean Benedicti, the parent-child relationship was emblematic of *all* social and political alliances. Benedicti commented that the fourth commandment teaches not only the deference "that children must show to their fathers and mothers . . . but also which the wife must show to her husband, servants

---

Marc Shell, *The End of Kinship: "Measure for Measure," Incest and the Ideal of Universal Siblinghood* (Stanford, Calif., 1988), p. 4. For changelings and inheritance issues in popular literature, see Stith Thompson, *Motif Index of Folk-Literature*, 6 vols. (Bloomington, Ind., 1955–58), under "Substituted Children" (K1920), "Deception by Substitution of Children" (K1847), and "Substitution of Children to Gain Inheritance" (K1847.1).

to their masters, and subjects toward their sovereign." In such a context, we can see how a nonhierarchically ordered family sphere—believed to result when children were moved between sets of parents through adoption—was perceived as menacing to the stability of both the domestic and the social realms.[127]

It is important to keep in mind that novelties in family law in these centuries were not introduced by a disembodied state acting independently of families themselves (at least not independently of families who had a direct impact in the legal and political spheres). As Sarah Hanley has shown, influential middling and noble families, working together with the Crown and forming what she has termed the "family-state compact," pressed for changes in civil law that ratified their desire to award parents greater control over their children's lives.[128] Barbara Diefendorf's study of the family life of Parisian city councillors in the sixteenth century also proposes a causal relationship between the model of the family nurtured by the upper classes and the nature of the changes in family law. Analyzing the new sixteenth-century marriage laws, which allowed parents to disinherit children who married without their permission, Diefendorf argues that the impetus for change came primarily from the parliamentary officers: "Pressing for further legislation, they encouraged the monarchy in its concern for public order to entertain a more authoritarian and patriarchal view of both state and family."[129] Viewed in this light, early modern laws touching upon adoption, like those pertaining to marriage and reproduction, should be viewed as ratifying a model of the family nourished primarily (although not exclusively) by the elite families of early modern Paris—families that were increasingly concerned to fix more securely the biological boundaries of privilege around the domestic as well as the social estates.

CONCLUSIONS: CIVIL LAW AND POPULAR PRACTICE

To answer the question of why early modern French customary law rejected adoption as a legitimate strategy of heirship requires a multifaceted response. From the perspective of the evolution of adoption laws in west-

[127] Royal declaration of November 1639, cited in *La famille, la loi et l'état de la Révolution au Code civil* (Paris, 1989), p. 507. In Jean Benedicti, *La somme des péchez et le remède d'iceux* (Paris, 1545), bk. 2, chap. 1, p. 90. On the family envisioned as a microcosm of the state in early modern France, see the discussion by Hanley, "Engendering the State." For a comparative look at this issue in early modern England, see Gordon J. Schochet, *The Authoritarian Family and Political Attitudes in Seventeenth-Century England: Patriarchalism and Political Thought* (New York, 1975; rev. ed., New Brunswick, N.J., 1988).

[128] Hanley, "Engendering the State."

[129] Diefendorf, *Paris City Councillors in the Sixteenth Century*, p. 301.

ern Europe from antiquity to the early modern period, we have seen that commencing in late antiquity new Christian notions of the family and kinship served to weaken Greco-Roman traditions of adoption. While early Germanic law carried on traditions of adoption in practices such as *affatomia*, the earliest codes of French customary law from the twelfth and thirteenth centuries discouraged the creation of a fictive heir by fixing the principle of devolution of family property firmly within the confines of consanguinity. Although initially barred only from inheriting a fief, by the sixteenth century the customary law system of succession had excluded adopted children from the system of natural succession by which one inherited *ab intestat*.

Alongside the progressive erosion of adoption laws since late antiquity, we have also seen that factors specific to sixteenth-century France influenced the law's rejection of adoption. For instance, the process of legal codification was governed by a growing Gallicanism, which served to discredit adoption, increasingly condemned as a foreign, Roman institution representing anachronistic family values. In addition, when viewed in the context of sixteenth-century legislation in other areas of family law such as reproduction, marriage, and inheritance, we have seen that adoption threatened the structure of the family grounded in biological reproduction and sanctioned by legal marriage.

A history of adoption based exclusively on a reconstruction of changing legal codes presents only one side of the story, however. Considering the odds against it, we have seen that adoption did not disappear completely from the law codes or from popular practice in late antiquity and the Middle Ages. In part, the legacy of Roman law worked to ensure the survival of adoption in areas of southern France ruled by traditions of written law. We have also seen that the Christian theology of "adoption through baptism" might very well have aided in sustaining adoption traditions for families interested in having a non-natal child to stand as their heir. Additionally, medieval charters and notarial evidence have demonstrated that adoption practices also endured in customary law areas of France, such as Brittany and Paris. Most important from the perspective of popular practice, we have seen that even in the face of the law's rejection of adoption, individuals such as the marquis d'Allègre and Augustin de Champagnon turned to adoption in order to perpetuate their family lines into the next generation. Finally, although the Parlement of Paris concurred with the revised Custom of Paris in insisting that adoption did not create legal ties of filiation, the high court also made clear that strategies such as the *inter vivos* donation and testamentary legacies constituted legally valid means of passing on family property to adopted children.

An examination of fluctuating laws of adoption from antiquity has offered us one avenue into understanding the construction of parenthood, childhood, and the family. The remainder of the book, however, moves beyond the texts of written law and the perspective on adoption offered by the jurists and legislators and seeks to explore the role played by adoption in the daily lives of families in sixteenth- and seventeenth-century Paris. By looking beyond the normative picture of the family outlined in the prescriptive texts, we are able to gain a new perspective on blood ties, fictive ties, and family life in the early modern period.

CHAPTER THREE

The Family and the Neighborhood: Adoptions of Children between Two Households

ON MARCH 5, 1605 Marie Sauron, who lived in the faubourg St. Germain in Paris with her husband, Jacques Gaugin, went before a notary in order to seal formally the adoption of her three-month-old goddaughter, Thiomette de la Salle, who was orphaned of her father and whose ailing mother, Jehanne Choutiante, was on the verge of passing away. Marie adopted her goddaughter "due to the good friendship" she felt toward Thiomette, and, as she noted, because "it was her pleasure and will to do so." Marie promised to raise, educate, apprentice, and dower her adopted daughter. Although Marie and Jacques were still married, Marie had undergone a legal procedure to separate her property from the marital community of property that her husband otherwise controlled. Because Marie had gained control over her dotal property she was able to make an irrevocable "gift" (a *donation entre vifs*) of all of her property to her adopted daughter, Thiomette. In promising to pass on all of her property to Thiomette, Marie, who had no children, adopted not only a daughter to raise as her own, but a future heir as well.

The Parisian candlemaker Nicholas Cantineau and his wife, Jacqueline Faron, signed a contract before a notary in their parish of St. Etienne-du-Mont on 31 August 1607 by which they adopted a child to raise "like their own child." Interestingly, the couple's future adopted child had not yet been born on that August day. However, Nicholas and Jacqueline brought with them to the notarial office a young, pregnant, and unmarried woman, Jehanne Le Long, who was living with them in their house on the rue St. Victor. The contract does not enlighten us about the exact nature of the ties between the married couple and Jehanne, but we are told that if "it pleased God" that Jehanne's child were born alive and healthy, then Nicholas and Jacqueline would take the infant "as soon as it was born," and immediately arrange to have the child baptized and wet-nursed. Further, the couple promised to care for their future adopted child for the rest of its life as they would do "for their own child."[1]

[1] AN, MC, Et. XVII, 145 (31 August 1607).

Marin le Prevost, a dealer in braid and trimmings, and his wife Marye Lescripvain from the parish of St. Medard, recounted that because they had "always wanted little children" and "had no living children of their own," they had arranged to adopt a one-year-old boy, Jehan Fournet, from his unmarried mother, Marye Le Maire. In a notarized contract signed on 27 May 1627 with the biological mother, Marin and Marye pledged to raise Jehan as their own child "as if he had been born from them." The couple promised to provide for Jehan, to teach him a trade, to instruct him in the Roman Catholic religion, and to raise him until he reached the age of twenty-five and was capable of earning his own living. This contract of adoption also entailed a formal renunciation of parental rights by Jehan's biological father, Nicholas Fournet, a merchant living in Paris, who, by the terms of an earlier contract, had taken charge of the young boy from his biological mother to whom he was not married. By the terms of the adoption arrangement, Fournet was released of any future obligations toward the young Jehan.[2]

These sample cases of adoptions illustrate that a history of adoption in early modern France told solely from the perspective of the customary law codes and judicial commentaries that herald the demise of adoption hides just as much as it reveals about family life in this period. Once we look beyond the legal texts to the evidence of the adoption laws as they were interpreted by the Parisian notaries and individual families, it becomes clear that adoption practices remained a viable part of family life. An examination of thirty-seven notarized contracts of private adoption spanning the period 1545–1690[3] indicates that, even given the obstacles placed in

[2] AN, MC, Et. XIII, 5 (15 May 1627).

[3] François Olivier-Martin uncovered one case of "private" adoption from fifteenth-century Paris. This case from 4 August 1484 relates that "Today before us stands the honorable Alain Martin, in the service of the very distinguished and powerful prince, the duke of Bourbon, who has declared that he has given away forever his son (and of his deceased wife, Alizon Duchat), Nicholas Martin, four years old, to the honorable M. Jehan Bay, secretary to the same duke of Bourbon. The aforementioned Jehan Bay adopts Nicholas as his son [*iceluy a adopté*], and promises to feed, take care of, educate, and treat him as a father is bound to do for his son. He also consents that after his death that Nicholas will inherit all of his movable and immovable properties, all as if Nicholas were his own son born in legal marriage." This case is cited in François Olivier-Martin, *Histoire de la coutume de la prévôté et vicomté de Paris* (Paris, 1922), 1:151; the text of the document is also reproduced in Paul Gonnet, *L'adoption lyonnaise des orphelins légitimes (1536–1793)* (Paris, 1935) 1:49n.13. Jean-Pierre Gutton reproduces three additional fifteenth-century charitable pensionings of children from the

the way of adoption by customary law, parents such as Marie Sauron, Nicholas and Jacqueline, and Marin and Marye found alternative avenues to adopt formally children to raise "like their own children." The scope of such private adoptions is somewhat variable, ranging from full-scale integration of a child into the new home complete with inheritance promises, as in the three stories described here, to arrangements by which the child was cared for until the age of marriage and then given a small donation of property. I have reserved the use of the word "adoption" for those cases in which parental authority is clearly transferred from the natal to the adoptive parents, who take on the full range of parenting duties extending from the child's infancy until adulthood.

The notarial contracts of private adoption offer a glimpse into the variety of circumstances that induced some natal parents to place a child in adoption and motivated other households to take in a child. In the first case, Marie's decision to adopt formally her goddaughter, Thiomette, as her child and heir reveals the practical role played by ties of spiritual kinship in this period. In this case and others, we see godparents acting as a safety net, willing to formally adopt a godchild when the natal parents could no longer care for him or her. The story of Marie Sauron and Thiomette also demonstrates the striking possibility that a married woman could arrange an adoption independently, passing on only her lineal property to her adopted daughter. The second story involving Nicholas and Jacqueline, who contracted to adopt the future child of an unmarried woman living with them, demonstrates the innovative strategies developed by would-be adoptive parents (which, at least in this instance, appear to foreshadow contemporary surrogate-parenting arrangements). In this case the contract is silent about the exact nature of the ties binding Jehanne and the adoptive married couple. Might Jehanne have been a servant in the employ of the married couple and possibly carrying the illegitimate child of Nicholas? An additional issue raised by this case is whether Jehanne effectively sold her unborn child to Nicholas and Jacqueline. A closer look at the contract, in fact, outlines the opposite scenario: it was the biological mother, Jehanne, who promised to pay the adoptive parents the sum of thirty livres for the first year to contribute to the child's upkeep. The same was true of all the private adoptions; the notarized contracts show no evidence that the natal parents sold their children outright to the adoptive parents. Rather, as in the preceding case, it was often the birth parent who made a small payment to the adoptive family as a contribution to the upbringing of the child in its new home. The third story of adoption outlined

---

records of the Parisian Châtelet who were taken in "pour l'amour de Dieu" in his recent survey of adoption practices in France. See Gutton, *Histoire de l'adoption en France* (Paris, 1993), pp. 74–75.

here underscores the depth of the desire evidenced on the part of some childless families in early modern Paris to bring children into their homes. In this instance, Marin and Marye state explicitly in the contract that the reason they arranged to adopt the one-year-old son of the unmarried, and presumably indigent, Marye Le Maire was because they had "always wanted to have little children," but so far had been unsuccessful in raising a child who survived past infancy.

RAISING AN ADOPTED CHILD

The contracts allow us to paint a portrait of the care provided for the adopted child by her or his new family. The extent of nurturing under-taken by the adoptive parents was determined primarily by the age of the child at the time of the adoption. In the first case, Marie Sauron adopted Thiomette at the age of three months, and thus her first obligation was to arrange for the infant to be wet-nursed. Similarly, in the case involving the adoption of the unborn child of Jehanne Le Long, one of the first duties of the adoptive parents would have been to employ a wet nurse immediately after the birth. Once the child was weaned, the adoptive parents were bound to take care of the daily needs of their adoptive children. In this light, Marie Sauron promised "to raise, nourish, and house" Thiomette, to keep her "in sickness and in health, and to provide her with all of her clothing." Similarly, in a case of adoption from 1603 in which a widow, Marguerite Choquet, adopted Jacqueline Forestier, the eleven-year-old daughter of a Parisian couple, Jehan Forestier and Nicolle Richard, the adoptive mother promised to provide Jacqueline with "new clothing and to dress her as if she were her own natural daughter."[4]

As we see in this last case, the language employed to characterize the care promised to the adopted children indicates the desire on the part of adoptive parents to treat the adopted child "like their own child" *(comme leur propre enfant)*.[5] In one case, we saw that Marin Le Prevost and his wife Mayre Lescripvain pledged to adopt Jehan Fournet "as if he had been born from them."[6] Similarly, in an adoption from 1552, Etienette Ysambert was to be raised by her adoptive parents as if she "were their own daughter, born from their bodies."[7] In a case from 1603, an adop-

[4] AN, MC, Et. XXIII, 105 (14 April 1603).

[5] The use of the phrase "comme leur propre enfant" might have also alluded to the creation of the same incest norms that held for biological parents and children.

[6] AN, MC, Et. XIII, 5 (15 May 1627): "En faire du mesme que sil estoit né et procuré d'eulx."

[7] AN, Series Y 97 (1552): "nourrir et entretenir . . . comme si ladite fille estoit leur pro-pre fille."

tive mother promised to give her adopted daughter, Loyse, new clothes and "all that she needed," including caring for her "in sickness and in health, as if she were her own natural daughter."[8] In 1627 Marguerite Tourcheron adopted Denyse Roussel, the three-year-old daughter of the widow Marie Cerisier, promising to "care for [her], raise her, and instruct her in the fear of God like her own child."[9] In an adoption contract from 1628 Pierre Thiou, a tailor visiting Paris from Senlis, adopted Pierre Lavasseur, the four-year-old illegitimate son of Marguerite Bailly and Jacques Lavasseur, to raise "as his own child." Pierre pledged to raise Pierre as a Roman Catholic, to take care of him "in sickness and health," and to teach him a trade.[10] In 1649 Pierre Chevrel, a wholesale merchant who lived on the rue vielle du Temple in the parish of St. Paul, promised along with his wife, Bonne Nerat, to raise their five-year-old adopted daughter, Anne David, "as their daughter and as their own child." Anne's adoption had been arranged and overseen by her tutor, Pierre Leger, who had taken over guardianship of Anne upon the death of her biological parents, Guillaume David, a journeyman woodworker, and Jehanne Daumont.[11]

The adoption contracts demonstrate that contemporary notions of good parenting included such tasks as raising the child "in good morals," "honestly," and "in the love and fear of God" so that, as several of the contracts explain, the child might become a "virtuous adult." In this regard, the adoptive father of Michelle Tondeur promised to care for her "within his capacity and as a father is bound to do for his child" and to "instruct her in good morals as he would do for his own children."[12] While early modern treatment of children might have allowed a greater use of corporal punishment than is typical of modern French society, parents were nonetheless expected to treat their children gently and humanely. Several contracts bind the adoptive parents to treat the child "gently . . . in sickness and in health."[13]

In addition to providing for the essential needs of their new children, adoptive parents were expected, as were biological parents, to play an educative role. The primary educational duty of all parents was to ensure a religious and moral upbringing for their children. The children were to be guided toward a life of "good morals" and taught to "love and fear

[8] AN, MC, Et. XXIII, 105 (14 April 1603).

[9] AN, MC, Et. XXXIX, 59 (November 1627).

[10] AN, MC, Et. XXXIX, 60 (28 May 1628).

[11] AN, MC, Et. XIX, 439 (27 May 1649).

[12] AN, MC, Et. XXXIII, 35 (October 1550): "à son pouvoir et que père peult estre tenu à son enffan" and to "instruire en bonne moeurs comme à ses propres enffans."

[13] AN, MC, Et. XVII, 144 (1606): "la traiter doulcement comme il appartient tout en santé que malady."

God."[14] Not surprisingly, in an era of religious war between a French Catholic majority and a feared Calvinist minority, the contracts stipulate that the child be raised according to the doctrines of the Roman Catholic Church (the phrase employed bound the parents to teach the children in the "beliefs of the Roman, catholic, and Apostolic church").[15] Many of the contracts specify that the children were to begin their religious training upon reaching the "age of understanding" or, as a case from 1606 informs us, when the child "reached the age when she was prepared to be instructed in the love and the fear of God, and to be schooled in the commandments and beliefs of the Roman Catholic Church."[16]

Following a religious education, all of the adoptive parents promised to apprentice the child in a trade at the appropriate age. The language of the contracts indicates that for both boys and girls the learning of a trade ensured that they might "earn their own living in the future." Marie Sauron promised to instruct Thiomette "so that she would be able to earn her own living when she reaches the age of reason."[17] Similarly, Marin and Marye promised to have their adopted son, Jehan Fournet, apprenticed in a trade when he matured.[18] In a case from 1600 François Ponart, the adoptive father of Charles Brunce, "the poor son of the deceased Charpentier Brunce," promised to apprentice the boy "as best he could" in his own trade of masonry so that in the future he could "earn his own living."[19] The fact that most of our adoptions took place before the age of apprenticeship makes sense when we consider that many private adoptions involved a move from the household of impoverished natal parents into the home of more prosperous adoptive parents. We can assume that many of the parents who gave their children in adoption could not afford to have the child apprenticed in a trade, yet they desired that their child have such an opportunity provided by another family.

Along with promises of daily provisions, a religious education, and apprenticeship in a trade, many of the contracts contain pledges of secular education for the children, including instruction in literacy. In 1606, for example, the Parisian adoptive father of a young Scottish girl, Michelle Douglas, promised to "send her to schools."[20] In another contract from

[14] This language is found, for example, in a case from 1601—AN, MC, Et. XXIII, 158 (5 July 1601).

[15] AN, MC, Et. XXIII, 112.

[16] AN, MC, Et. XVII, 144 (6 July 1606): "quand elle sera venue en âge capable de la faire instruire en l'amour et crainte de dieu en observant de ses commandements et en la croyance de l'église catholique apostolique et romaine."

[17] AN, MC, Et. III, 476 (5 March 1605).

[18] AN, MC, Et. XIII, 5 (15 May 1627).

[19] AN, MC, Et. XXIII, 157 (9 December 1600).

[20] AN, MC, Et. XVII, 144 (6 July 1606): "l'envoyer aux escoles."

1606 an adopted son was to be taught to "read and write."[21] In the mid-seventeenth century we find a promise to an adopted daughter to "instruct her and school her according to the condition of her birth."[22]

The majority of the contracts disclose that the adoptive parents agreed to keep the children "with them" (that is, in the household) until they reached their majority and the age of marriage, at which time the parents also promised to provide a dowry. We have seen that Marie Sauron undertook to provide Thiomette with a dowry when she "reached the age of capacity."[23] Similarly, the parents of Marguerite Denys stated that she was to "live with them until she reached the age to be provided for marriage."[24] For girls, the age of maturity seems to have arrived in the early twenties. The widowed Marguerite Choquet promised to care for her adopted daughter, Jacqueline Forestier, until "she reached the age for marriage and until she reached the age of twenty."[25] For girls, the promise to provide for them when they reached the age of marriage might also mean placing them in a convent to lead a religious life. As an early sixteenth-century contract tells us, Michelle Tondeur was to stay in her new household until she was old enough to be provided for "in marriage or in a religious life."[26] Boys seem to have reached the age of independence a few years later than girls. We have seen, for instance, that Marin Le Prevost and Marye Lescripvain promised to keep and raise their adopted son, Jehan Fournet, "until he reached the age of twenty-five and was capable of earning his own living."[27]

The voices of the adopted children appear rarely in the adoption contracts. Several contracts, however, include a pledge made by the children (or on their behalf if they were too young), to treat their adoptive parents as a child would his or her biological parents. Marguerite Denys, for example, who was six years old when her contract of adoption was signed, pledged to obey her new parents "in all licit and honest affairs."[28] Another

---

21 AN, MC, Et. XXIII, 112 (6 July 1606): "lire et escrire."

22 AN, MC, Et. LIII (27 June 1648): "instruire et escholler selon sa condition de naissance."

23 AN, MC, Et. III, 476 (5 March 1605): "En tous qu'elle aura attainct l'âge de cappacité promest la faire pourvoire pour mariage au mieulx que luy sera possible."

24 AN, MC, Et. XLII, 85 (12 June 1634): "Vivre avec eulx jusques au qu'elle est attainct l'âge destre procurer par le mariage ou aultrement." AN, MC, Et. XC, 1 (1618). A contract from 1634 recounts that the parents will marry the child when she reaches the "age of reason."

25 AN, MC, Et. XXIII, 105 (14 April 1603): "Sera en âge de mariage et quelle atteint l'âge de vingt ans."

26 AN, MC, Et. XXXIII, 35 (October 1550): "Jusques à ce que ledit enfant soit pourvue par mariage, religion ou aultrement."

27 AN, MC, Et. XIII, 5 (15 May 1627).

28 AN, MC, Et. XC, I (1618): "en toutes choses licites et honnestes."

young girl promised to obey her adoptive parents "as she would her own father and mother."[29] A contract from 1634 pledges that an infant boy, Henry Barbier, adopted from his natal parents by a nobleman living outside of Paris, would obey his adoptive father, Charles de Pelerin, in the future "as he would his own father."[30] Five-year-old Anne David promised in a 1649 adoption contract that, when she became capable she would obey her adoptive parents as "her true mother and father."[31]

PRIVATE ADOPTION AND SOCIAL MOBILITY

The families involved in two-household adoptions, with the exception of one outstanding case to be discussed, came from the laboring, artisan, and minor merchant sectors of the Parisian working classes. Within this group the socioprofessional status of the adoptive fathers (and their widows) ranged from master artisans and merchants at the upper end of the social scale to journeymen, day laborers, and the unemployed at the other end. A consistent feature of two-household adoptions finds children moving from a financially or otherwise incapacitated family to a new home that both desired a child and possessed the requisite financial resources. Viewed in this light, we can suggest that the two-household adoptions offered an alternative to abandonment or outright infanticide for indigent parents, while, at the same time, offering a child and an heir to families without children of their own. Adoption also offered a "second chance" to the children whose parents could no longer care for them.

A case of adoption from 1634 dramatically highlights the possibility for upward social mobility through adoption. In this instance, Charles de Pelerin, an esquire of Forteville who served in the court of the duchess of Angoulême in Burgundy, traveled to Paris to sign a contract with Jean Barbier, a master printer, and his wife Jehanne Rogier, which formalized Charles's adoption of Henry Barbier, the four-week-old son of Jean and Jehanne. By the terms of the contract Charles promised to raise Henry from infancy "as his adopted son," including a promise that Henry would become his heir. Charles pledged to transmit the inheritance to Henry through a testament "just as he would do for his own heir."[32] Although we do not know exactly why Henry's birth parents decided to place him in adoption (there is no indication of a payment made to the couple by Charles in the contract), this case underscores the potential for a child to

[29] AN, MC, Et. XIX, 439 (1649): "Quelle sera tenue porter honnestement auds. Chevrel et sa femme quant elle sera capable et de leur obeyir comme à ses propre père et mère."
[30] AN, MC, Et. XXIV, 340 (10 April 1634).
[31] AN, MC, Et. XIX, 439 (27 May 1649).
[32] AN, MC, Et. XXIV, 340 (10 April 1634).

ascend socially through adoption.[33] It should be stressed, however, that this case stands out as a striking exception to the normal patterns of private adoption in early modern Paris. Charles de Pelerin was the sole case I located of a nobleman who openly arranged to adopt a non-natal child (and from a non-noble family), to become his heir. We would not expect to come across many noble families adopting non-natal children as their heirs considering the centrality of the bloodline for the nobility and the general prejudice against adoption harbored by the upper classes. Excepting the de Pelerin case, the remainder of the families involved in the two-household adoptions came from the non-noble sectors of society.

MOTIVES FOR ADOPTION

The contracts reveal that childlessness was the primary factor motivating a family to adopt a child from a friend, a kinsman, or a neighbor. In 1627, when Marin le Prevost and Marye Lescripvain adopted Jehan Fournet, they indicated to the notary that they "had always wanted to have little children" but that they had not been successful in raising a child past infancy.[34] The language employed in another case of adoption mentioned earlier from 1649 suggests that childless couples turned quite regularly to adoption in order to reproduce the family into the next generation. In this instance Pierre Chevrel and Bonne Nerat recounted that since they had no biological children, they had decided—"*according to the customary practice*"—to adopt a six-year-old orphan, Anne David, from her tutor, Pierre Leger.[35] The language employed in this case is significant for a social history of adoption practices in early modern Paris inasmuch as it suggests that, far from having disappeared, adoption remained a "customary" remedy for some childless couples.

It is worth pausing for a moment to ask what the adoption of a child

---

[33] The social movement inherent in the private adoptions concurs with the interpretive framework advanced by the anthropologist Grant McCracken, who places the custom of sending children away from their natal parents to be raised in other homes in early modern England in the context of theories of exchange and reciprocity formulated by Claude Lévi-Strauss, Marcel Mauss, and Marshall Sahlins, among others. McCracken suggests that the exchange of children as servants fostered a degree of unity between households of varying socioeconomic status. At the same time, however, social boundaries were not completely obscured and the exchange of children also served to differentiate givers from receivers, thereby reinforcing the existing social hierarchy. See Grant McCracken, "The Exchange of Children in Tudor England: An Anthropological Phenomenon in Historical Context," *Journal of Family History* 8 (winter 1983): 303–13.

[34] AN, MC, Et. XIII, 5 (15 May 1627).

[35] AN, MC, Et. XIX, 439 (27 May 1649). Emphasis added.

meant to couples such as Pierre Chevrel and Bonne Nerat and Marin Le Prevost and Marye Lescripvain and why they went to so much trouble to adopt? In answering these queries it is helpful to envision the phrase employed in the contracts by which the adoptive parents promised to treat the child "like their own child" (*comme leur propre enfant*), as reflecting the establishment of a mutually beneficial relationship between the adoptive parents and their adopted children. From the perspective of the adopted child, we have already seen some of the concrete benefits that resulted from an adoption—from the basic necessities, an education, and an apprenticeship to a dowry and an inheritance. In return for the care and provisions provided for the adopted children, the adoptive parents gained a child to "honor" them as parents, help with work around the house (labor that biological children also would have performed), and care for them in their old age, as well as a child and heir to carry on the family name, property, and traditions.

We may also speculate that adoption was motivated by a desire to establish the same affective bonds that were formed between biological parents and children. The literature on the history of the family in early modern France has for the most part reserved the formation of affective ties between parents and children, as distinct from the view of children as mere objects of exchange or labor, for the upper classes.[36] Yet, the fact that many childless families from the artisanal classes chose to adopt nonbiological children, often from infancy, suggests that children were desired for a wide variety of reasons by these families. We see indications of the desire to forge emotional bonds in an adoption case that appears in an early seventeenth-century manual for notaries. In this instance Marie la Rousse, a married woman who had no biological children of her own, recounted that "out of divine love, she has always wanted to adopt a daughter whom she could treat as her own."[37] Moreover, several adoption contracts refer explicitly to preexisting emotional bonds that led a family to arrange to adopt a particular child they were fond of. In a case already mentioned from 1618, Pierre Chevreu and his wife Claude Ducloz adopted the young daughter of a poor widow they knew and made clear that their decision to adopt Marguerite Denys "grew from a particular affection that they held for Marguerite."[38] Affective bonds also influenced a case of adoption from 1624 in which grandparents took over custody of

---

[36] See Phillipe Ariès, *Centuries of Childhood: A Social History of Family Life*, trans. Robert Baldick (New York, 1962), and Lawrence Stone, *The Family, Sex and Marriage in England, 1500–1800* (London, 1977; abridged paperback ed., New York, 1979).

[37] This case appears as a model contract in a manual for notaries: Philippes Cothereau, *La théorique et pratique des notaires* (Paris, 1632), pp. 62–63. This treatise is discussed in more depth later in the chapter.

[38] AN, MC, Et. XC, 1 (1618).

their two-year-old granddaughter, Anne Le Tanneur, due to the "bonne amitié" they held for her.[39]

ADOPTED CHILDREN AS HEIRS: CUSTOMARY LAW AND POPULAR PRACTICE

How could families rest assured that the adoptions they contracted were secure and binding, considering the customary law's refusal to recognize adoptive kinship as forming a legal tie of filiation complete with inheritance rights? In this context, the most significant, and surprising, section of the contracts is that which addresses the problematic matter of inheritance. We find diverse avenues selected by the adoptive parents to transmit all or a portion of their property to their adopted child. Because an adopted child's inheritance was not regulated by Parisian customary law (other than to deny them traditional inheritance privileges), it was up to the individual adoptive parents to decide how much of the property they wished to pass on to the child and through which channel: an *inter vivos* donation, a testamentary legacy, or through a more general promise to provide an inheritance for the adopted child in the future.

Not all of the adopted children were lucky enough, however, to be promised an inheritance at the time the adoption contract was signed. When Blaise Breton, a master racket maker living in Paris, contracted in 1606 with his friend Leonarda Girante, a domestic servant, to "take forever" Leonarda's young, illegitimate daughter Michelle Douglas "as his own child," he made no specific promises to provide her with an inheritance.[40] The same was true for the six-year-old Marguerite Denys who was adopted from her mother, Jehanne Faverolle, the widow of a day laborer, by a married couple, Pierre Chevereu, a master ropemaker, and his wife Claude Ducloz. While the couple promised to raise Marguerite, to care for her in sickness and in health, to instruct her in the Catholic religion, and to treat her "gently and kindly," the contract contains no clause relating to inheritance.[41] Although the absence of an inheritance provision does not necessarily indicate that the children would not be provided for, we have no way of knowing for certain whether they ultimately received a portion of the family's property.

Some adopted children were more fortunate and were provided a modest donation from the family property. In 1600 François Ponart a mason and his wife Marguerite Le Brun made a small donation to their new son,

[39] AN, MC, Et. CV, 529 (3 April 1624).
[40] AN, MC, Et. XVII, 144 (6 July 1606).
[41] AN, MC, Et. XC, 1 (1618).

Charles Brunce, whom they adopted from the widower Charpentier Brunce. Charles was sixteen at the time of the adoption and had already been living with the couple for two years when the contract was signed. Perhaps a small donation rather than a full inheritance seemed enough to Charles, who thanked his adoptive parents for "pulling him out of a life of poverty and mendicancy" and promised never to leave them.[42] In 1606 a small donation of property was also given to the six-year-old Claude Tougart who had been adopted from his biological mother, Jehanne Prevost, the widow of Jehan Tougart, by Nicholas Rhut, a master tailor, and his wife Marie Mynette. The adoptive parents promise to raise Claude, to teach him to read and write, and to apprentice him in the father's trade of clothes making, in addition to making him a small donation of property.[43]

Many of the children adopted between private households were fortunate enough, however, to be named the full heir of their new adoptive parents in the contracts. In light of the customary law's denial of inheritance rights to adopted children, most of the contracts that name the children as complete heirs employ the legal channel of the *donation entre vifs* to transmit the totality of the family property as "a gift" during the lifetime of the adoptive parents. By the terms of these gifts the donors would normally retain usufruct of the property until their deaths. Thus, a contract of adoption from 1552 makes clear that although the adoptive parents, Robert Dumont and his wife made an "irrevocable donation of all of their goods" to their adopted daughter, Etiennette Ysambert, the couple would "retain for themselves usufruct of the said goods during their lifetime."[44] Many of the adoptive parents chose to employ such donations. In a case cited at the outset, Marie Sauron made a donation to her adopted daughter, Thiomette, of all her "movable and immovable goods that belong to her now and will belong to her in the future."[45] Similarly, in 1603 the widow Marguerite Choquet made a gift to her adopted daughter Jacqueline Forestier "as if she were her own, natural daughter" of "all of her movable and immovable property."[46] In a contract from 1634 Julian Vivier, a horse merchant, and his wife Charlotte Le Tas made a *donation entre vifs* to their adopted daughter and Charlotte's niece, Anne Le Tas, of "all and everyone of their movable and immovable goods . . . as if she were their own daughter."[47] In 1649 Pierre Cheval, a wholesale merchant, and his wife Bonne Nerat made an irrevocable donation of all their property to their adopted daughter, five-year-old Anne David. The adoptive parents

[42] AN, MC, Et. XXIII, 157 (9 December 1600).
[43] AN, MC, Et. XXIII, 112 (6 July 1606).
[44] AN, Series Y (Insinuations) (1552).
[45] AN, MC, Et. III, 476 (5 March 1605).
[46] AN, MC, Et. XXIII, 105 (14 April 1603).
[47] AN, MC, Et. XLII, 85 (12 June 1634).

explained further that their donation to Anne was made out of the affection ("bonne amour d'association") that they felt for her.[48]

It is worth pausing for a moment to explore in greater detail the history of the *donation entre vifs*. The donation was a conveyance from Roman law where it evolved in order to give those normally deprived of the right to draw up a will (such as slaves and foreigners) the opportunity to dispense of their property through "gifts" during one's lifetime. Until the twelfth century the donation was used primarily for charitable bequests to the church made during one's lifetime. Subsequently, in the late medieval and early modern periods, the donation took on a new role as a means of exchanging property between private persons. For example, an elderly couple might make a small gift of property to an individual who was expected, in return, to care for them in their old age.

Yet this new use of the donation ran counter to the spirit of the evolving continental legal systems, which were based on the principle of lineage property or "forced heirship," as it is often termed. In this system an individual's leeway in dispensing of property was limited to guarantee close kin their share in any estate. In addition to being viewed as potentially damaging to close kin, the donation was also viewed as risky for the donor since the donor technically had to divest claims on the property at the moment of the gift (one sixteenth-century proverb warned in this regard that "He who gives before he dies soon learns to suffer").[49]

What we see in the adoption contracts, however, goes far beyond the traditional uses of the donation. The notaries' employment of the donation to effect the transmission of the totality of the adoptive parents' property to create an heir is unprecedented. Although the donation was not originally intended as an avenue to create an heir, it makes perfect sense for the notaries to have selected the lifetime gift as a means to ensure an inheritance for the adopted children. Property in early modern French law was divided into two categories of movable and immovable goods. Movable goods (*meubles*) were traditionally defined by the adage "movable goods follow the body"[50] and referred to "personal property," whereas immovable goods (*immeubles*) referred to "real property" such as land, rents, and, beginning in the mid-sixteenth century, hereditary offices.[51] According to the Custom of Paris, immovable goods were further divided into two distinct categories when it came to matters of inheritance: property

---

[48] AN, MC, Et. XIX, 439 (27 May 1649).

[49] Antoine Loysel, *Institutes coutumières* (Paris, 1846), s.v. "donation."

[50] See Loysel, *Institutes coutumières*, p. 221: "Le meuble suit le corps et l'immeuble le lieu où il est assis."

[51] On the category of *propres*, see Ralph E. Giesey, "Rules of Inheritance and Strategies of Mobility in Pre-Revolutionary France," *American Historical Review* 82 (1977): 271–89; Olivier-Martin, *Histoire de la coutume*, 1:201ff. 2:430–47.

acquired during an individual's lifetime due to the fruits of his or her labor (the *acquêts* and the *conquêts*),[52] and the lineage property (the *propres*), the family heritables that had been handed down from generation to generation. It followed that immovable acquisitions handed down from parents to their children became part of the lineage property from then on. Unlike *conquêts, acquêts,* and movable property, which could be freely donated or willed to nonfamily members, the *propres* normally followed distinct rules of devolution intended to keep them within the family line.[53]

Unlike restrictions placed by the Custom of Paris on testaments (by which only one-fifth of the lineage property could be alienated), the *inter vivos* donation remained largely exempt from the constraints of the *réserve héréditaire*.[54] The latitude regarding disposition of one's property offered by the donation allowed adopted parents to pass on the lineal property traditionally reserved for collateral heirs in the absence of a child to their adopted child.[55] How secure were these *donations entre vifs* for ensuring a future inheritance for the adopted children? To answer this question fully, we would need to follow a few select adoption cases through to the moment of actual transferral of the property to ascertain whether, for instance, the adoptive parents had rescinded the donation or whether the collateral heirs attempted to block the inheritance. Unfortunately, this information is difficult to obtain due to the near impossibility of tracing these laboring and artisan families in the archives in the years following the adoptions. In theory, all donations were irrevocable (the contracts routinely state that the donations "cannot be revoked or taken back by any

---

[52] *Conquêts* referred to goods acquired during the community of marriage, whereas *acquêts* were goods acquired before marriage. See Paul Viollet, *Histoire du droit civil français,* 3rd ed. (Aalen, 1966), p. 772.

[53] Technically four-fifths of the *propres,* known as the *réserve héréditaire,* had to be reserved for the family line (New Custom of Paris, 1580, art. 292). The remaining one-fifth could be disposed of freely, as with all personal property and lifetime acquisitions. See Olivier-Martin, *Histoire de la coutume,* 2:316–17.

[54] On the *réserve,* see Olivier-Martin, *Histoire de la coutume,* 2:315. The freedom to alienate one's property through lifetimes gifts had been secured in the thirteenth century. Although the Paris region did not technically know the form of burgage tenure characteristic of Normandy and England, restrictions on alienation of property in the town of Paris from the late Middle Ages on were minimal. On the question of burgage tenure in Normandy, see Robert Génestal, *La tenure en bourgage: Etude sur la propriété foncière dans les villes normandes* (Paris, 1900). On the freedom to alienate urban property through *inter vivos* donations in early modern Paris, see Olivier-Martin, *Histoire de la coutume,* 1:377–78.

[55] Title 13 of the New Custom of Paris (1580) states that: "It is licit for any person over the age of twenty-five who is of sound mind to give and dispose by means of a donation *entre vifs,* all of the movables, héritables, *propres,* acquisitions and conquests, to any other capable person." Those incapable of receiving such gifts were concubines and illegitimate children. If a couple had children, however, they were protected from disinheritance by the *légitime,* which safeguarded a certain amount of the lineal property for them.

means or in any manner" or that the donors "have no intention or desire
to ever revoke the donation"). By the terms of the Custom of Paris, however, such gifts of property could be revoked by the donor due to "ingratitude" displayed by the individual who received the gift, or in the case of a
childless couple who subsequently had a child. The central reason that the
notaries employed the donation, however, was to protect the adopted children not from the donors, but rather from future competitive claims to the
property made by collateral heirs. In this regard the donations served their
purpose; by the terms of the Custom of Paris donations of property made
by competent and mature individuals were legally binding and could be
revoked only by the donor.

THE PARISIAN NOTARIES AS LEGAL MEDIATORS

The question still remains as to how the Parisian notaries reconciled the
inheritance clauses in the contracts they penned with the customary law
dictum that "adopted children cannot inherit"? Although the employment
of the *donation entre vifs* and the testamentary legacy did not technically
transgress the guidelines of customary law, the private adoptions nonetheless challenged the spirit of customary law by upholding the legitimacy of
constructing familial alliances and channels of inheritance outside of blood
and marriage. How, then, did the Parisian notaries navigate between official legal proscriptions and the evident desire of households to adopt children as full and legitimate heirs? The best sources for answering such
questions are contemporary manuals for notaries, which elaborate the role
of the notary in society in addition to offering the novice notary a selection
of sample contracts. The best known of these manuals, *La science parfaite
des notaires*, written in the seventeenth century by Claude de Ferrière,
offers an image of the notary guided primarily by local customary law and
parliamentary precedent:

> It is not sufficient to have models to be copied down word by word; instead
> an act must be drawn up with judgment, following the ordinances and the
> customary law of the region in which one is working, otherwise one risks
> drawing up odious acts, which happens frequently to those who follow no
> other guidance than that which they find in a notarial "Style" or "Practice."[56]

[56] Claude de Ferrière, *La science parfaite des notaires* (Lyon, 1695), p. 51. On the use of
notarial formularies as evidence for the professional identity of early modern notaries, see
Jean-Paul Poisson, "L'apport des formulaires notariaux à la connaissance de la vision des
notaires sur eux-mêmes et sur la société aux XVIe et XVIIe siècles," in Jean-Paul Poisson,
Notaires et société: Travaux d'histoire et de sociologie notariales (Paris, 1990), 2:21–53.

De Ferrière's notarial manual did not include a contract of adoption among its sample contracts, perhaps because he deemed adoption one of the "odious acts" prohibited by customary law. I did, however, ultimately locate two early modern notarial formularies that included sample adoptions. A late sixteenth-century treatise on the notarial profession, translated from Latin by the Lyonnais jurist Pardoux du Prat, contains a Roman-style adoption contract in which an adult male is adopted as an heir by a childless man.[57] This sample contract was clearly intended to show one of the two kinds of adoption under Roman law (adrogation in this case since the man adopted was an adult and under his own *potestas*). This contract concerns us less than a sample adoption contract from an early seventeenth-century manual composed by a Parisian notary that outlines the adoption of a young girl by a childless couple. It is worth citing the contract in its entirety, particularly as the section on inheritance states explicitly that the adopted daughter would inherit from her new mother even in the advent of future biological children:

> The honorable Marie la Rousse, wife of Gilles du Puy, a merchant and bourgeois of Paris, who has authorized her to undertake what follows declares that she has no children, and that due to the charity and divine love that inspired her, she has always wanted to adopt a daughter whom she could treat as her own daughter. Thus, she has recognized and confessed to having adopted and chosen . . . as her daughter and own child, Claire le Roy, young daughter of Pierre le Roy, a merchant of hats living in Paris and of Avoye Caillet his deceased wife, as Pierre le Roy has at present said and confirmed. Pierre le Roy has given and now voluntarily gives his daughter to the aforementioned Marie, who has taken her as her adopted daughter, considering that the said Pierre le Roy, due to his present state of indigence, does not have the means to earn a living for himself and his daughter. Marie la Rousse promises to instruct Claire during her lifetime in good morals, according to the catholic, apostolic, and Roman church, to raise her well and properly as her own daughter, and to provide for her as best she can. In the case that the said Marie has a child or children in the future, she wishes that Claire partake in her property by head [*par teste*] along with any biological children. If, however, Marie does not have any children, she intends that any property she has at the time of her death be passed on to the said Claire, after the fulfillment of her testament and the payment of her debts, just as if she were her own daughter.[58]

[57] Pardoux de Prat, *Théorique de l'art des notaires pour cognoistre la nature de tous les points de droit qui concernant l'estat, et office de notariat, nouvellement traduite de latin en francoys et succinctement adaptée aux ordonnances royaux* (Lyon, 1572), pp. 414–15.

[58] Philippes Cothereau, *La théorique et pratique des notaires par Maistre Philippes Cothereau, Notaire au Chastelet de Paris—Reveuë, corrigée et augmentée de nouveau, pour la quatriesme édition* (Paris, 1632), pp. 62–63.

Because Cothereau was a notary at the Châtelet of Paris, where all donations of property were ultimately registered, this model contract is
important in revealing that the Parisian notaries did indeed have
models for drawing up contracts of adoption complete with inheritance
clauses.

Jean-Paul Poisson has suggested that while notaries were concerned to
fulfill their role as "emissaries of royal justice" and to follow legal prescriptions, they were also conscious of cultivating a less dogmatic interpretation
of the law inasmuch as they perceived themselves as more connected to the
realities of daily life than their more illustrious judicial colleagues.[59] Several studies of notarial practices in early modern France have supported
Poisson's claim and have underscored the relative independence of notarial procedures in relation to the guidelines laid down by the regional customary law codes.[60] The situation of adoption is somewhat mixed,
however, when it comes to assessing the relationship of the notarial practice to the Parisian customary law; while the adoption contracts might
have contradicted the spirit of the law in terms of inheritance law, they did
not technically contradict the letter of the law. As noted earlier, the Custom of Paris did not ban adoption per se, it merely banned a particular
method of transmitting property to adopted children. Moreover, commentators on the Custom of Paris and the Parlement of Paris both suggested alternative routes, such as the testamentary legacy and the *donation
entre vifs*, for transmitting property to adopted children. We may conclude, then, that adoption was neither an illicit nor even an impractical act
in sixteenth- and seventeenth-century Paris. By improvising and finding
new uses for legal mechanisms such as the donation, the Parisian notaries
acted as critical mediators navigating between the demands of the popu-
lace on the one hand and the official tenets of written law on the other
hand. In its broadest sense, the evidence of adoption suggests that the
"law of adoption" was not a static entity imposed from above by the
drafters of the newly codified customary law codes. Rather, like many
other areas of civil and criminal law in the early modern period, the law of
adoption appears as an adaptable and fluid construct whose terms were
regularly altered by notaries responsive to the demands of individual families confronting the realities of daily life.

[59] See Jean-Paul Poisson, *Notaires et société: Travaux d'histoire et de sociologie notariales*,
vol. 1 (Paris, 1985); vol. 2 (1990). We should also consider the fact that these notaries had a
professional interest in catering to the wishes of their clients, regardless of whether these
desires—such as naming an adopted child as an heir—were compatible with regional customary law.

[60] See, for example, Jean Hillaire, "Coutumes rédigées et gens du champs (Angoumois,
Aunis, Saintonge)," *Revue historique de droit français et étranger* 4 (1987):545–73.

KINSHIP TIES AND PRIVATE ADOPTIONS

How did the households involved in adoptions, in an era without adoption agencies, manage to arrange for the transfer of a child from one family to another? The contracts reveal that the bond of kinship appears as the primary tie linking the two households involved in the private adoptions. In the case of Marie Sauron and her adopted goddaughter Thiomette, ties of godparenthood, or spiritual kinship, bound the two households together and facilitated the adoption of a soon-to-be orphaned child. The archives furnish other instances of godparents who formally adopted a godchild. In a case from 1609 Jeanne Gauthier, the widow of Amiot Bail and a servant living in the house of her employer, the lawyer M. Rigault of Paris, decided to give over the care of her four-year-old son, Toussaintz Bail, to his godfather, Jehan Allait. Jehan, a master ropemaker also living in Paris, promised to take in his godson in order to "house, feed, and raise him . . . for the rest of his life." Jehan promised to raise Toussaintz in the Catholic religion, and to apprentice him in the leather trade when he was older, all "as if Toussaintz were his own son."[61] The contract tells us that Jehanne Gaultier was a widowed domestic servant at the time of the adoption, a status that might have influenced her decision to place her son in his godfather's home (although the contract reveals that she did arrange to pay Jehan twelve livres tournois per year). If Jehanne found herself unable to care adequately for her son, the boy's godfather, Jehan, was in a position (and willing) to house, feed, educate, apprentice, and raise Toussaintz "as his son."

These instances of adoptions between spiritual kin stand in marked contrast to the statements of many early modern jurists who asserted that godparents were not held responsible for the real work of raising their godchildren. While godparents were expected to contribute to their godchildren's religious and moral education, the promises made at the baptismal font were not binding in secular law. The seventeenth-century jurist Brillon concluded quite succinctly that "godfathers and godmothers are not bound to raise their godchildren. Either they are to be placed in hospices, or alms may be sought for them."[62] As we have seen, however, early modern notions of godparenthood envisioned the ties between spiritual kin as constituting a form of adoption.[63] Accordingly, in a case involving a

---

[61] AN, MC, Et. LXXIII, 272 (26 October 1609).

[62] P. J. Brillon, *Dictionnaire des arrests ou jurisprudence universelle des Parlements de France* (Paris, 1711), 1:260: "Parrains et marraines ne sont tenus de nourrir les enfants. Ou ils sont mis à l'Hôpital, ou l'on permet des quêtes pour eux."

[63] Claude Henrys, a sixteenth-century jurist, spoke of "spiritual adoption" and "spiritual affiliation" as the status "we acquire through the grace of baptism which renders us the children of God," in *Les oeuvres de M. Claude Henrys* (Paris, 1708), p. 976.

donation of property made by a godfather to his godson in 1603, the young boy is described as "a spiritually adopted son."[64] This case appears in the legal record because the godfather's collateral heirs disputed the donation on the grounds that it alienated the family property to a "stranger." The donation was upheld by the courts, however, due to the association made between spiritual kinship and adoption: "This boy is not a stranger, but a kind of son: *est filius adoptivus spiritualis*."[65] Marie Sauron's adoption of her goddaughter Thiomette and Jehan Alliat's adoption of his godson Toussaintz Bail reveal that a "spiritual adoption" might be translated into a civil adoption at a time of crisis for the natal family.

Adoptions between two households were also contracted between close biological kin. In 1545 the widow Jacqueline Petit adopted her deceased husband's twelve-year-old niece, Mathurine le Roy. Although Jacqueline officially adopted Mathurine in 1545, she had taken the young girl into her home more than two years before, when her husband, Pasquier le Roy, a journeyman dyer was still alive. Mathurine's parents, Jean le Roy, a merchant, and his wife Guillemette lived in Normandy. The contract does not tell us why Mathurine originally came to live with her uncle and his wife in Paris—perhaps it was to find work in the city—or why, in the end, she was adopted by her aunt, although this is likely another case in which the natal parents were too poor to raise her.[66]

In another case of kin adoption, Jehan de la Borne a mason from the parish of St. Eustache, adopted Ysabel Dode, an eight-year-old orphan, promising to treat her "gently and humanely as his own child." The adoption was authorized by Ysabel's tutor, Pierre Morin, another mason living in the parish of St. Sauveur. Ysabel was, in fact, the sister of Jehan de la Borne's wife, Marguerite Dode, and thus Jehan's sister-in-law. Ysabel and her sister Marguerite were the heirs of their parents, Pierre Dode, a wine merchant, and Adriane Reguard. In this case, ties of marriage and consanguinity were not the only connections between these two households. Notarial records show that Pierre Morin, Ysabel's tutor who authorized the adoption, and Jehan de la Borne not only shared the same trade of masonry but signed many business contracts together over the years.[67] Many of these contracts involved the property included in the inheritance of the Dode sisters. In 1601, for example, Pierre Morin, again in his capacity as Ysabel Dode's tutor, authorized a five-year "title of rent" for a house included in Ysabel's inheritance to Jehan de la Borne. In the same year Pierre

---

[64] "Filius adoptivus spiritualis," in *Arrests de la Cour, questions tant de droict que de coustume, prononcez en robbes rouges* (Paris, 1702), p. 3.

[65] Ibid.

[66] This case appears in Ernst Coyecque, *Receuil d'actes notariés relatifs à l'histoire de Paris au XVIe siècle* (Paris, 1905), vol. 1 [1498–1545], no. 3128 (ca. 1545).

[67] AN, MC, Et. LXVII, 61 (1603).

and Jehan authorized a six-year lease of another house included in the Dode inheritance.[68] The elements of this private adoption illuminate the intersection of several networks—kinship, marital, professional, and inheritance—that framed the adoption of Ysabel Dode.

In several kin adoptions, the arrangements were drawn up when the natal parents could no longer care for the child and had consequently turned to other family members for assistance. Circumstances of poverty might have provided the context for the adoption of Catherine le Doux, a four-year-old girl, by her cousin Claude Roger in 1621.[69] Catherine's mother had died by the time the adoption took place and it was her father, Jehan le Doux, a gardener from Colombes, who signed the contract. Claude Roger promised to take and keep Catherine with him "as his child" and to provide her with all of her necessities. In 1638 Fleurance Bourdy, the widow of Noël Rigaud from the parish of St. Etienne-du-Mont in Paris, pledged to Jehan du Courq, a master chef, to take in, raise and educate his son, also named Jehan du Courq. In this instance Jehan's deceased wife, Jacqueline Rigaud, was Fleurance Bourdy's sister-in-law.[70] In a case from 1634, a widowed mother who was "in great need" and could no longer care for her daughter, gave her daughter in adoption to the girl's aunt.[71]

Another pattern of kin adoption entailed grandparents formally adopting a grandchild when the parents had died or been rendered incapacitated in some way. In one instance from 1605 Jean de Sève, a merchant, arranged along with his wife Louise Sevin to adopt formally their six-year-old granddaughter, Marguerite de la Place, from Marguerite Dumont who was Louise's daughter from a previous marriage. The adoptive parents recount in the contract that they had taken the young Marguerite into their home three years before and that they now desired to formalize the arrangement.[72] In another case involving grandparents from 1627 Nicholas le Tanneur and Anne Montallier adopted their two-and-a-half-year-old granddaughter Anne. The couple's daughter, also named Anne, was living with them at the time of the adoption. As no father is named for the child, it is likely that Anne was a minor and a single mother. Almost certainly, she did not feel capable of maintaining full responsibility for raising her child and thus transferred the legal duty to her own parents. The grandparents in this case promised to raise their granddaughter, to provide her with all of her necessities, and to give her a religious education.[73]

---

[68] Ibid.

[69] AN, MC, Et. CV, 343 (27 September 1621).

[70] AN, MC, Et. XXIX, 178 (5 April 1638).

[71] The widow found herself "en la grande nécessité." AN, MC, Et. XLII, 85 (1634).

[72] AN, MC, Et. XVIII, 140 (3 December 1605).

[73] AN, MC, Et. CV, 345 (1627).

Adoptions between kin might also be supervised by the Hôtel-Dieu. This hospice arranged to place some of the orphans left to its care (most often when their mothers died in childbirth) in adoption with members of the same kin group. In 1670 Jacques Salebourse, a master leatherer who resided on the rue St. Victor, arranged with the governors of the Hôtel-Dieu to adopt "forever" his nephew, Jacques Louis, whose mother, Françoise, had died giving birth at the hospice. Jacques pledged that he would take full responsibility for Jacques and raise him in the Roman Catholic religion "like his own child."[74] In a similar case from 1676 Marin Fontaine, a day worker, and his wife Catherine Moytié from the faubourg St. Germain, arranged with the governors to adopt their granddaughter, Marie-Jeanne Roger, already orphaned of her father and whose mother Marie Fontaine had recently died at the Hôtel-Dieu. Fontaine and his wife adopted their granddaughter pledging to raise her in the Roman Catholic religion "as their daughter" and to "provide for her as their own child."[75]

As many of the above cases disclose, households often adopted kin when the natal parents had died or were otherwise prevented from providing adequately for the child. In many cases the inclination to come to the aid of a relative in need was reinforced by the fact that the adopting household had no biological children. This combination of factors provided the impetus for Julien Vivier and Charlotte Le Tas to adopt their niece, Anne Le Tas, from her widowed mother, Magdeleine Papelart. Magdeleine was most likely a destitute widow as her husband had been a day worker. The adopting couple recounted that, "considering that they have no children" they decided "out of charity and love . . . to adopt and choose Anne Le Tas, niece of the said Charlotte Le Tas, to take in their charge as their own child."[76] For her part, Magdeleine gave her daughter to the couple to raise as their "adopted daughter . . . in a good manner according to the Roman Catholic faith." The adoptive parents promised Anne a donation of their immovable and movable goods "as if she were their own daughter."[77] In the 1690s Nicholas Capelain, a master distiller and merchant of eau-de-vie, made a donation of property to Marie and Christophe Ponce, the nephew and niece of his deceased wife, Marie Grisollet, who had named the children as her heirs. In the contract Nicholas noted that he and Marie had produced no children in twenty years of marriage, but that they had always taken particular care of the education of Nicholas and Marie, whom they "considered to be their own children [*comme ses propres enfants*]."

74 AP, Fonds de l'Hôtel-Dieu, liasse 877.
75 AP, Fonds de l'Hôtel-Dieu, liasse 877 (last day of June 1676).
76 AN, MC, Et. XLII, 85 (12 June 1634).
77 Ibid.

Nicholas noted further that the children had been raised in his home "just as if he had adopted them."[78]

Ties of kinship and the networks of support created by such bonds have been portrayed as significant primarily to the upper classes of early modern French society. As the preceding stories of kin adoption suggest, however, ties of spiritual, affinal, and consanguineous kinship formed strong and enduring bonds for artisan and laboring families, ties that ensured the intervention of kin in critical moments for some families. There are several reasons why adoptions between kin formed the most common type of private adoption. Recalling the strong prejudice against adoption found in many quarters of early modern French society, we can imagine that the adoption of child from the kin group might have posed less of a threat to the family lineage than would the adoption of a child from outside of the kin group, such as an abandoned child of unknown lineage or the child of a neighbor. In addition, because the biological heritage of the child was a matter of "public record" in cases of kin adoption, the fear that the child would become embroiled in a future incestuous union with unsuspecting kin was minimized.

The question still remains, however, as to why these families bothered to undergo the process of formalizing the adoptions in front of a notary, rather than simply taking in the children of their relatives on an informal fostering basis? One possible explanation is that even kin adoptions could provoke resistance from collateral heirs who hoped to inherit any family property in the absence of children. In a court case cited earlier, we saw that a donation from a godfather to his godson was attacked by the donor's collateral heirs as alienating the patrimony to a "stranger." A court case from the late sixteenth century supplies additional evidence of the pattern of collateral heirs challenging, although not always successfully, donations made to adopted children from the same kin group. In this instance Nicholas le Gras and his wife Anne Guymier made a donation in 1583 of all of their movable and immovable property to their nephew, the son of Nicholas's brother. The donation was subsequently challenged by collateral heirs, and it was left to the Parlement of Paris to pronounce on the validity of the nephew's inheritance. The record of the case recounts that Nicholas and Anne had no biological children and, "despairing of ever having any," decided not to "adopt a stranger," but rather to select a kinsman "whom nature presented to them." Long before the donation was made, Nicholas and Anne had taken care of their nephew's upbringing and education, sending him to "college and university." In return, the nephew had aided his uncle in his business affairs, which further solidified the bond

---

[78] BN, Ms. fr. Clairambault, 771, fols. 113–23 (I thank Sarah Hanley for pointing out this interesting case to me).

between uncle and nephew. The court ultimately upheld Nicholas's donation to his nephew based on the fact that the bond between Nicholas and his nephew stretched back many years, was grounded in the services they provided for one another, and was fortified by the "deep-rooted love they felt for one another."[79] Such examples of resistance by collateral kin helps to explain why even families adopting a child from the same kin group found it expedient to seal the act in front of a notary.[80] We can speculate, moreover, that the tougher restrictions on adoption and inheritance in the revised Custom of Paris made it even more important for adopting families to seal the arrangements before a notary. Rather than risking future challenges by collateral kin, many adoptive parents opted to pass on their property to adopted kin through a *donation entre vifs* sealed in front of a notary in order to ensure that the adopted child would inherit in the future "like their own child."

PRIVATE ADOPTIONS FROM OUTSIDE OF THE KIN GROUP

In addition to kinship networks, a wide range of other bonds facilitated two-household adoptions. Several contracts reveal that neighborhood ties linked the two households involved in private adoptions. In 1552 Robert Dumont and his wife from the faubourg St. Honoré adopted Etienette Ysambert, the daughter of Gilles Ysambert who was also from the faubourg St. Honoré. Gilles Ysambert was a fugitive from Paris, which led Robert and his wife to adopt Etienette "in good faith and with goodwill and considering that they had no children from their marriage." The contract reveals that Robert and his wife, after having "found the girl abandoned by her father," had taken her in and cared for her for a year before signing the contract to adopt her.[81] Although the two fathers did not share the same profession—Dumont was a horse merchant and the fugitive Ysambert a journeyman papermaker—the two households most likely had some contact prior to the adoption inasmuch as they lived in the same neighborhood and the couple took in Etienette immediately after her father had first fled Paris. Neighborhood ties seem also to have been a factor in a case from 1627 involving two widows, Marguerite Tourcheron who

---

[79] This case in discussed in Loys Servin, *Arrests notables et plaidoyez de M. Loys Servin* (Rouen, 1629), pp. 558–68.

[80] It is interesting that, although the great majority of the households contracting adoptions were illiterate (the contracts often note that they could not "write or sign their names"), they nonetheless decided that it was expedient to have a *written and notarized* record of the adoption and the transferral of property.

[81] AN, Series Y 97 (1552).

adopted the daughter of Marie Cerisier, both of whom lived in the parish of St. Germain l'Auxerrois.[82]

In addition to adopting neighborhood children directly from their biological parents, households also fostered or adopted orphaned children from their neighborhoods who were under the care of one of the city's charity hospices. For instance, in 1605 the Bureau of the Poor authorized the adoption by Thomas Dyot and Marguerite Raundy of Marguerite Auffroy, a four-year-old orphan. Before the death of her parents, the young girl's biological parents had lived on the same street, the rue Montmartre, as Thomas and Marguerite.[83] The Hôtel-Dieu also arranged adoptions for orphans whose fathers shared the same profession. In a case from 1540 a young orphan girl named Baptiste Bernard whose parents had died at the Hôtel-Dieu in Paris was adopted by Guillaume Percheron and his wife, Jeanne Gorret. Baptiste's deceased father, Symon Bernard, and Guillaume were both manual laborers and this work-related bond may have led Guillaume to adopt Baptiste from the orphanage. The contract recounts that Baptiste's adoptive parents promised to furnish her with her drink and food, to raise her in good morals, to furnish her with clothing, to provide for her marriage "as if she were their own child."[84]

The decision to take another person's child into one's home also stemmed from ties of friendship and a desire to aid the child of a friend in need of assistance. Bonds of friendship were operative in the 1606 adoption of Michelle Douglas, the illegitimate daughter of Leonarda Girante and Jacques Douglas, a domestic servant originally from Scotland. Michelle was adopted "forever . . . as his own child" by Blaise Breton, a merchant living in the faubourg St. Marcel. Blaise promised to care for, apprentice, and send Michelle "to schools," stating that he undertook the adoption "out of pleasure and due to the assistance and friendship [amityé] that he owed the aforementioned Girante."[85] Ties of friendship seem to have inspired a married couple from Paris, Pierre Chevreu, a master ropemaker, and his wife Claude Ducloz, to adopt Marguerite Denys, the six-year-old daughter of Jehanne Faverolle who was the widow of a day laborer. The adoptive parents clarified that the reason they adopted the young girl from her impoverished mother was because they held a "particular affection for Marguerite Denys."[86] Sharon Kettering's useful definition of "social friendship" (as opposed to a patron-client relationship) in early modern France describes a relationship based on voluntary assistance exchanged among individuals of equal social status: "Social friendships

[82] AN, MC, Et. XXXIX, 59.
[83] AN, MC, Et. III, 487.
[84] AN, MC, Et. XXXIII, 25 (1540).
[85] AN, MC, Et. VXII, 144.
[86] AN, MC, Et. XC, 1 (1618).

supplemented family resources, and provided what they could not as an individual made his way in the world."[87] Although Kettering's conclusions regarding social friendships derive from the experiences of the upper classes, the evidence of children being adopted by "friends" of a family too poor to continue the responsibilities of child care suggest that we may extend this notion of social friendship to the artisan stratum of early modern French society.

Confessional ties—in this case, Protestant—also created networks of child care that facilitated the movement of a child from one household to another. In 1606 Nicholas Rhut, a tailor and resident of Paris, and his wife Marie Mynette offered to adopt a six-year-old boy named Claude Tougart from his widowed mother, Jeanne Prevost. The couple promised to care for and raise Claude "in the fear of God according to the Holy Scripture [*Saincte Evangile*]." The reference to the Holy Scripture, especially in juxtaposition to all of the other contracts that state clearly that the child be raised according to the "apostolic, catholic, and Roman faith," alerts us to the Protestant leanings of the two households. In this case the adoptive parents promised to teach the young Claude to "read and write," to apprentice him in the tailor's trade, and to donate a portion of their property to him.[88]

WOMEN AND ADOPTION

Widows appear frequently in the network of private adoptions, as biological mothers giving up children for adoption or as adoptive mothers. These cases bring to light a previously unexplored side of family life in which women managed to build families outside of marriage and biological reproduction. In 1603, for instance, Marguerite Choquet, the widow of an ironmonger, adopted the eleven-year-old daughter of Nicolle Ricard and Jehan Forestier, a shoemerchant. The biological parents confessed to having "placed and left [*delaissée*] from now and forever" their daughter, Jacqueline, in the care of Marguerite. Marguerite lived in the parish of St. Barthelemy and accepted Jacqueline as "her adopted daughter whom she now adopts" and pledged to raise her "as her very own and natural daughter."[89] In 1629 another widow named Marguerite Toucheron adopted a three-year-old girl named Denyse Roussel from her biological mother, the

---

[87] Sharon Kettering, "Friendship and Clientage in Early Modern France," *French History* 6, no. 2 (1992): 150. See also M. Amyard, "Friends and Neighbors," in Roger Chartier, ed., *A History of Private Life*, vol. 3, *Passions of the Renaissance*, trans. Arthur Goldhammer (Cambridge, Mass., 1989), pp. 477–92.

[88] AN, MC, Et. XXIII, 112 (1606).

[89] AN, MC, Et. XXIII, 105 (14 April 1603).

widow Marie Cerisier. Marguerite pledged to "care for, raise, and instruct" Denyse "in the fear of God as her own child." The contract explains that the biological mother had undertaken this action because she "recognized that she did not at the present time have any means to care for or raise the said child."[90] Another widow, Nicolle le Noble, adopted the three-month-old daughter of Michel Granval and Fleurance Callerante in 1631. Michel Granval signed the contract while a prisoner at St. Eloy and it seems likely that Michel's imprisonment had rendered it financially impossible for his wife Fleurance to continue to raise their infant daughter.[91] In 1643 a widow named Jeanne Billon adopted Anne Charon, the two-and-a-half-year-old daughter of another widow named Claude Gaye, to raise as her child.[92]

Alongside widows, the contracts show us women who had undergone a legal procedure to separate their dotal property from their husband's control and who, in turn, arranged to adopt daughters as heirs. We have already met Marie Sauron who had gained control over her lineal properties and who had, in turn, arranged in 1605 to adopt her goddaughter, Thiomette de la Salle, as her daughter and heir.[93] This form of legal separation, the *séparation de biens*, was granted to women whose husbands threatened to squander their dotal properties that were reserved for their widowhood, or, in the case that the couple did not have any children, reverted to the collateral heirs on her side of the family.[94] The separation of property did not mean that women such as Marie were living apart from their husbands (this would entail another legal process of separation, the *séparation de corps*, normally granted in cases of repeated domestic violence). The separation did, however, permit women to authorize adoptions without the presence of their husbands.

What do these cases of women adopting daughters independently (and, in some cases, with their husband's permission) suggest about women and family life? The standard definition of adoption describes it as an act that creates "an artificial line of paternity" linking adoptive fathers and sons (hence Robert Estienne in his French-Latin dictionary of 1549 defines adoption as "taking a son").[95] The instances of women adopting daughters to be their heirs, however, suggest the existence of informal traditions

---

[90] AN, MC, Et. XXXIX, 59 (29 November 1629).

[91] AN, MC, Et. CV, 381 (7 July 1631).

[92] AN, MC, Et. XIX, 426 (2 May 1643).

[93] AN, MC, Et. III, 476 (5 March 1605).

[94] On the process of the *séparation de biens* and on women and property more generally in early modern France, see Wendy Gibson, *Women in Seventeenth-Century France* (Basingstoke, 1989), esp. pp. 84–96.

[95] Robert Estienne, *Dictionnaire francoislatin, autrement dict les mots francois* (Paris, 1549), p. 15, s.v. "adoption": "prendre un fils."

of "matrilineal descent". Indeed, these matrilineal traditions figure prominently in several of the contracts involving couples whose marital community of property remained intact. In a few instances the contracts make
clear that the main impetus behind the adoption came from the wife.
Moreover, in many contracts it was the wife's property (her "movables"
and "immovables") that was pledged to the adopted daughter. Thus, in an
early seventeenth-century case in which Marie la Rousse was authorized by
her husband, Gilles du Puy, to sign a contract to adopt Claire le Roy, the
contract makes clear that the adoption was primarily Marie's concern. Ex-
plaining why she had turned to adoption, Marie recounted that she had
"always wanted to adopt a daughter whom she could treat as her own
daughter." Furthermore, the contract outlines that Marie's adopted
daughter, Claire, would inherit only her property, suggesting that the lines
of filiation were forged primarily between mother and daughter.[96]

We can imagine that in addition to providing a licit avenue to pass on
the mother's property, these notarized arrangements provided the pathway for the transmission of less tangible "inheritables" such as knowledge
of the mother's trade, family traditions, and even women's "secrets."[97]
The adoptions granted these women daughters who would "honor" them
as mothers, help them around the house, assist in their trades, and succor
them in their old age. In exchange, the adopted daughters received from
their mothers general care and nurturing, the promise of an apprenticeship
in a trade, the pledge of a dowry, the gift of an inheritance, and, we can
speculate, the maternal love and affection they otherwise would not have
experienced had they grown up in the foundling hospice or in one of the
city's orphanages.

What were the legal and cultural precedents for women adopting
daughters as heirs in sixteenth- and seventeenth-century Paris? Early Roman law had argued that unmarried women could not adopt since women
remained in perpetual *potestas* and thus were not in a position to wield
parental authority over others. Justinian's legal reforms of the sixth century, however, opened up the possibility for childless widows to adopt
children to console them in their old age. Medieval French law chose to
follow earlier Roman law, however, maintaining that women were not legally capable to adopt. The fourteenth-century jurist Bouteillier, in his
Somme rurale summed up a woman's relationship to her children: "A
woman cannot adopt or recognize a child. Because women's own, natural

[96] Cothereau, *La théorique et pratique des notaires*, pp. 62–63.

[97] On the role of mothers in passing on work traditions to their daughters and the role of
work in shaping the mother-daughter bond in early modern France, see Olwen Hufton,
"Women, Work, and Family," in Arlette Farge and Natalie Z. Davis, eds., *A History of Women: Renaissance and Enlightenment Paradoxes* (Cambridge, Mass., 1994),
pp. 15–45.

children are not under their authority [*poteste*], they could not have others as such."[98]

Given the background of a legal tradition that denied women the potential to forge familial ties on their own, what are we to make of the evidence of women adopting daughters as heirs? Viewed from a legal perspective, the cases of adoption echo the findings of a growing body of research suggesting that, in practice, women retained a good deal of autonomy with regard to their property, even while in theory women were steadily losing legal ground.[99] The work of Barbara Diefendorf and Evelyne Berriot-Salvadore, for instance, has demonstrated that contrary to reigning cultural assumptions about women's inherent frailty and need to be guided by male rationality, the status of widowhood in early modern Paris offered women an important social and economic role, as well as providing women with many freedoms barred to married women.[100] Unlike married women, widowed women were given important responsibilities as heads of households regarding the guardianship of their children and the management of the family properties. As an extension of their role as household managers, widows were able to sign contracts on their own dispensing of the family property as they saw fit, provided that the children were not disadvantaged.[101] Like widows, women who had separated their lineal property from the marital community of property and mature unmarried women (*filles majeures*) were also given greater independence in terms of managing property than were married women.[102] Thus, the un-

---

[98] "Item femme ne peut avoir fils adoptif ni advoüé. Cars leurs fils mesmes naturels n'ont elles pas en leur poteste, ergo n'en peuvent elles avoir autres." In Jean Bouteillier, *La somme rurale ou le grand coustumier général de pratique civil et canon* (Paris, 1603), p. 536, under title "Que femme ne peut prendre fils adoptif."

[99] See, for example, Barbara B. Diefendorf, "Women and Property in Old Regime France: Theory and Practice in Dauphiné and Paris," in John Brewer and Susan Staves, eds., *Early Modern Conceptions of Property* (New York, 1995), pp. 170–93 and Amy Louise Erickson, *Women and Property in Early Modern England* (London, 1993).

[100] On the advantages of widowhood in terms of property management and in terms of acting as heads of households, see Barbara Diefendorf, "Widowhood and Remarriage in Sixteenth-Century Paris," *Journal of Family History* 7 (winter 1982): 379–95; Evelyne Berriot-Salvadore, *Les femmes dans la société française de la Renaissance* (Geneva, 1990). For a slightly different view of widowhood, see Julie Hardwick, "Widowhood and Patriarchy in Seventeenth-Century France," *Journal of Social History* 26 (fall 1992): 133–48.

[101] The working women of the markets in Paris, such as Les Halles, as well as merchant women were also able to sign contracts on their own in order to conduct business. See the royal edict of December 1683—which mentions a lost edict of 1606—regulating this issue in François-André Isambert, *Recueil général des anciennes lois depuis l'au 420 jusqu'à la Révolution de 1789*, 29 vols. (Paris, 1821–33), 19:438–39.

[102] During the marriage, the husband retained control over the community property and could alienate it at will, excepting the woman's lineage property—including the *propres*, acquisitions made before the marriage, and certain gifts received by either spouse during marriage. On marital property in the Custom of Paris, see Olivier-Martin, *Histoire de la coutume*, 2:210–11, 214–15.

attached and separated women who adopted daughters to treat "like their own" and name as their heirs, formed part of this somewhat paradoxical sociocultural system that positioned widows and other unmarried women as female heads of households, while women were officially denied an independent role in economic, legal, and political spheres. Clearly, this model of "adoptive reproduction" offered women who could not marry, or did not want to, an alternative avenue to creating a family and ensuring the passage of their property into the next generation.

In early modern France the family lineage was traced traditionally through the father's side and rendered legitimate through legal marriage. In these contracts, however, we see informal lines of matrilineal descent traced through "fictive" bonds that were rendered legitimate through notarized contracts.

In its broadest terms, the evidence of households composed of adoptive mothers and daughters highlights the wide range of family forms forged at this time. In an era when the family was increasingly being defined in legal, religious, and moral treatises in patriarchal terms, this model of adoptive reproduction reveals the potential for alternative domestic arrangements centered on the figure of the mother and on the strength of the mother-daughter bond. In searching for the broader sociocultural context in which to place these female-oriented families, we can point to the variety of ways in which unmarried women took on roles of nurturing and educating children—from the women in enclosed religious orders such as the Ursulines, who were in charge of educating young girls, to lay women working in hospices and in charitable confraternities who also cared for destitute girls. Parisian society was also familiar, of course, with the model of families headed by widowed mothers who chose not to remarry. We can imagine that such examples of women who took on maternal roles outside the institution of marriage helped, in turn, to facilitate the acceptance of the households composed of adoptive mothers and daughters in the neighborhoods of early modern Paris.[103]

THE CIVIL STATUS OF THE ADOPTED CHILDREN

The language employed in many of the two-household contracts indicates that the adoptive parents wanted to ensure that their adopted children were brought into their new households as fully "legitimate" family members. Although most privately adopted children were born to legally married parents, when this was not the case it appears that the act of adoption constituted a form of legitimation. For instance, when Marin le Prevost and his wife Marye Lescripvain adopted Jehan Fournet, whose biological

---

[103] For a discussion of the spectrum of "nurturing" roles for women in Renaissance France, see Berriot-Salvadore, *Les femmes dans la société française de la Renaissance.*

mother was unmarried, the couple promised to raise him as if he were "*born from their bodies in legal marriage.*"[104] The language of a renewed birth employed in this contract suggests that Jehan was granted the status of "legitimate son" by his adoptive parents. The use of a language of legitimate procreation in this contract appears to signal a rebirth of the adopted child, indicating a transition in civil status from an "illegitimate and biological" child to a "legitimate and adopted" child.[105] Similar language of legitimate procreation was employed even in cases where the adopted child was "legitimate." In a case from 1552, the adoptive parents of Etienette Ysambert, Robert Dumont and Jeanne Courtois, promised their daughter a future inheritance of all of their movable and immovable property "as if [she] had been *born and procreated from their bodies in legal marriage.*"[106] Similar language was employed in 1603 when Marguerite Choquet, a widow, promising to care for Jacqueline Forestier "as *her own, natural daughter,*" granted her a future inheritance of "all and each of her movable and immovable goods."[107]

In these instances the language of legitimate birth seems to have been used to signal the legitimate nature of the ties binding the adoptive parents and their children. The language of rebirth in the adoption contracts echoes that employed in royal letters of legitimation, which granted illegitimate children rights of succession. In a letter from 1566, for example, the king legitimated Nicholas Richer, the "natural son" of Mathurin Richer and Jehanne Lethillier, "as if he were born in true and legitimate marriage." The act of legitimation accorded to Nicholas rights to the family property that he had not previously possessed, stating that now "he can succeed to the goods of his mother and father and *amys charnelz,* providing that it is the desire of the aforementioned parties."[108] The granting of a new civil status through an act of adoption also parallels popular ceremonies undertaken when a child was legitimated through the subsequent marriage of the biological parents. In such ceremonies the child was often passed under a veil (*voile*) and symbolically reborn as a legitimate member of the family. In a case of legitimation "under the veil" from 1568, Antoine Carron and Ambroise Bitouzet from the parish of St. Merry in Paris were wed on Saturday, 14 February, at which time they placed their three daughters, Suzanne, Marie, and Perette Carron "under the veil." The three girls were then considered to have been reborn as legitimate in

[104] AN, MC, Et. XIII, 5 (15 May 1627).

[105] On illegitimacy in the early modern period, see Renée Barbarin, *La condition juridique du bâtard d'après la jurisprudence du Parlement de Paris du Concile de Trente à la Révolution française* (Mayenne, 1960).

[106] AN, Series Y 97 (1552). Emphasis added.

[107] AN, MC, Et. XXIII, 105 (14 April 1603). Emphasis added.

[108] AN, Series K, no. 172 (17 January 1566).

1568.[109] The terms of legitimation embedded in the contracts of private adoption in many respects, then, mirrored the transformative power of this early modern ritual of rebirth through subsequent marriage.

THE FLEXIBILITY OF EARLY MODERN ADOPTION

A number of the private adoption contracts conclude with a clause outlining procedures to be followed in the event that the natal family desired to reclaim the biological child at some future date. In a case introduced previously, from 1634, the contract concludes by stating that should either of the birth parents wish to recover four-week-old Henry in the future they would be obliged to reimburse the adoptive father, Charles de Pelerin, for all of his expenses incurred up until that point.[110] Similar reversal clauses appear in other contracts. In another case of adoption from 1634, Charlotte Papelart, a poor widow who gave her daughter in adoption to the young girl's aunt, promised not to ask for the child back. The contract stipulated, however, that if such a reclamation were to occur Charlotte would have to reimburse the adoptive couple for the care given to Anne.[111]

Why might both sets of parents have desired the inclusion of such reunion clauses in the adoption contracts? One possible answer to this query is that these clauses served as a form of legal protection for the natal parents. Early modern law banned the disavowal of children and in this context the reversal clauses might have been added as a measure of protection for the natal parents who gave away their child to the care of adoptive parents.[112] The addition of a reversal clause also reflects the fact that most households gave up a child in adoption due to some incapacity, most often economic, which precluded them from continuing the task of raising their child. Consequently, many of these families hoped that in the future they

109 From the parish registers of St. Merry (Thursday, 12 February 1568). Cited in Ernst Semichon, *Histoire des enfants abandonnés depuis l'antiquité jusqu'à nos jours* (Paris, 1886), appendix, p. 314.

110 AN, MC, Et. XXIV, 340 (10 April 1634).

111 Many other contracts contained such a "clause": in a case from 1606 (AN, MC, Et. XVII, 144) in which Michelle Douglas was adopted by a friend of her mother, Blaise Breton, the contract stated that, if the father wanted to reclaim Michelle in the future, he would have to pay Blaise the costs he had spent in raising her. For other examples of such reclamation clauses, see AN, MC, Et. XVII, 144 (6 July 1606); CV, 343 (27 September 1621); XLII, 85 (12 June 1634).

112 It could be that this model of adoption alleviated some of the fears associated with adoption. Because the children's natal family was known to the new parents, and we can speculate, to many of the adopted children as well, fears of future accidental incestuous unions would be minimized.

would find the means to bring the child back into the natal home. For instance, such circumstances of poverty shaped an adoption from 1554 in which Guy Le Fèvre and his wife adopted a young girl, Perrine, from the girl's indigent mother, Jehanne Gandellet, "for the honor of God."[113] Jehanne gave away Perrine in adoption as she "did not have at present any means to care for her children due to her poverty and indigence." Although Guy promised to provide Perrine with all of her necessities, including providing her for marriage, the terms of the adoption remained somewhat flexible in light of the future reversal clause, which obligated Jehanne to reimburse Guy for his expenses if she claimed Perrine in the future. Jehanne might have hoped that at some point in the future she would find the means enabling her to take back Perrine to raise her on her own. The inclusion of such reversal clauses suggests that early modern adoption departed in significant ways from the model developed in the early twentieth century in Europe and in the United States, which insists that an adopted child undergo a complete and permanent break with the natal parents. In contrast to the demand for a complete transfer of familial identity inherent in most modern legal adoption codes, the model of private adoption from early modern Paris appears adaptable to changing circumstances, allowing for the possibility of a future reclamation by the biological parents (although we may also conjecture that such reversals were extremely rare).[114]

CONCLUSIONS

In the end, the case studies of adoptions privately contracted between two households highlight the multiplicity of models of parenthood that shaped family life in early modern Paris. The dominant pattern of parenting emanated from biological generation, and formed part of a larger cultural system of marriage, the "conjugal debt" and inheritance laws in which lineage was traced through a legally constituted bloodline. A second, and

---

[113] AN, MC, Et. CXXII, 1365 (28 February 1554).

[114] Customs of abandonment also reveal that many parents hoped for future contact, and even reunion, with the child they had left to the fortunes of charity. Abandoned children were often found with trinkets or "name tags" attached to their clothing, suggesting that parents hoped that, someday, if they had the means and wanted to reclaim their children, they would recognize them as their own. Such identity markers may have also been placed by parents in order to prevent future incestuous unions between the foundling and blood kin. For seventeenth-century Paris, see the Registres des enfants trouvez, AN, Y 743, where entries often refer to identifying objects left with the child: "Un garçon âgé d'environ deux jours a esté exposé rue St. Roch sur le pas de la porte des Soeurs de la Charité ayant un billet" (18 June 1699). Yet, actual reclamations, so far as can be determined, were extremely rare.

lesser known, model of parenthood derived from what can be termed "adoptive reproduction," which was grounded in a legal contract linking adoptive parents and their adopted children in mutually beneficial arrangements of obligations and benefits.[115] This model of parenthood formed part of an alternative, though complementary, culture of family life, which, while not entirely divorced from the criteria of blood and marriage, was characterized by flexible domestic boundaries by which a child from another family could become an affiliated family member and an heir to the family name and property.

With few exceptions, due to the concrete legal obstacles and to their firm belief in the biological basis of family lineage, noble families rejected this model of adoptive reproduction. Sarah Hanley has demonstrated the lengths to which some childless noble families might go in order to solve the problem of heirship while still conforming to the model of biological reproduction.[116] In an intriguing case from the eighteenth century, a noblewoman named Barbe-Françoise Digard des Meulettes was determined to avoid becoming a childless widow, in which case much of the marital property would revert to collateral relatives. To avoid such a fate, Barbe-Françoise collaborated with a midwife to acquire a newborn orphan from the Parisian Hôtel-Dieu and to bring it, stained sheets and all, to Barbe-Françoise's house to stage a birth (such an action was technically a crime, known as a *supposition d'enfant*).[117] Although Barbe's unsuccessful ruse stands out as an exceptional case, her story signals the depth of attachment on the part of noble families to conform (at least publicly), to the model of biological reproduction. In contrast to the nobility, however, many laboring, artisan, and merchant families created an alternative avenue of reproduction through adoption. Rather than bringing a non-natal child into the home clandestinely to pose as the family's biological heir, the families we have met in this chapter openly negotiated and sealed adoptions of non-biological children before a notary. As we have seen, the offering of a child in adoption to another household often occurred when the natal parents were no longer capable of raising their child. For their part, the majority of the households taking in a child had no biological children and turned to adoption in order to continue the family line into the next generation. In the context of the history of the law and of family life, the private adoptions arranged between two households reveal that even in a society in which upper-class families and civil law rejected the validity of adoptive

[115] I would like to thank Sarah Hanley for initially urging me to analyze the adoption contracts as forming an alternative culture of parenting based on "adoptive reproduction."

[116] Sarah Hanley, "Engendering the State: Family Formation and State Building in Early Modern France," *French Historical Studies* 16, no. 1 (1989): 4–27.

[117] Ibid., p. 20.

ties, families built on such ties found an acceptable place among the artisan and merchant classes. We can attribute the endurance of adoption in this period to the combined efforts of the individual Parisian families who desired to adopt children and to the skill of the local notaries who were adept at interpreting the law in such a way to meet the needs of their clients.

CHAPTER FOUR

Parisian Charity Hospices and the Care of Orphans and Foundlings

These little ones, barely clothed,
Have only Dame Barbe for their mother
For support, the public is their father
Barbe sees their troubles, but what to do?
She is poor and extra clothing is dear;
The Chapter can do little to help
The poor little ones, born of anonymous authors,
Who know neither parents nor kin,
And have nothing besides the grace of God
To keep them warm.
   (*Gresset, description of the Parisian*
     Foundling Hospice,
   Conte du Lutrin Vivant, *1735*)

IN MEDIEVAL and early modern Paris, many of the city's charity hospices routinely placed some of the children under their care as servants, apprentices, and foster children in private Parisian households. Although these arrangements were typically short-term and thus do not fall under the rubric of "adoption," they are important to our exploration of formal adoption practices in highlighting a central—and often overlooked—feature of poor relief. Rather than merely retaining the city's destitute children behind institutional walls, many of the charity hospices worked to reintegrate them into the Parisian community to be raised by "surrogate families" until adulthood.

Like many cities in sixteenth- and seventeenth-century France, Paris experienced an urban crisis characterized by population growth (the city's population rose as high as 250,000 or 300,000 by midcentury),[1] an increase in immigration from regions outlying the city, periodic plagues, food shortages, and, in its public manifestation, a crisis marked by a greater visibility of poverty. City officials responded to these changes in the

---

[1] On the population of Paris in this period, see Jean-Pierre Babelon, *Nouvelle histoire de Paris: Paris au XVIe siècle* (Paris, 1986); Jean Jacquart, "Le poids démographique de Paris et de l'Ile-de-France au XVIe siècle," *Annales de démographie historique* (1980): 93–94.

urban climate by reworking and expanding the city's programs of public assistance. It was in this context that François I ordered a reorganization of the Parisian charity hospices in 1520, a reformation aimed at "correcting the great disorder . . . and evident abuses which up until now have been committed and perpetrated."[2] This renewal of public assistance prompted both a reorganization of several of the city's existing orphanages as well as the establishment of several new institutions oriented toward the care of orphans.

ST. ESPRIT

One of the oldest orphanages in the city was the hospice founded at the place de Grève in 1363 by the confraternity of St. Esprit. This hospice opened its doors to orphans, "born in legal marriage . . . who had neither father nor mother, nor *amys charneulx*[3] or others who could provide for them."[4] Once admitted, infant orphans were sent out to be wet-nursed, while older children were cared for within the hospice. Both boys and girls were taught from the age of five or so by teachers who resided in the hospice. The primary goal of their education was to school them in the "Catholic beliefs and faith" in order to "learn to praise and serve Our Lord."[5] In addition to a religious education, boys were routinely instructed in reading, writing, arithmetic, and grammar.[6] Both boys and girls were schooled until they reached the age where they could be apprenticed in a trade, in order, as the regulations of 1363 stated, to "learn to work and to be able to earn their own living."[7]

Parliamentary edicts awarded the administrators of St. Esprit the title of

[2] "Et pour ce faire réformer et corriger le grand désordre, evidans abbuz et malversacions que par cy-devant se y sont faiz, commis et perpétré," from the confirmation of powers given by the king (1 March 1520) to Jean Briçonnet and Pierre du Val. Cited in Marcel Fosseyeux, "L'assistance parisienne au milieu du XVIe siècle," *Mémoires de la société d'histoire de Paris de l'Ile de France* 43 (1916): 84. The reform of Parisian hospitals envisioned by the king formed part of a broader process of laicization of public assistance in the early modern period. Each Parisian establishment, for example, was to be overseen by a lay as well as a religious administrator. For a comparative look at these trends in the town of Lille, see M. J. Desnoyers, "Les dépenses faites par la ville de Lille pour les enfants trouvés au XVe et au XVIe siècle," *Bulletin du comité de la langue, de l'histoire et des arts de la France* 3 (1855–56): 444–80.

[3] On the role of *amis charnels*, see J. M. Turlan, "Amis et amis charnels d'après les actes du Parlement au XIVe siècle," *Revue historique du droit français et étranger* 47 (1969): 645–98.

[4] See Joseph Berthelé, "La vie intérieure d'un hospice du XIVe au XVIe siècle: L'hôpital du Saint-Esprit-en-Grève à Paris," *Revue de l'hôpital et l'aide sociale à Paris* 5 (1961). For the full text of the 1363 règlement of St. Esprit, see BN Ms. 11778, fol. 53.

[5] Berthelé, "La vie intérieure," p. 694, and BN Ms. fols. 63–64.

[6] Berthelé, "La vie intérieure," p. 695, and BN Ms. fol. 65.

[7] Berthelé, "La vie intérieure," p. 695, and BN Ms. fol. 65–65v.

"adoptive parents" to the orphans under their care. This title granted them, alongside the traditional parental obligation to raise the children, rights to usufruct of an orphan's property before the age of marriage, and, by a royal edict of 1566, rights to succession to the movable property when a child died.[8] Additionally, as an extension of their duty to raise, educate, and provide for the orphans under their care, the governors of St. Esprit frequently placed the orphans into service and foster care in private households throughout Paris. In 1605, for instance, the governors gave approval to Charles Charbonnier, a counselor to the king, and his wife Marie Louet to take into their home for six years an eighteen-year-old orphan named Marie Fourniton. The couple promised to provide her with clothing, food and drink, a room with a bed and a light, and all other things she might require for the time she spent with them "in their service." At the end of her six years of service, the couple promised Marie a payment of fifty-five livres tournois to be managed for her by the administrators of St. Esprit.[9] In another case from 1605 Cecile Blondeau, the wife of a wine merchant in Paris, arranged with the governors of St. Esprit to "take into her service" a twelve-year-old orphan named Magdeleine Potier. In return for serving Cecile and her husband Jehan in "all licit and honest matters" Magdeleine would be provided with all of her necessities and would be "instructed in the Roman Catholic faith."[10]

The regulations of St. Esprit explicitly excluded the foundlings, the children left anonymously in public places by their natal parents, from the charity of the hospice.[11] To ensure the legitimate status of the orphans, beginning in the sixteenth century the hospice required that the relatives of the orphan wishing to be placed in St. Esprit had to "bring in front of two notaries of the Châtelet any godfathers, godmothers, uncles, aunts, or

---

[8] On the title of the administrators of St. Esprit as "adoptive parents" and the parallels with the directors of the Aumône générale in Lyon, who also stood as "adoptive parents" to the children under their care, see Paul Viollet, *Droit privé et sources. Histoire du droit civil français . . . 3 éd. du Précis de l'histoire du droit français* (Paris, 1905), 2:407, and Paul Gonnet, *L'adoption lyonnaise des orphelins légitimes (1536–1793)* (Paris, 1935), 1:223–45, on St. Esprit, and 2:151–59, for the royal letters confirming the full succession rights of the rectors of the Lyonnais Aumône as "adoptive parents" to the property of the orphans under their care.

[9] AN, MC, Et. III, 487 (December 1605) For other similar cases involving orphans from St. Esprit, see Et. III, 487 (December 1605), (July 1605), (13 October 1605), (27 October 1605). In several of the servant and apprenticeship cases, the master or mistress promised to give the children a religious education or to provide them with a dowry. In these cases, then, the lines between master or mistress and parent and between servant and child are somewhat fluid. See, for example, a contract from St. Esprit in Et. III, 476 (27 October 1605).

[10] AN, MC, Et. III, 487 (October 1605).

[11] The regulations of 1363 restricted entrance to the hospice to orphans of one or both parents and made it quite clear that "the foundlings, which are left in the churches and parishes or in the streets, will not be allowed in this hospice." Berthelé, "La vie intérieure," p. 688, and BN Ms. fol. 61.

other neighbors who can attest to the fact that these children were born in legal marriage and in the city and faubourgs of Paris."[12] Despite the hospice's refusal to admit foundlings, infants were nonetheless abandoned regularly at the doorways of the orphanage. These practices induced the governors to obtain royal letters from Charles VI in 1409 reaffirming their right to deny charity to abandoned children.[13] The administrators argued that the girls raised in the hospice, who were sought in marriage by the "honorable people" of Paris, would never contract suitable marriages if their legitimate origins were in doubt.[14] The governors also maintained that for the hospice to receive the foundlings would be tantamount to condoning extramarital sex.[15] When a child of unknown parentage was abandoned at the hospice the administrators informed the officers of the Châtelet who had the infant taken to the foundling hospice run by the Chapter of Notre-Dame.

THE HÔTEL-DIEU AND THE HOSPICE OF THE ENFANTS-DIEU

The Hôtel-Dieu, the primary hospital in the city located adjacent to the Cathedral of Notre-Dame, also served as a place of refuge and care for the orphaned children of Paris, primarily those children whose parents had died while residing at the Hôtel-Dieu. A royal investigator described the experiences of Cécille la Maraschalle, a sister at the Hôtel-Dieu, in 1531:

> During her time at the Hôtel-Dieu she has seen a large number of infants brought to the hospice by their sick mothers, or who were born there to poor women who came to give birth at the hospital. These children, in turn, were left behind by their mothers after they gave birth or because they had died in childbirth.[16]

Sister Maraschalle recounted further that children also were abandoned clandestinely to the care of the Hôtel-Dieu, noting that "swaddled infants

[12] "Meinent devant deux notaires du Chastellet les parrains, marraines, oncles, tantes ou autres voisins attester que les ditz enfants sont nez en loyal mariage en la ville ou forsbourgs de Paris." Cited in Berthelé, "La vie intérieure," p. 691 and BN Ms. fol. 60.

[13] *Lettres patentes* of Charles VI (29 July 1409), cited in Berthelé, "La vie intérieure," pp. 688–89.

[14] The *lettres patentes* of Charles VI remarked that, "plusieurs bons varlez sont venus, ou ont envoyé plusieurs bons gens, au dict hospital, pour demander les filles du dict lieu en mariage—pour ce qu'ils tiennent et sçaivent qu'elles sont nées en loyal mariage." Ibid., p. 688.

[15] Cited in ibid., p. 689, and BN Ms. fol. 201–2. The hospice of St. Esprit also pleaded a lack of funds as a reason for not extending charity to the infants left at its doorstep.

[16] AP, Fonds des Enfans Rouges, "Information de Pierre Carrel sur le sort des enfants à l'Hôtel-Dieu," (1531), fol. 10r.

were brought and abandoned at night in front of the two portals of the hospital. In the case that no one else took them, the sisters took them in out of pity and charity."[17]

Sixteenth-century records indicate that, like St. Esprit, the Hôtel-Dieu relied on the participation of the Parisian community to help raise the orphans and foundlings under its care. In 1501 Brother Jehan le Feure reported to the royal commissioner, Bureau Boucher, that the Hôtel-Dieu encouraged charitable people to come to the hospital to take home one of the foundlings left to its care. Le Feure reported that, when an abandoned child was found at the doors of the Hôtel-Dieu, he would often "leave the said child near the door until the evening with the hope that some good person would come by who, through an act of charity, would want to take the child and care for it."[18] More humane procedures seem to have prevailed in 1531 when Sister Hélène la Petite, the prioress at the Hôtel-Dieu, told another royal commissioner, Pierre Carrel, that many married couples without children arrived at the hospice to select a child "for the love of God."[19] Sister Cécille la Maraschalle revealed to Carrel that notables from the city who came to tour the Hôtel-Dieu and who saw "the children crowded together and sleeping in large numbers in the same bed, asked for a boy or girl if they had no children of their own." La Maraschalle added that the children would be given to those who it seemed would be able to offer them suitable care and good treatment.[20]

Because it ministered in large part to victims of the plague, the Hôtel-Dieu evolved into a sort of deathtrap for the ever increasing numbers of orphans and foundlings consigned to the hospice's care.[21] The deteriorating conditions at the hospice led Marguerite d'Angoulême, the sister of King François I, to oversee the creation in 1536 of a separate Hôpital des Enfants-Dieu in the quartier du Temple, which was dedicated to care of the city's orphans. The children of the hospice were known as the "enfants rouges" due to the color of their uniforms. Initially, the hospice received only legitimate orphans whose parents had died at the Hôtel-Dieu, but in

[17] Ibid.

[18] AN, L553b, "Information de Bureau Boucher," n. 29 (1501), fol. 8v. Francis I made reference to these traditions of adoption from the Hôtel-Dieu in a royal decree of 1541: "Nous avons été averti que ceux qui ont été tirés jusqu'ici, nos bons Bourgeois & Bourgeoises de Paris en prennent beaucoup, tant pour s'en servir, que pour apprendre leur métier; & quelquefois en doüent quand ils n'ont point d'enfans, pour les nourrir pour l'amour de Dieu." *Déclaration du Roy François Ier* (22 June 1541), AP, Fonds de l'Hôp. gén., liasse 3.

[19] "Information de Pierre Carrel" (1531), fol. 4v.

[20] Ibid., fol. 11r.

[21] In Paris the plague struck in almost every year of the sixteenth century. One of the most virulent outbreaks occurred between 1531 and 1533 and inspired a new series of edicts of the Parlement. The plagues of these years left many children orphaned, especially at the Hôtel-Dieu, and was an important factor behind the creation of the hospice of the Enfants Rouges.

1541 its doors were opened to all the legitimate orphans of the city and suburbs of Paris. As in the case of St. Esprit, however, the hospice of the Enfants Rouges closed its doors to the city's foundlings.[22] When children of unknown parentage were left at the portals of the hospice, the administrators promptly turned the infants over to the "Couche," or Cradle, of the Poor Foundlings, the sole home for abandoned children in the city.

THE TRINITÉ

Another hospice serving the needs of the poor and orphaned children of Paris in the sixteenth century was the Trinité, located on the rue St. Denis in the neighborhood of St. Sépulcre. Founded in the twelfth century, the Trinité was run until 1545 by the order of the Premontés as a shelter for pilgrims and other itinerants.[23] In 1545, by order of the Parlement of Paris, the Trinité was transformed into a hospice for the "male children of the poor" and served as a place of refuge and instruction for boys above the age of seven. Soon thereafter the hospice extended its services to poor girls and, finally, to orphans of both sexes. Due to the color of their outfits, the orphans of the Trinité were known as the "enfants bleues." The children were given a religious education and taught to read, sing, write, and recite the psalms.[24] At the age of seven the children were instructed in various branches of the textile trades in apprenticeship houses run by the hospice, or they were sent out of the hospice to apprentice with masters in the city.[25] As in the cases of St. Esprit and the Enfants Rouges, the Trinité refused to extend its charity to include the city's abandoned children. In 1552, however, the city of Paris mandated that the Trinité participate in the care of the foundlings by taking them from the Couche once they reached the age of seven or eight.

THE GREAT BUREAU OF THE POOR

In 1531 the city of Lyon, where the urban authorities were concerned with eradicating the growing numbers of beggars[26] and staying the tide of

---

[22] The *lettres patentes* of François I marking the foundation of the hospice stated explicitly that its doors were closed to the foundlings. The full text of the letters is found in AN, Series KK 334.

[23] See Fosseyeux, "L'assistance parisienne," p. 106.

[24] See Fosseyeux, "L'assistance parisienne," p. 108.

[25] See Marcel Fosseyeux, "Les maisons d'apprentissage à Paris au XVIIe et XVIIIe siècles," *Bulletin de la société historique de Paris* 40 (1913): 36–56.

[26] Prohibitions against begging for alms appeared in many cities beginning in the sixteenth century, signaling a change from the medieval toleration of public forms of begging.

food riots, founded a centralized public welfare organization called the Aumône générale. The work of the Lyonnais Aumône included providing for the city's orphans and foundlings, many of whom were fostered or formally adopted by families from Lyon and its surrounding areas.[27] Paris had founded a similar welfare organization one year before the establishment of the Lyonnais Aumône, though we know little of its structure until 1544 when the Parlement of Paris oversaw its reorganization in conjunction with the reformation of the city's programs of public assistance. The refurbished organization was named the Great Bureau of the Poor (Le Grand Bureau des Pauvres) and was situated at the place de Grève not far from the Hôtel de Ville. The bureau was run by a combination of religious and lay urban notables whose central duty was to supervise the poor relief rolls for the sixteen principal neighborhoods of the city.[28] In addition, as we saw in the preceding chapter, the bureau oversaw the formal adoption of some of the orphans by relatives, neighbors, and friends who had known the child's natal parents. Notarial records reveal that the bureau also routinely arranged apprenticeships and short-term foster care for many of the poor and orphaned children under its care. In a case overseen by the bureau in 1605, a young girl named Denise Jehan who was orphaned of father, was taken in as a servant and an apprentice for six years by Marie Maurion, a hatter, who had been authorized by her husband Baltazard du Sainctequitte, a journeyman tailor, to arrange the apprenticeship. Marie promised to teach Denise "all aspects of her trade of hat making, and also to provide her with drink and food, her bed and room and light, and to treat her as is customary" (in this case the bureau provided Denise with her clothing and linen). To help Marie care for Denise during her apprenticeship, the bureau gave her fifteen livres tournois.[29] As far as can be

See Natalie Z. Davis, "Poor Relief, Humanism, and Heresy," in *Society and Culture in Early Modern France* (Stanford, Calif., 1975), pp. 17–64. On changes in systems of poor relief in Europe as a whole in this time, see Michel Mollat, *Etudes sur l'histoire de la pauvreté: Le moyen-âge–XVIe siècle* (Paris, 1974).

[27] See Gonnet, *L'adoption lyonnaise*, and Jacqueline Roubert, "L'adoption des enfants par des particuliers à Lyon sous l'ancien régime," *Société française d'histoire des hôpitaux* 36–37 (1978): 3–30.

[28] An office of the bureau was set up in each neighborhood. In order to be placed on the poor-relief role, the administrators would first visit the individual's home to attest to his or her indigent state. On the Grand Bureau des Pauvres, see Fosseyeux, "L'assistance parisienne," as well as the contemporary account of the structure and function of the bureau in *La police des pauvres à Paris* by Montaigne, attorney of the cardinal of Tournon and of the Abbey of St.-Germain-des-Prés (Paris 1555 or 1560). The text appears in *Bulletin de la société de l'histoire de Paris* (1888): 105.

[29] AN, MC, Et. III, 476 (20 January 1605). For more examples involving the Bureau des Pauvres, see AN, MC, Et. III, 476 (January 1605), Et. III, 487 (15 September 1605), Et. XXIX, 158 (1606), and Et. XXIX, 170 (1619). In addition, see the cases of apprenticeship found in Ernst Coyecque, *Recueil d'actes notariés relatifs à l'histoire de Paris au XVIe siècle*, vol. 1 [1498–1545] (Paris, 1905), no. 1410 (May 1540), and no. 1413 (May 1540).

gathered from its records, the Bureau of the Poor, like the city's orphanages, did not extend its charity to the foundlings of Paris.

THE COUCHE

If the majority of the hospices in early modern Paris limited their assistance to legitimate orphans, what, then, was the fate of the children abandoned in the streets and at the portals of the churches and hospices in the city? The movement to reform the system of Parisian poor relief did not initially include a project to expand or improve on the care offered to abandoned children. This lack of interest in the foundlings stemmed in part from the stigma they carried of near-certain illegitimate birth. The city elders feared that expanding the network of care offered to the foundlings would only serve to encourage the extramarital sexual liaisons, which often ended in the abandonment of an infant.[30] We can safely assume, in fact, that the majority of the infants abandoned in the sixteenth century were indeed illegitimate. The parents—or, more likely, an unwed mother[31]—moved to abandon an illegitimate child would do so for two reasons: an unstable economic condition and fear of public censure for having given birth to a

[30] Studies of abandonment patterns reveal that contemporaries were most likely correct in assuming that the majority of foundlings were illegitimate. The *procès verbaux* of the Foundling Hospice, which begin only in 1639, have allowed historians to determine that between 70 and 80 percent of the children abandoned to the foundling hospital in the seventeenth and eighteenth centuries were illegitimate. See Léon Lallemand, *Un chapitre de l'histoire des enfants trouvés: La maison de la Couche à Paris (XVIIe–XVIIIe)* (Paris, 1885), p. 37. Lallemand supplies numbers at the Couche for the year 1760, which show that out of 5,032 children abandoned to its care, 4,297 were illegitimate. On the issue of illegitimacy and abandonment in early modern Paris, see also Claude Delasselle, "Les enfants abandonnés à Paris au XVIIIe siècle," *Annales: E.S.C.* 30 (1975): 187–218; Rachel G. Fuchs, *Abandoned Children: Foundlings and Child Welfare in Nineteenth-Century France* (Albany, N.Y., 1984). A study of the Foundling Hospital of St. Yves in Rennes also found that legitimate children formed only 27 percent of those admitted. See Sonoko Fukita, "L'abandon des enfants légitimes à Rennes à la fin du XVIIIe siècle," *Annales de la démographie historique* (1983): 151–62. Richard Trexler, in his study of the foundling hospice in Florence in the fifteenth century, also concludes that the majority of the children admitted were illegitimate; see "The Foundlings of Florence, 1395–1455," *History of Childhood Quarterly* 1 (1973): 259–84.

[31] Véronique Demars-Sion connects the growing numbers of illegitimate children abandoned by their mothers from the late sixteenth century onward to the overall deterioration in women's position in society in addition to growing public censure regarding illegitimacy: "Moins bien protégées juridiquement, discréditées socialement, les mères illégitimes cherchent à se débarasser de cet enfant dont on leur impose de plus en plus souvent la charge alors qu'il constitue avant tout à leurs yeux la preuve vivante de leur déshonneur," in "Illégitimité et abandon des enfants: La position des provinces du Nord, 16e–18e siècles," *Revue du Nord* 65 (1983): 482.

child out of wedlock.[32] As noted, the mark of illegitimacy served further to exclude the foundlings from entrance to the majority of the orphanages in the city, which accepted only orphans born to legitimately married parents. In the end, Paris counted only one hospice oriented toward the care of abandoned children, the Couche of the Poor Foundlings.

The question of exactly who was responsible for the care of the foundlings was asked frequently by religious and civil authorities throughout the sixteenth century and proved to be a source of conflict between the city's charity hospices and the Crown. For the most part, the responsibility for abandoned children rested with the seigneur, lay or ecclesiastic, in whose fief or jurisdiction a child was found. In return for his general protection, the seigneur retained legal claims over "strays" and treasures found within his jurisdiction, as well as rights of escheat in cases of disinheritance and bastardy. For the local seigneur, an abandoned child was considered a "burdensome stray" for whom he provided himself or, more likely, took to the nearest foundling hospice.[33] If the seigneur defaulted on this duty, as was often the case, the Crown ordered that the child be cared for by the parish of the child's origin.[34] In Paris, the seigneurs, or ecclesiastical high justices traditionally associated with caring for the foundlings, were the canons and deans of the Chapter of Notre-Dame. The *lettres patentes* of François I, which marked the establishment of the Enfants Rouges in 1536, made explicit reference to the chapter's role as the primary caretakers of the foundlings. The letters, which restricted the charity of the Enfants Rouges to legitimate orphans, thereby excluded "the illegitimate children [*bâtards*], whom the deans, canons, and Chapter of Notre-Dame of Paris are accustomed to receiving for the honor of God."[35]

The duties of the chapter extended beyond its immediate territorial jurisdiction to include children abandoned in other areas of the city. It is unclear exactly when the Chapter of Notre-Dame became the primary caretaker of the foundlings. The chapter's work could very well have begun in the fourteenth century when other European cities established institutions specifically oriented toward the reception and care of abandoned children. As early as 1392, the registers of the Châtelet tell of an aban-

---

[32] Turning again to the eighteenth century, studies reveal that illegitimate children were usually abandoned in the first weeks of life—indicating that the decision to abandon them had already been made—while legitimate children were abandoned within a wider span of time from birth, and often at times that corresponded to general economic hardship and a rise in grain prices.

[33] Léon Lallemand, *Histoire des enfants abandonnés et délaissés* (Paris, 1885), pp. 110–11, describes the seigneur's obligation to care for the children abandoned within his jurisdiction as a logical extension of his rights of justice. In some regions of France, such as Brittany, the parish, not the seigneur, was held responsible for the foundlings.

[34] *Ordonnance du Moulins sur la réforme de la justice* (February 1566), art. 73.

[35] See the royal *lettres patentes* of January 1536.

doned child sent to the Couche of Notre-Dame.[36] By the late fourteenth century the registers of the chapter regularly record funds spent for the care of the children, the *pueri reperti*, left in and around the Cathedral of Notre-Dame.[37] References to the Couche continue to appear regularly in the chapter's records in the fifteenth century; in an entry from 1451, for instance, an abandoned child is described as a *filia de la couche*.[38] By this point, the foundlings of the Couche also appear routinely as recipients of charitable donations in private wills: in 1431 Isabeau de Bavière donated "eight francs to the poor foundlings of Notre-Dame."[39] By the sixteenth century commentators recount that the chapter "had always" played the role of ministering to the foundlings, or that it had done so "since time immemorial."[40]

Infants were routinely abandoned at the steps of the cathedral as well as inside the church in stone cradles provided for this purpose.[41] The Cathedral of Notre-Dame, which represented the center of Parisian religious life, and the area in front of the church known as the *parvis*, had long served as popular locales of abandonment for parents unable, or unwilling, to care for their children.[42] Recalling the representation of the Virgin as a universal mother sheltering a multitude of poor and needy children below her cloak, we see how the Cathedral of Notre-Dame was connected in the popular imagination with the reception of unwanted children.[43] Consid-

[36] Cited in Henri Duples-Agier, *Registres criminels du Châtelet de Paris du 6 sept. 1389 au 18 mai 1392* (Paris, 1861–64), 2:530.

[37] See AN, Registres Capitulaires de Notre-Dame, Series LL 105–47. AN, Series LL 295 (fol. 410–30) is an eighteenth-century compilation by the canon Sarasin, which contains extracts (from the fourteenth to the eighteenth century) of the cartularies regarding the *pueri reperti*.

[38] AN, Series LL 117, fol. 240.

[39] "Aux pauvres enfans trouvez de Nostre-Dame de Paris huit francs." Cited in Félibien, *Histoire de la ville de Paris*, (Paris, 1725), 3:554.

[40] See, for example, the *Extraits des registres de Parlement* (11 December 1546), BN Ms. 21802, Collection Delamare (enfants trouvés et exposés), fol. 376v.

[41] See Albert Dupoux, *Sur les pas de Monsieur Vincent: Trois cents ans d'histoire parisienne de l'enfance abandonnée* (Paris, 1958), p. 26.

[42] On abandonment customs in early modern France, see the special issue "L'enfant abandonné," *Histoire, économie et société* 2 (1987); Lallemand, *Histoire des enfants abandonnés et délaissés*; Ernst Semichon, *Histoire des enfants abandonnés depuis l'antiquité jusqu'à nos jours* (Paris, 1886); Fernand Boussault, *L'assistance aux enfants abandonnés à Paris du XVIe au XVIIIe siècle* (Paris, 1937); Jehanne Charpentier, *Le droit de l'enfance abandonné: Son évolution sous l'influence de la psychologie (1552–1791)* (Paris, 1967); Delasselle, "Les enfants abandonnés à Paris au XVIIIe siècle," 187–218; Fuchs, *Abandoned Children*.

[43] Even at churches named after other saints, the special role of the Virgin as receptor of foundlings stands out. In a case from Béthune in 1564 an infant was left at the altar of "la Vièrge Marie" in the church of St. Barthélemy. Case cited in "Documents inédits pour servir à l'histoire des usages et des moeurs aux XIVe et XV siècles," *Annuaire bulletin de la société de l'histoire de la France* 2 (1864): 97. On the role of the Virgin, see also "La Vierge au grand

ered in this light, we can imagine that, by leaving their children to be taken in and raised in the institutional setting of the city's principal cathedral, these families may have believed that they were somehow giving their children to the "family" of the church and to the service of God.

The abandonment of infants at churches such as Notre-Dame constituted a public form of abandonment, which, as John Boswell's work has demonstrated for the ancient and medieval periods, must be placed in a separate category from infanticide.[44] When infants were left in public locales such as churches, charity hospices, and the homes of fellow citizens— where they could be found in a short period of time—the biological parents hoped that, with some luck, the child would be taken in and provided for. Boswell has found such beliefs reflected in high medieval tales of abandonment, which, for the most part, recount hopeful stories of the fate of the foundlings.[45] Rather than narrating the demise of the children, these tales often culminate in dramatic successes by which the abandoned child grows up to become a pope, a saint, or a prince. Boswell explains that behind this positive view of abandonment lay the need of medieval society "to believe that abandonment could result in a better life for their children, a need obviously created . . . in the absence of any other acceptable means of family limitation."[46] Civil and canon law, in fact, distinguished between abandonment in a public place where the child could be found readily by passersby and clandestine abandonment, which was considered tantamount to infanticide. While infanticide was universally condemned and punished by death,[47] both religious and secular authorities displayed a

---

manteau," in Jean Delumeau, *Rassurer et protéger: Le sentiment de sécurité dans l'Occident d'autrefois* (Paris, 1989), pp. 261–92. The Catholic Church stood as the traditional caretaker of orphans and foundlings inasmuch as destitute children fit into the category of *miserabiles personae* protected by the church. See Olivier-Martin, *Histoire de la coutume*, 1:150n. 1.

[44] On the differences between child abandonment and infanticide, see John Boswell, *The Kindness of Strangers: The Abandonment of Children in Western Europe from Late Antiquity to the Renaissance* (New York, 1988).

[45] Ibid., chap. 10: "Literary Witnesses." Versions of the tales outlined by Boswell certainly continued to circulate in the early modern period. For such tales, see, for example, "The Little Lad Who Became a Bishop," in *Folktales of France*, ed. Geneviève Massignon, trans. Jacqueline Hyland (Chicago, 1968), pp. 78–79. See also Stith Thompson, *Motif Index of Folk-Literature* (Bloomington, Ind., 1955–58), S354.1, "Abandoned child adopted by queen"; N836.1, "Adoption of hero by king"; K2015 "Adoption by rich man." Barbara L. Estrin found for Renaissance English tales of foundlings, however, that the standard plot involves an exposed aristocrat raised by peasants. See Barbara Estrin, *The Raven and the Lark: Lost Children in Literature of the English Renaissance* (London, 1985).

[46] Boswell, *The Kindness of Strangers*, p. 394. Similarly, Estrin remarks that foundling tales in Renaissance England provided the perfect "wish fulfillment" in a society that practiced child abandonment; see *The Raven and the Lark*, p. 26.

[47] The secular authorities' harsh treatment of infanticide was connected to a fear of its clandestine and suspected occult circumstances. See the 1556 Edict of Henri II which con-

certain degree of leniency in the treatment of public abandonment.[48] In cases where the parents of an abandoned child were located and judged to be indigent, no punishment would be accorded and the infant would be sent to the appropriate hospice. In this light, the sixteenth-century Catholic theologian Jean Benedicti concluded that the act of abandonment was considered sinful only if the parents were considered to have sufficient means to raise the child: "He who exposes his children, whether it be in a public or private place, and who possesses the means to raise them, sins."[49]

The records of royal investigations in 1501, 1531, and 1546 into the condition of the foundlings helps us to piece together the methods employed by the chapter to care for the infants in the early part of the sixteenth century. When an infant was discovered abandoned at Notre-Dame, the first obligation was to arrange for the child to be sent to a wet-nursing family.[50] In 1501 the royal commissioner Bureau Boucher interviewed a wet nurse he encountered near the Cathedral of Notre-Dame "who was holding in her arms a child of about a year old and had another, about six months old, in a cradle." When asked to whom these children belonged, she informed him that they had been found abandoned in a doorway of the cathedral and had subsequently been given to her by M. Mathieu, a canon of the Chapter of Notre-Dame, who supervised the care of the foundlings.[51] This same woman reported that she knew of at least ten children who were given out to be fostered with wet-nursing families "here and there throughout Paris."[52]

---

demned "Toute femme qui se trouvera duement atteinte et convaincue d'avoir celé, couvert et occulté dans sa grossesse et son enfantement, sans avoir déclaré l'un et l'autre et avoir pris témoignage de la vie et de la mort de son enfant, et après se trouve l'enfant avoir été privé tant du St. Sacrement de baptême que sépulture publique et accoutumé, soit tellement tenue et réputée avoir homicidé son enfant, et pour réparation sera punie de mort." For a full text of the edict see François-André Isambert, *Recueil général des anciennes lois depuis l'an 420 jusqu'à la Révolution de 1789*, 29 vols. (Paris, 1821–33), 13:471–73.

[48] Fernand Boussault notes that "On ne trouve trace d'aucun édit et d'aucune lettre patente émanant de l'autorité royale interdisant et condamnant l'exposition pure et simple, c'est-à-dire, non assimilable à l'infanticide," in *L'assistance aux enfants abandonnés à Paris du XVIe au XVIIIe siècle*, p. 123. The customary punishment for abandonment was whipping (*la foüette*). In 1576, for example, a young servant girl who had abandoned an illegitimate child she had conceived with another servant was condemned by the criminal lieutenant of the Châtelet to be whipped in front of the house where she had left the infant. In L. Bouchel, *La bibiliothèque ou trésor du droit français* (Paris, 1629), s.v. "exposez."

[49] "Celuy qui expose ses enfants, soit en lieu particulier ou public, ayant les moyens de les nourrir, pèche." J. Benedicti, *La somme des péchez et le remède d'iceux* (Paris, 1595), bk. 2, chap. 2, no. 19, p. 143.

[50] Regular entries of payments made to wet nurses appear in the "Registres Capitulaires de Notre-Dame," found in AN, Series LL.

[51] "Information de Bureau Boucher" (1501), doc. 34, fol., 7v.

[52] Ibid.

What happened to the foundlings once they left the care of the wet nurses? In the first half of the sixteenth century the weaned foundlings were tended to in a house located near the cathedral which was known alternately as the "Couche" or the "Crèche" and was staffed by charitable women, usually widows, from the neighborhood. Until 1570 the Couche had no permanent location; it moved between houses depending on which charitable family from the neighborhood was willing to house the foundlings. Accordingly, in the first decades of the sixteenth century we do not have much information regarding the fate of the foundlings once they reached the age of seven or eight. An examination of the fifteenth-century cartularies of the chapter reveals, however, that some of the foundlings were given over to the care of local foster parents. One such entry from the cartularies tells of a young foundling, baptized at the church as "Nicholas," who was taken from the Couche in 1444 by a Parisian merchant named Colin le Mercier. The entry notes that le Mercier received from the Chapter of Notre-Dame a "poor little boy, about two months old, who had been brought to the cathedral and left there in January." In the contract, Le Mercier promises to raise Nicholas "like his own child" (*de suo proprio filio*) at his own expense. Employing the language of charity common to medieval fosterings, le Mercier promises to care for Nicholas "for the love of God" (*ob amorem dei*).[53]

Descriptions of the Couche from the sixteenth and seventeenth centuries reveal that the hospice went to great lengths to encourage private households to foster one of the foundlings. On holidays some of the foundlings were placed in cradles inside the cathedral to announce their plight to the community and encourage the donation of alms. This ritual does, in fact, seem to have inspired some families to foster an abandoned child. The seventeenth-century jurist Laurent Bouchel described this process:

[53] "Hodie Colinus le Mercier laborator nuper commerans in ville de la Rothoginon nunc vero parisiensis in domo de la Riviere prope domuum de Clichon confessus est accepisse adversus de capitulo parisiensis unum parvum puerum masculinum etatum II mensum vel circa nuper ad januam ecclesie parisiensis missum apportandum et repertum et postmodum cum aliis pueris in dicta ecclesia repertis missum et receptum atque hodie baptizatum et supra fontes per dictum Nicolaum in ecclesia Sancte Johannis Rotundi tentum hoc modum quod ipse Nicolaum promisit et juravit etiam ipsum infantem quamdiu vixerit bene et sufficiendum nutrire alimentare vestire et alia sibi necessaria quaerere et ministrare suis sumptibus et expensibus et de ipso puero facere sicut facere posset de suo proprio filio ob amorem dei." AN, Registres Capitulaires de Notre-Dame, Series LL 115, fol. 691 (February 1444). It is striking how similar this fifteenth-century "adoption" contract is to the formal contracts from the Couche from the sixteenth and seventeenth centuries: although the word adoption is not found in this contract (the marginal notation reads "De puero reperto tradito ad regendum etiam"), many of the promises made to the child—to provide for him "de suo proprio filio"—appear in a similar format in the later contracts of adoption from the Couche.

Inside the great church of Notre-Dame, to my left, sits a cradle made of wood, in which the foundlings are placed on feast days in order to move the people to charity. Several nurses stand alongside in order to receive alms from the charitable passersby. It often occurs that good people who have no children of their own ask for and take in the foundlings, promising to care for and raise them as their own children.[54]

The public display of the foundlings at the cathedral alerts us to the fact that Parisians living near Notre-Dame were aware that the Couche received abandoned children and that, in their turn, the canons encouraged the fostering of the foundlings by private families "for the honor and love of God." Presumably, if the children were not sought by foster parents, the chapter paid for them to be apprenticed in a trade and provided the girls with dowries for marriage.

As early as the first years of the sixteenth century the chapter began to rebel actively against its role as the sole benefactor of the foundlings. The quarrel between the chapter and the Crown over responsibility for the foundlings stemmed in large part from the perception that abandonment of children was on the rise in the sixteenth century. In this regard, Maître Jehan Larchier, who had worked at the Châtelet from 1474 or 1475, compared abandonment rates from the beginning of the sixteenth century with those from the last decades of the fifteenth century, alerting a royal investigator in 1501 that "there was not such great abandonment [then] as exists now."[55] Similarly, in 1508 the canons of the Chapter of Notre-Dame spoke of the foundlings "in magno numero," and a 1514 entry in the registers remarks on the "multitudini puerorum" received by the chapter.[56] Witnesses interviewed at the Hôtel-Dieu in 1531 by the royal commissioner also remarked on the growing numbers of infants being abandoned to the care of that hospice.[57]

---

[54] "Dedans la grande église de Notre-Dame à ma gauche, il y a un bois de lit qui tient au pavé, sur lequel pendant les jours solemnels on met les enfans trouvez, afin d'exciter le peuple à leur charité. Auprès duquel sont deux ou trois nourriciers et un bassin pour recevoir des aumônes des gens de biens. Lesdits enfans trouvez sont quelquefois demandez et pris par bonnes personnes qui n'ont point d'enfans, en s'obligeant de les nourrir et élever comme leurs propres enfans." In Bouchel, *La bibliothèque ou trésor du droit français*, p. 1013.

[55] "Lors n'y en avait grant abondance comme on dit qu'il y en a à présent." See "Information de Bureau Boucher" (1501), fol. 5v.

[56] AN, Registres Capitulaires de Notre-Dame, Series LL (27 June 1508): 295 fol. 418v and Reg. 23, p. 345; 14 Maiji 1514: Series LL 132 B fol. VI(xx)VIII. Figures on the numbers of foundlings cared for by the chapter are also found in Paule Bavoux, *Les orphelins et les enfants trouvés à Paris à la fin du moyen-âge*, Mémoire maîtrise lettres (Paris, 1967), and her article "Enfants trouvés et orphelins du XIVe au XVIe siècle à Paris," in *Actes du 97e congrès national des Sociétés Savantes (Nantes, 1972)* (Paris, 1979), pp. 359–70.

[57] "Information de Pierre Carrel" (1531).

Were these witnesses correct in assuming a rise in abandonment of children in their time? Immigration to Paris and a general growth in the population in the sixteenth century—slowed temporarily by the devastation wrought during the worst decades of the Wars of Religion—no doubt contributed to elevated rates of abandonment. Paris presented an attractive place of temporary or permanent resettlement for the young and unmarried of both sexes in this period.[58] Historians have emphasized the overwhelmingly youthful character of the rising tide of immigration to the capital as poor young men and women came to Paris from the countryside with the aim of finding work as domestic servants or manual laborers.[59] The individuals who immigrated to Paris inevitably left behind support networks of kin and neighborhood ties in their native towns and villages. Although new networks and ties would eventually be formed, life in Paris surely presented the newcomers with a wealth of obstacles to be confronted without the aid of familial and communal systems of support.[60] In this context, an unexpected and unwanted pregnancy for a young servant girl or a prostitute might easily have led to a child being abandoned at the doorways of the Hôtel-Dieu or on the steps of Notre-Dame.

As the numbers of abandoned children increased, the chapter turned to the Crown for assistance, claiming that the king himself as well as the other high justices of the city should participate in caring for the *enfants trouvés*. In the ensuing legal proceedings between the chapter and the Crown, the canons complained that they were unjustly receiving growing numbers of children abandoned in jurisdictions other than their own who were subsequently sent to them by the lieutenants of the Châtelet. In a typical scenario from 1501, a lawyer from the Châtelet discovered an infant abandoned in front of his house, prompting him to parade the child around the parish in the hopes that someone might recognize the infant.[61] In this case, as in many others, no information about the natal parents could be ferreted out from the neighbors, and the infant was taken to the Couche

---

[58] It is not until the mid-seventeenth century that the archives furnish reliable demographic material, due to the loss in 1871 of most of the Parisian parish records. Yet, the notarial records show a steady flow of immigration to the city beginning in the mid-sixteenth century. On demographic trends in early modern Paris, see Jacques Dupâquier, ed., *Histoire de la population française*, vol. 1, *Des origines à la Renaissance* (Paris, 1988); Georges Duby, ed., *Histoire de la France urbaine*, vol. 3, *La ville classique de la Renaissance aux Révolutions* (Paris, 1981); Michaël Flinn, *The European Demographic System* (Brighton, 1981).

[59] See René Pillorget, *Nouvelle histoire de Paris: Les premiers Bourbons, 1594–1661* (Paris, 1988), p. 98.

[60] On immigration to Paris in the late Middle Ages and the lack of traditional family ties experienced by the "marginals" of the city, see Bronislaw Geremek, *The Margins of Society in Late Medieval Paris*, trans. Jean Birrell (Cambridge, 1987).

[61] See the case in "Information de Bureau Boucher" (1501), doc. 34, fol. 1v. The goal of such inquests was to find the natal parents and urge them to take back the child.

to be provided with a wet nurse.[62] The chapter also complained that it
was illegally receiving children abandoned in areas beyond its jurisdiction.
The canons alleged that seigneurs from other quarters paid women to
bring the foundlings to Notre-Dame to be abandoned, clandestinely, for a
second time.[63]

It is difficult to assess exactly how many children were under the care of
the chapter during the sixteenth century. Tentative figures can be gathered
from records of the chapter as well as from the royal inquests. Figures on
the number of children abandoned each year include the children abandoned within the jurisdiction of the chapter as well as the children sent to
the Couche from the other quarters of the city. We find that between 1512
and 1518 the chapter declared 78 children found abandoned in its jurisdiction, or, on the average, 13 children a year. In addition, during these
same years Notre-Dame received an average number of 48 children per
year from the other jurisdictions of Paris.[64] A rough estimate, then, is that
in the first decades of the sixteenth century the chapter found itself responsible for no fewer than 70 infant foundlings per year. These figures proba-
bly fall short, however, of the actual numbers of children abandoned to the
care of the Couche. Richard Trexler has shown that the foundling hospice
in the city of Florence, the Innocenti, received as many as 900 children
annually during the same decades.[65]

In an attempt to justify their refusal to aid the chapter in ministering to
the foundlings, the high justices of Paris claimed that the chapter possessed a special fund for the care of the foundlings, which exempted all
others from financial responsibility. The chapter vigorously denied the ex-

[62] In times of famine and plague, when mothers were too ill to breast-feed and wet nurses
were scarce both at the Hôtel-Dieu and at the Couche, the infants were fed goat's or cow's
milk from a bottle. Sister Helaine from the Hôtel-Dieu informed the royal commissioner,
Pierre Carrel, in 1531 that, although they employed this as a last resort, "Elle en a veu
advenir plusieurs inconveniens de mort ausdictz petiz enfans qui meurent à faulte de nourriture de mamelle et ne peuvent ladicte dépposant ne autres religieuses audict hospital y pour-
veoir ne donner ordre à leur dicte nouriture sinon que leur donner du laict de vache ou de
chèvre en ung biberon d'estain ou de terre en cornette ou enveloppe de quelque petit drap-
peau que lesdictz enfans sussent par le bout dudict biberon." "Information de Pierre Carrel"
(1531), fol. 3r. Another witness from the same inquest, Sister Alips la Lambine, reported
that, again as a last resort, the sisters would give the infants a baked apple or pear to suck on
(fol. 7r).

[63] See AN, L553b (n. 35): "Inventaire de la production que mectent par divers bons nos
seigneurs tenant le Parlement du Roy nostre sire en son Parlement à Paris les doyens et
chapître de l'église de Paris deffendeurs d'une part à l'encontre de monsieur le procureur
général du Roy demandeur" (1519–36), fols. 16r-16v.

[64] See the "Inventaire de la Production," fols. 18v–19r. In addition, for a discussion of
the battles between the chapter, the ecclesiastical high justices, and the Crown over the fate
of the foundlings, see Bavoux, Les orphelins et les enfants trouvés, pp. 72–73.

[65] See Trexler, "The Foundlings of Florence: 1395–1455," 263.

istence of such a fund; the royal attorney eventually determined, in fact, that the chapter possessed no special fund, save for the chapter's holding of a few vineyards outside of Paris, the meager proceeds of which went toward the care of the foundlings. The findings of the royal inquests culminated in the Royal Edict of 1552, which commanded the other ecclesiastical high justices of Paris[66] to pay a combined annual tax (of 960 livres parisis), to be put toward the care of the foundlings. The money was ordered managed by the governors of the hospice of the Trinité, where the abandoned children were to be sent once they returned from the care of their wet nurses at the age of six or seven. Even in light of the new role accorded to the hospice of the Trinité, however, the Chapter of Notre-Dame and the Couche continued to act as the principal caretakers for the foundlings of Paris.[67] Although the chapter was successful in compelling its seignorial colleagues to share the financial and administrative burden for its charitable work, the cradles (*berceau* or *bouëtte*) that received the abandoned infants were ordered by the Crown to remain within the cathedral. In addition, the chapter continued to pay the wages of the wet nurses and the lay women from the neighborhood near the cathedral who ministered to the infant foundlings at the Couche. Thus, toward the close of the sixteenth century, after nearly a century of altercations over the responsibility of the abandoned children of Paris, the Chapter of Notre-Dame continued to stand as the primary benefactor of the foundlings. As we shall see in the following chapter, many of the sixteenth- and seventeenth-century adoption contracts from the Couche show that the canons of the Chapter of Notre-Dame frequently served as governors of the Couche.

The Couche finally gained a settled locale in 1570 when the chapter was ordered by the Parlement of Paris to use two of its houses at the Port St. Landry (the present-day Quai-aux-Fleurs) as the new locale for the abandoned children. At St. Landry the Couche was run by a lay person, who, in turn, was overseen by three widows (originally Marie de la Croix, Anne Guyon, and Catherine Mousy). In addition, Pierre Hotman, a gold merchant, was named as the Couche's first treasurer giving the fledgling hospice at St. Landry the beginnings of an autonomous administration.[68] The Couche remained at the Port St. Landry from 1570 until its management

---

[66] The other ecclesiastical high justices of the city mentioned in the edict included "L'Evesque de Paris, les Religieux, Abbé et Couvent de Saint Denis en France, de St. Magloire à Paris, de Ste. Geneviefve à Paris, de St. Victor de Paris, de St. Germain des Prez de Paris, de Tiron à Paris, les Religieux Prieur et Couvent de St. Martin des Champs et le Grand Prieur de France Commandeur du Temple de cette Ville." BN, Ms. "Anciens petits fonds français" 21802, Collection Delamare, "Extraits des registres de Parlement," fol. 375r.

[67] The full text of the edict appears in Dupoux, *Sur les pas de Monsieur Vincent*, pp. 25–26.

[68] For the text of the 1570 edict, see ibid., p. 27.

was taken over in the 1640s by Vincent de Paul.[69] Guided by a reinvigorated Counter-Reformation zeal to perform charitable works such as ministering to destitute children, St. Vincent founded a charitable order of lay women, the Order of the Ladies of Charity (Dames de la Charité), run by influential lay women who solicited funds and guided work on the parish level ministering to the poor and sick. The superiors of the order included noblewomen such as Madame de Lamoignon, Richelieu's niece the duchess of Aiguillon, and Louise-Marie Gonzague, the future queen of Poland. In 1629 under the guidance of St. Vincent, the widow Louise de Marillac established the auxiliary charitable order of the Daughters of Charity (Filles de la Charité), lay women who took vows to work inside various charity hospices with the poor and the sick (these women would become the future order of the Soeurs de Saint Vincent de Paul).

Alerted to the deteriorating conditions at the Couche by the Ladies of Charity and the chapter itself, St. Vincent made a visit there in 1638 and left horrified at the poor conditions in which the children were kept. Working together with the Ladies and the Daughters of Charity, St. Vincent embarked on a crusade to ameliorate the care of the foundlings. In addition to the funds provided by the *hauts-justiciers*, St. Vincent was aided in his work by a generous donation from the Crown of 4,000 livres to supplement an annual royal donation of 8,000 livres.[70] In 1645, after a long search for new quarters, St. Vincent moved the site where the weaned foundlings were cared for to the larger quarters of thirteen houses located near the priory of St. Lazare in the faubourg St. Denis. The relocated hospice at St. Denis was known throughout the seventeenth century as the Hôpital des Pauvres Enfants Trouvés. Here, the "Daughters of Charity" worked in the hospice to care for the Parisian foundlings.[71] Even after the foundlings were moved to St. Denis, however, a reception house for abandoned children, known as the le dépôt de la Couche des enfants-trouvés continued to operate near the Cathedral of Notre-Dame. The commissioners of the Châtelet brought the abandoned infants to the Couche to be placed with wet nurses before they were sent on to St. Denis.

In 1670 the Couche was incorporated under the umbrella administration of the Hôpital général (founded in 1656), under a royal edict issued by Louis XIV.[72] A few years after the 1670 edict, the hospice was moved

---

[69] On the work of Vincent de Paul on behalf of the foundlings of Paris, see ibid. Other than Albert Dupoux's work, which does not deal in depth with the sixteenth century, there is no comprehensive study of the Couche for the late medieval and early modern period.

[70] Ibid., p. 34.

[71] Ibid., p. 37.

[72] Louis XIV seems to have harbored some less-than-charitable motives for seeing to the welfare of the abandoned children of Paris; a royal edict from 1670 (7 January) reads: "Combien leur conservation était avantageuse puisque les uns pouvaient devenir soldats et servir

once again and its tasks divided between two locations: the Maison de la Couche, on the rue Neuve-Notre-Dame near the Hôtel-Dieu, received the infant foundlings and arranged for them to be sent to wet nurses, while the Maison de faubourg St. Antoine housed the children after they had returned to Paris from their wet nurses. Even after 1670 when the Hôpital des Pauvres Enfants Trouvés officially became a secular institution funded by the state, the Sisters of Charity continued to play a central role in the care of the foundlings at the hospice, including, as we shall see, arranging for the adoption of some of the children by private families.[73]

CONCLUSIONS

The fostering traditions employed by many of the charity hospices in late medieval and early modern Paris encourage us to view the assistance given to the city's orphans and foundlings as constituting a community affair. Indigent parents who abandoned infants at churches, in the city streets, and at the portals of the charity hospices did so believing that the children might eventually be taken in to be raised by local foster families. Indeed, while many of the children were raised inside the confines of the hospices, many orphans and foundlings were placed as apprentices, servants, and foster children with families throughout the city. The system of fostering was particularly expedient for the Couche inasmuch as it was the only hospice in Paris that ministered to the otherwise reviled foundlings. The fostering customs employed by the Parisian charity hospices prove significant for the history of adoption and family life in early modern France; by absorbing indigent children into their care and, in turn, by fostering the children out to local families, charity hospices such as St. Esprit, the Trinité, the Hôtel-Dieu, and the Couche provided visible models of non-biological parenting. Indeed, by the mid-sixteenth century several of the charity hospices, notably the Couche and the Hôtel-Dieu, expanded the types of assistance they extended to the destitute children to include placing some of them in permanent adoption arrangements with families from Paris and its outlying areas; it is to these stories of formal adoption which we now turn.

---

dans nos troupes, les autres ouvriers et habitants des colonies que nous établissons." Cited in Muriel Jeorger, "Enfant-trouvé-enfant-objet," *Histoire, économie et société* 3 (1987): 373–86.

[73] For the history of the foundling hospital in the modern period see Fuchs, *Abandoned Children*.

CHAPTER FIVE

The Adoption of Children from the Couche of the Poor Foundlings and the Hôtel-Dieu

ON 22 MAY 1589, Jehan Damiot, a merchant of linen and cotton from the parish of St. Eustache, went with his wife Marguerite Fleuryet to the Couche of the Poor Foundlings to adopt one of the *pauvres enfants trouvez,* as the children were known. In this period the Couche comprised two houses located at the Port St. Landry along the Seine, not far from the Cathedral of Notre-Dame, whose religious order ran the hospice. Jehan and Marguerite signed an adoption contract before a notary with Jacques de la Forestz, the master of the Couche. By the terms of the contract the couple arranged to adopt a seven-year-old girl named Claudine des Petitz Champs, a young foundling whose surname, like many of the children's names, reflected the site in Paris where she had been abandoned.[1] Jehan and Marguerite, who had no biological children of their own, promised to care for Claudine "from today and forever" and to provide for all her needs "as they would for their own child." The couple also promised to teach Claudine "an honest trade" in the future "to help her earn a living and become an honorable woman." The couple pledged further to provide Claudine with a dowry when she reached the appropriate age. Finally, Jehan and Marguerite pledged that if they died without biological children Claudine would become the sole heir to their movable and immovable property.[2]

---

[1] The last names of some of the foundlings offer clues to the children's origins. When first brought to the Couche, most of the foundlings were given surnames based on the location in the city, or its surrounding areas, where the children were found abandoned. Claudine des Petitz Champs was most likely found in the area of Paris known as the "Petits Champs" (we see a similar naming pattern with foundlings such as Magdeleine de la rue Perpignan, Jehanne des Halles, Nicolle de l'Hostel Dieu, and Jehanne de la Rue des Deux Portes).

[2] AN, MC, Et. XXIII, 152 (22 May 1589). Claudine had been adopted almost one year before (24 October 1588) by Marie Filleyet from the parish of St. Eustache in Paris. Although Marie was legally married at the time of the adoption to Marquin du Chesne, a mason, she contracted the adoption on her own since the two held their properties separately. Marie explained that, because she had "no children of her own nor any heirs who might take and enjoy her inheritance after her death," she decided to adopt Claudine "as her child and as her principle heir." Due to the "great affection" she held for Claudine, Marie promised to raise Claudine "as her own child," to provide her with food and drink, to send her to school, to teach her a trade, and to provide for her marriage when she reached matu-

On 23 April 1599, Marie Poussin, from the rue St. Honoré in the parish of St. Germain l'Auxerrois, went to the Couche to adopt a child. Marie had no children from her marriage with her husband, François Pointel, a cart driver. Even though legally married at the time of the adoption, Marie arranged the adoption and authorized the contract independently because she had earlier separated her lineal property from the marital community of property held with her husband. Marie signed a contract at the Couche with Jacques Dieu, a canon from St. Denis-du-Pas and the current "commissioner of the poor foundlings," to adopt as her daughter a five-year-old girl named Magdeleine de la rue Perpignan. Marie promised to feed and to care for Magdeleine, to raise her "honestly" as a Roman Catholic, and to teach her a trade to help her earn a living in the future, "all as if she were her own natural and legitimate child." Because Marie also desired that Magdeleine become her full heir in the future, she made a *donation entre vifs* of her movable and immovable property to her adopted daughter, which was accepted on behalf of the young girl by Jacques Dieu.[3]

On 12 December 1605, Thomas Vaucombert, a master harness maker from the parish of St. Sulpice in Paris, went to the Couche with his wife Suzanne Cousteau to adopt a young boy named Claude, identified in the contract by the adoptive father's surname of Vaucombert (which was penned in a different hand). Thomas and Suzanne explained to the notary that they had no biological children of their own and that they had taken Claude into their home from the Couche four months earlier, for what appears to have been a trial period. The couple had subsequently decided

---

rity. Finally, Marie made a *donation entre vifs* to Claudine of a portion of all of her property. We can only speculate as to why Claudine ended up back at the Couche to be adopted again; perhaps Marie Filleyet died and her husband broke the original contract. AN, MC, Et. XXIII, 149 (24 October 1588).

   [3] AN, MC, Et. XXIII, 157 (1599). In 1605 Marie Poussin adopted another young girl, Jehanne des Halles, from the Couche (at this later date she was no longer separated in goods from her husband). The couple, who had moved to the parish of St. Lazare, declared "to having adopted and now adopting [Jehanne] for their own child, seeing that they have no children born of the two of them." AN, MC, Et. XXIII, 162 (12 April 1605). It seems likely that Magdeleine, the young girl adopted by Marie in 1599, had died and the reconciliated couple decided to adopt another child. Both contracts were witnessed by Jacques Dieu, canon at the church of St. Denis-du-Pas and "commissioner of the high justices of the city of Paris and receiver of the poor foundlings of Paris," which, apparently would mean that this couple had been deemed worthy of adopting another child from the Couche.

to return to the Couche to formalize the adoption. In addition to promising to educate and raise Claude as a Roman Catholic, the couple pledged that when Claude came of age they would leave him their movable and immovable goods "as if he were their own legitimate child." To seal their good intentions on this point, Thomas and Suzanne made an immediate and irrevocable donation to Claude of 300 livres. The contract was witnessed by Simon Qualt, a surgeon, and by Jacques Dieu, the "commissioner of the poor foundlings."[4]

The adoptions of foundlings such as Claudine, Magdeleine, and Claude from the Couche bring to light a second model of adoption that we can place alongside adoptions arranged between two families. Throughout the sixteenth and the seventeenth centuries married couples and individuals came from the city of Paris and its immediate outlying regions to the sole foundling hospice in Paris, the Couche of the Poor Foundlings (known after 1645 as the Hôpital des Enfants Trouvés) to adopt one of the abandoned children. As we have seen, many Parisian charity hospices such as the Couche, St. Esprit, the Trinité, and the Hôtel-Dieu had long employed fostering practices as one means of ministering to the destitute children of the city. The sample cases of adoption outlined here reveal that beginning in the mid-sixteenth century the Couche added formal adoption arrangements (complete, in most instances, with inheritance clauses) to the spectrum of ways in which the foundlings were integrated into Parisian society.[5]

[4] AN, MC, Et. XXIX, 157 (12 December 1605).

[5] In contrast to the evidence from the Parisian Couche, Phillip Gavitt's study of the foundling hospice of the Innocenti in Florence found that adoptions of the abandoned children became less common in the sixteenth century than had been the case in the fifteenth century: "In the fifteenth century . . . the hospital relied on adoptive parents to lead the hospital's boys to an important religious or secular post, or to lead a girl to honor and provide her with a dowry. By the sixteenth century the Innocenti had acquired a more recognizably residential character." See *Charity and Children in Renaissance Florence: The Ospedale degli Innocenti, 1436–1536* (Ann Arbor, Mich., 1990), p. 301. The Florentine example aside, it is clear that in a variety of countries throughout early modern Europe traditions of adoption were kept alive due to the existence of foundlings and orphans without families of their own, on the one hand, and families without children of their own, on the other. For customs of adoption at foundling hospices in Italy, see Volker Hunecke, *Die Findelkinder von Mailand: Kindaussetzung und aussetzende Eltern vom 17. bis zum 19. Jahrhundert* (Stuttgart, 1987); Lucia Sandri, *L'Ospedale de S. Maria della Scala di S. Gimignano nel Quattrocento: Contributo alla storia dell'infanzia abbandonata* (Florence, 1982). For Spain, see Leon Carlos Alvarez Santaló, *Marginación social y mentalidad en Andalucía Occidental: Expósitos en Sevilla, (1613–1910)* (Seville, 1980), esp. chap. 2, 4.2.

The evidence of adoption from the Couche is clustered in three periods in the sixteenth and seventeenth centuries that correspond to modifications in the hospice's institutional structure. The first record of formal adoption practices from the Couche appears in 1541. Although the 1541 contract represents an isolated case, we shall see that its central characteristic—a childless family approaching the Couche to adopt one of the foundlings— would remain constant. In the 1541 case Simmone Tareau received permission from her husband, Simon de Souville, a master hatter in Paris, to make an irrevocable donation of property to her adopted daughter, seven-year-old Jeanne Helloye, a foundling from the Couche who had been living with the couple for several years. Simmone clarified in the contract that the immovable property she pledged to Jeanne was her own lineal properties (and not the joint marital properties she held with her husband). Simmone pledged, moreover, that the gift would hold even if she and Souville had biological children in the future. As a final note, Simmone explained that she made this donation to Jeanne due to the "love" that she felt for her young adopted daughter.[6] After the 1541 case, the next substantial group of cases of adoption from the Couche emerges in the 1580s in the period after the Couche had moved in 1570 to new quarters at the Port St. Landry and had been endowed with a fledgling administration. The twenty cases of adoption from the period 1588–1613 offer the only information we have concerning the daily operation of the Couche at the close of the sixteenth century; histories of poor relief in Paris have assumed that the ravages of the wars of religion forced the Couche to cease functioning altogether in this period.[7] The contracts from this period were drawn up by four separate notaries who worked closely with the Chapter of Notre-Dame: Martin Jacques and Mathieu Bontemps, both with offices in the Cité, and François Chauvin and Etienne Corrozet, with offices on the rue de la Vielle Drapperie. As a testament to the regularity with which these notaries drew up adoption contracts for the Couche, the 1605 notarial register of Martin Jacques, who notarized the majority of the adoptions in this period, contains a formula for an adoption from the Couche— complete with blank spaces to be filled in with the names of the future adoptive parents and child.[8]

Additional evidence of adoption from the foundling hospice surfaces in two contracts from 1645, the period after the Couche was reorganized under the guidance of Vincent de Paul and the Ladies and Sisters of Char-

---

6 AN, Series Y 87 (20 January 1541).

7 The principal historian of the Couche, Albert Dupoux, notes that for almost a century after 1571 when the chapter donated the two houses to the foundlings at St. Landry, "nous ignorerons tout du fonctionnement de la Couche." Cited in Dupoux, *Sur les pas de Monsieur Vincent: Trois cents ans d'histoire parisienne de l'enfance abandonnée* (Paris, 1958), p. 28.

8 AN, MC, Et. XXIII, 162 (1605).

ity and relocated to the faubourg St. Denis. An additional fifteen adoption contracts emerge in the 1670s and 1680s after the merger of the hospice's administration with the Hôpital général in 1670. Another ten cases of formal adoption from seventeenth-century Paris derive from the records of the Hôtel-Dieu. Beginning in 1656 the Ladies of Charity of the Hôtel-Dieu, an order linked with Vincent de Paul and comparable to the "Sisters of Charity" who worked at the Couche, placed in adoption orphans whose parents had died at the Hôtel-Dieu and foundlings who had been abandoned at the hospice. Our exploration of the central features of the adoptions from the charity hospices begins with the contracts overseen by the Couche from the period 1588–1613.

RAISING THE FOUNDLINGS "LIKE THEIR OWN CHILDREN"

The ties of familial association established in the adoption contracts overseen by the Couche presuppose a long-term commitment to care for the child on the part of the adoptive parents. Thus Jehan de la Borive and Laura Combaultz adopted Barbe Trouvez from the Couche to "raise, take care of, and nourish" her for "her entire life."[9] Similarly, the widow Charlotte Gandellet promised to care for her adopted son Pierre de la Rue Bourtibourg "for life."[10] The life-long bond established is encapsulated in the pledge found in the majority of the contracts by which the parents promise to raise the foundlings "like their own children" (*comme leur propre enfant*). For instance, Marie Poussin pledged to care for her adopted daughter Magdeleine "as if she were her own natural and legitimate child,"[11] and Thomas Vaucombert and Suzanne Cousteau adopted Claude "to be their own child."[12] Similarly, in a contract from 1604 Jehan Collin, a barber from Beauvais living temporarily in Paris, promised to care for his adopted daughter, Nicolle de l'Hostel Dieu, "as if she were his own legitimate daughter."[13]

The contracts bind the adoptive parents to fulfilling the same duties expected of biological parents. The first parental duty inherent in the pledge to raise an adopted child "like one's own" entailed providing the basic necessities for the child's survival such as food and drink, clothing, a bed and linen. Additionally, if a foundling was adopted in infancy, the

---

[9] AN, MC, Et. XXIII, 152 (20 May 1589).

[10] AN, MC, Et. XXIII, 152 (24 May 1589).

[11] "Tout comme sy estoit son enffan propre et légitime." AN, MC, Et. XXIII, 157 (1599).

[12] AN, MC, Et. XXIX, 157 (1605).

[13] AN, MC, Et. XXIII, 161 (1604).

adoptive family would first arrange for a wet nurse. This was the case for the widow Vincente Hondeau who adopted a fifteen-day-old abandoned girl in 1610, and whose first duty after having the infant baptized was to provide her with a wet nurse.[14] We can also speculate that if an adoptive mother had just lost an infant of her own, she might also decide to nurse the infant herself. In addition to providing the children with essential items for daily living, the adoptive parents were also expected to supply the children with a religious education. All of the contracts contain the phrase stipulating that the child be raised in the precepts of the "catholic, Roman, and apostolic faith." It should not cause surprise that it was the precepts of Roman Catholicism that were to be taught to the children considering that these adoptions were overseen by the Chapter of Notre-Dame during the era of the French religious wars. If the abandoned children were to be reintegrated into Parisian society, the canons of Notre-Dame wanted to ensure that they were reintegrated as Catholics.

After a religious education, the subsequent duty of an adoptive parent was to provide the child with an apprenticeship in a trade once she or he reached the customary age of eleven or twelve. A child's apprenticeship was most often in the adoptive father's (or perhaps mother's) trade, or in another occupation outside of the household. The parental obligation to teach a child a trade held true for both boys and girls, and its main purpose, as numerous contracts tell us, was that every child be able to earn his or her own living in the future. The chapter seems to have been particularly concerned that the girls be taught a trade that would maintain their honor. Jehan Damiot and Mary Fleuryet promised to teach their adopted daughter Magdeleine an "honest" trade in order to "aid her later on in gaining her livelihood and in becoming a virtuous woman."[15] The language stressing "virtue" might reflect the chapter's fears that the girls adopted from the Couche would be forced into a life of prostitution if placed into the wrong hands. Following their apprenticeship, all of the adopted girls were to be provided a dowry for marriage "or otherwise," which most likely meant a donation of property or perhaps placement in a convent when they reached the age of maturity. In 1604, Robert Procelier, a weaver of linen and cotton from Lormaison, in his name and in the name of his wife, promised his adopted daughter Jehanne de la Rue des Deux Portes that she would receive a portion of his movable property as her dowry "when she came of age . . . as if she were his legitimate child"[16] Similarly, the adoptive parents of Jehanne des Halles promised that, when

---

[14] AN, MC, Et. LXXIII, 273 (26 March 1610).

[15] "Et luy faire apprendre à l'advenir en quelque honneste mestier pour ayder à pouvoir à ladite après gaigner sa vye et estre fille et femme de bien." AN, MC, Et. XXIII, 152 (22 May 1589).

[16] AN, MC, Et. XXIII, 161 (25 June 1604).

she came of age, they would "provide her for marriage as if she were their own child born to them in legal marriage."[17]

The final provision in the contracts pledged an inheritance to help support the children after the parents' deaths. As with private adoptions arranged between two households, we find a wide spectrum of inheritance arrangements in the adoption contracts from the Couche. The lack of uniformity in the inheritance provisions of the contracts derives primarily from the absence of guidelines on adoption and succession in early modern Parisian customary law. In such a nebulous legal context, the amount and type of property promised to the adopted children, as well as the avenue selected for passing it on, were left up to the discretion of each individual adoptive family. When the adopting family desired the child to be named its full heir, the notaries working with the Couche nearly always employed the *donation entre vifs* as the avenue for passing on the totality of the family property, including the lineal portion, the *propres*.[18] We have already seen that Marie Poussin made a donation to Magdeleine to ensure that her adopted daughter would "inherit all of her movable and immovable property in her possession at the time of her death."[19] Similarly, Thomas Vaucombert and Suzanne Cousteau, made an irrevocable donation to their adopted son Claude of "all of their movable and immovable goods."[20] In an adoption from 1605, Philippe Perlot, a merchant of used clothing, and his wife Jehanne Tresorier made an irrevocable donation of all of their property to their adopted daughter, Martine Dupont.[21]

While in these instances the *donation entre vifs* was employed to effect the transmission of all of the family property, several adoptive parents preferred to make a donation to their adopted child of merely a portion of the family property. We have seen that in 1541 Simmone Taureau was authorized by her husband to donate only her lineal property from the couple's community of goods to her adopted daughter, Jeanne Helloye.[22] Other adoption arrangements restricted the inheritance in a different manner by donating only the movable property and the nonlineal portions of the immovable property to the adopted child, in the process excluding the *propres*. A similar arrangement was forged by Charlotte Chatellet, who made a donation to her adopted son, Pierre de la Rue Bourtibourg, that

[17] AN, MC, Et. XXIII, 162 (1605).

[18] Following the regulations of the edict of Villiers-Cotteret of 1539 all donations of property had to be formally accepted. Since the foundlings were all minors, the donations were accepted in the contracts by the governor of the Couche, usually a canon from the Chapter of Notre-Dame.

[19] AN, MC, Et. XXIII, 157 (1599).

[20] AN, MC, Et. XXIX, 157 (12 December 1605).

[21] AN, MC, Et. XXIII, 162 (17 March 1605).

[22] AN, Series Y 87 (20 January 1541).

was limited to the movable property and to the immovable "conquests" and "acquisitions."[23] In yet another model, the adoptive parents restricted the donation to the movable property alone. Thus in 1604 Jehan Collin, a barber, made an irrevocable donation of his movable property to his adopted daughter, Nicolle de l'Hostel Dieu, "as if she were his own legitimate daughter."[24] Similarly, in 1606 Jacques du Rozay, a porter at the Porte de St. Denis, and his wife Françoise la Teu "adopted as their child" Geneviève Roger, promising to raise her, instruct her in the Roman Catholic faith, teach her a trade, and to provide her a dowry for marriage all at their own expense. Finally, the couple donated their movable property to Geneviève "since they had no children of their own."[25]

A few of the contracts fail to make any explicit provisions for the child's inheritance. When in 1589 Jehan la Borive, a cart driver from the faubourg St. Marcel, and his wife Laura Combaultz adopted Barbe Trouvez from the Couche for her "entire life," the contract they signed contained no inheritance clause. The couple promised to raise Barbe at their own expense, including apprenticing her in a trade when she was older and providing a dowry for her marriage.[26] In this case, considering the extent of the commitment made by the adoptive parents toward Barbe, it is difficult to assess whether the exclusion of a promise of inheritance should be read as an oversight or as an intentional omission.[27]

THE ADOPTIVE FAMILIES

The information contained in the contracts allows us to piece together a general portrait of the families who came to the Couche to adopt a foundling as their child and heir. Just as in the private adoptions, the families who adopted from the Couche came overwhelmingly from the laboring, artisan, and merchant sectors of Parisian society. The professions of the adoptive parents in the three sample cases outlined at the outset of the chapter are representative of the socioeconomic status of the entire group of adoptive families: Jehan Damiot was a merchant of linen and cotton,

[23] AN, MC, Et. XXIII, 155 (1589).
[24] AN, MC, Et. XXIII, 161 (25 June 1604).
[25] AN, MC, Et. XXIX, 158 (2 May 1606).
[26] AN, MC, Et. XXIII, 152 (20 May 1589).
[27] The *donation entre vifs* did not provide an infallible means of securing an inheritance for the children adopted from the Couche. Technically, a donation could be revoked for ingratitude or in the case of the birth of a biological child. In the latter instance the adopted child would most likely still be provided some form of inheritance: Simmone Tareau's donation of a portion of her movable and immovable property in 1541 to her adopted daughter Jeanne Helloye included the promise that Jeanne would inherit "even in the case that Simmone and her husband had other biological children." AN, Series Y 87 (20 January 1541).

Marie Poussin's husband was a cart driver, and Thomas Vaucombert was a harness maker. Other professions listed in the body of contracts from the sixteenth and early seventeenth centuries include several weavers, launderers, masons, carters, as well as a day laborer, a master hatter, a florist and gardener, a master shoemaker, a master carpenter, a barber, a rug maker, a clothier, a doorman, a valet de chambre, and a vinedresser, as well as their widows. The list of adoptive parents also includes several merchants: one of cotton and linen, two of wine, and two of used clothing, and a few individuals identified simply as urban "bourgeois."[28] While we can conclude that the adoptive families did not form part of the elite of early modern Parisian society, neither did they come from the poorest sections of the working classes. The families who adopted children from the Couche came more often from the master artisan, merchant, and upper-level domestic servant class (including their widows) than from the poorer journeymen or day-laborer class. Families from the poorer sectors of the Parisian working classes simply did not possess sufficient financial means to commit to the wide range of care that accompanied bringing an infant or a young child into the home to raise until adulthood (especially when we consider that the Couche did not pay families a stipend to adopt one of the children). In this light, the adoptions of foundlings from the Couche represented a unique, and as yet unexplored, avenue of social mobility for these destitute children who had been abandoned by their natal parents to a life of poverty and uncertainty. Through adoption, the more fortunate of the foundlings such as Claudine, Magdeleine, and Claude were adopted by families from the upper echelons of the Parisian artisanal class.

While adoption from the Couche remained by and large a local Parisian affair, with most of the families coming from the principal neighborhoods and outlying suburbs of the city,[29] several families came to the Couche to adopt from towns and villages outside of the city. For instance, Charlotte Chantellet came from Bretigny in 1589 to adopt Pierre de la Rue Bourtibourg to bring into her household as an adopted son and heir, promising

---

[28] On the breakdown of socioeconomic groups in early modern Paris according to profession, see Daniel Roche, *The People of Paris: An Essay in Popular Culture in the 18th Century*, trans. Marie Evans (New York, 1987); Albert Franklin, *Dictionnaire historique des arts, métiers, et professions exercés dans Paris depuis le treizième siècle* (Paris, 1906).

[29] The residences of the families who adopted children from the Couche were dispersed rather widely throughout the city. Jehan Damiot and Marguerite Fleuryet lived in the parish of St. Eustache, across the river from the île-de-la-cité, Marie Poussin lived on the rue St. Honoré in the neighborhood of St. Germain l'Auxerrois, and Thomas Vaucombert and Suzanne Cousteau lived in the parish of St. Sulpice. The remainder of the adoptive families were spread throughout the sixteen principal neighborhoods and faubourgs of Paris: we find several households from the faubourg of St. Germain as well as from the parishes of St. Eustache, St. Jacques de la Boucherie, St. Denis, St. Martin, St. Paul, St. Médard, and St. Marcel.

to "feed, raise, and care well for him, at her own expense, as if he were her own child, from today and for always." Charlotte also pledged to teach Pierre a trade, and to "provide for his marriage or otherwise, at her own expense."[30] In 1604 Robert Procelier and his wife adopted Jehanne de la Rue des Deux Portes from the Couche. The couple adopted Jehanne as "their child," to care for and raise in the Roman Catholic faith, to teach a trade, and to provide her with a portion of their movable property as her dowry when she married, "just as if she were their legitimate child."[31] Also in 1604 Jehan Collin, a barber from the Beauvais, adopted Nicolle de l'Hostel Dieu from the Couche "as his own legitimate daughter." Jean promised to feed and care for Nicolle, to raise and instruct in her in the Roman Catholic faith, to teach her a trade, and to leave her the movable goods he has at the time of his death "as if she were his own legitimate daughter." Jehan explained that he decided to adopt a child from the Couche considering that he had no children since the dissolution of his marriage and he did not want to die without any heirs.[32]

How might families from outside of Paris have known about the Couche and its traditions of adoption? Several contracts offer clues as to how news about the Couche was disseminated and how plans for adoption might have been formulated by families from outside of Paris. In one contract from 1604, Jehan Collin from the Beauvais recounts that he had originally encountered his adopted daughter, Nicolle de l'Hostel Dieu, at the home of her wet nurse, a woman named Charlotte Feullit who lived in Jehan's town.[33] Similar circumstances led to the adoption in 1604 of Jehanne de la Rue des Deux Portes by Robert Procelier and his wife, from Lormaison, who first encountered their adopted daughter while she was under the care of a wet nurse who also resided in Lormaison. In addition to wet nurses hired by the Couche, women hired by the Hôtel-Dieu also acted as informational links between the orphans placed in their care by the Ladies of Charity of the Hôtel-Dieu and families from outside of Paris who were interested in adoption.[34] Thus in 1669 Jean Barbereau, a valet de chambre from l'isle d'Adam in Picardy, acting in his name and the name of his wife Anne Barbereau, traveled to the Hôtel-Dieu in Paris to adopt formally a two-year-old orphan named Catherine Cointel who had been born at the Hôtel-Dieu and was the illegitimate daughter of Charles Coin-

[30] AN, MC, Et. XXIII, 152 (24 May 1589).

[31] AN, MC, Et. XXIII, 161 (25 June 1604).

[32] AN, MC, Et. XXIII, 152 (25 June 1604).

[33] AN, MC, Et., XXIII, 161 (1604).

[34] For the important mediating role played by wet nurses in sustaining informal networks of assistance among poor women in nineteenth-century Paris, see Leslie Page Moch and Rachel G. Fuchs, "Getting Along: Poor Women's Networks in Nineteenth-Century Paris," *French Historical Studies* 18 (spring 1993): 34–49.

tel and Gabrielle du Bout, both deceased. Jean recounted that he and his wife had "cast their eyes" on Catherine while she was under the care of a wet nurse named Marguerite Faroire in their town of l'isle d'Adam and that, due to the "affection" that they had developed for Catherine, they had taken her into their own home. Having been approved as "charitable people" by the governors of the Hôtel-Dieu, Catherine was given to the couple permanently to raise and to provide for "as they would for their own child."[35]

A few contracts also demonstrate that Parisian wet nurses hired by the Couche played the same role of matching the infant foundlings under their care with local prospective adoptive parents. In one instance Vincente Hondeau, the widow of Jehan Joly, a master harness maker from the faubourg of St. Germain, arranged in 1610 with the Couche to adopt a fifteen-day-old girl whom she had received that same day from a wet nurse named Germaine Gerard. Vincente promised to baptize the infant girl as a Catholic, to take care of all of her needs, and to teach her trade, all as if "she were her own child."[36] In 1613 Marguerite d'Allu, a *fille majeure* who lived on the rue St. Antoine in the parish of St. Paul signed a notarized contract to adopt a six-month-old girl named Marguerite who had been abandoned four months earlier at the church of St. Merry, and who subsequently had been given by the Couche to Peorette Paris to be wet-nursed. Marguerite had taken the child earlier from her wet nurse and now promised to feed and raise Marguerite and to teach her a trade in the future, all at her own expense as if "she were her own child."[37]

In addition to acting as links between prospective adoptive parents and the Couche, some wet nurses hired by the Couche made the decision themselves to adopt permanently an infant who had been placed under their care. In most of these cases the wet-nursing family had no biological children of its own. Thus in 1601 the childless couple, Nicholas Hoffeau, a carter, and his wife Nicolle Housset adopted Pierre de Bourges St. Jacques, a young boy from the Couche whom Nicolle had wet-nursed for three years.[38] Noël and Nicolle promised to "raise him and to provide him with all his necessities, to raise him in the Roman Catholic religion, and to teach him a trade." The couple also named Pierre as their heir, promising

---

[35] The original contract of adoption and subsequent documents relating to this case can be found in AP, Fonds de l'Hôtel-Dieu, liasse 877 (42 pieces), 10 December 1669. The list of orphans from the Hôtel-Dieu given to private families begins in 1656.

[36] AN, MC, Et. LXXIII, 273 (26 March 1610).

[37] AN, MC, Et. XIX, 380 (12 July 1613).

[38] Infants usually stayed with the wet nurse for one to two years, although, in some cases, the child might stay on longer after it was weaned. For a history of wet-nursing, see Valerie Fildes, *Wet-nursing: A History from Antiquity to the Present* (Oxford, 1988).

to leave him "their movable goods and immovable acquisitions . . . as they would do for their own legitimate child."[39]

Although it is not until the eighteenth and nineteenth centuries that we receive the horrifying images of cartloads of moribund foundlings being transported to and from wet nurses residing outside of Paris,[40] the traditional portrait of the profession of wet-nursing in the earlier centuries nonetheless portrays heartless and mercenary women who cared little for the infants and who only calculated the money each new infant would bring to the household. The stories of wet nurses who formally adopted the foundlings under their care illustrate that, at least in some cases, the infants were viewed as much more than a source of income, and that enduring emotional bonds might form between a wet nurse and the infant under her care—bonds strong enough for the child to be adopted formally and named as the family's heir. Indeed, we find evidence from other cities showing the same pattern of wet nurses adopting a foundling or an orphan placed in their care by a local charity hospice. In her work on poor relief in early modern Toulouse, for instance, Barbara Beckerman Davis located cases of wet nurses adopting abandoned children from the city's foundling hospice.[41] Similarly, Jacqueline Roubert's study of adoptions of orphans from the Aumône générale in seventeenth-century Lyon brings to light several cases of wet nurses who requested to adopt one of the infants under their care.[42] Prost de Royer, an administrator of the Lyonnais Aumône in the eighteenth century, relates the tale of a wet-nursing family that requested to adopt a young boy, named Pierre, they had earlier fostered. Soon after the family had returned Pierre to the Aumône, at the customary age of seven, the foster family suffered the misfortune of seeing all three of their children die. The foster father then returned to the Aumône with his wife, who had wet-nursed Pierre, asking to take Pierre back. Royer recounts the peasant's plea: "My son, my poor Pierre, give him back to me! Hélas! While he was with us the heavens blessed us and since you have taken him back, I have lost all three of my children . . . we are alone, my poor wife and I; what will become of us? Give him back to me, my Pierre, he will be our child, and we will provide him with everything." Royer relates further that Pierre arrived and threw himself into the arms of his

[39] AN, MC, Et. XXIII, 158 (11 October 1601).

[40] See George Sussman, *Selling Mother's Milk: The Wet-nursing Business in France* (Urbana, Ill., 1982).

[41] Barbara Beckerman Davis, "Poverty and Poor Relief in Toulouse, 1474–1560: The Response of a Conservative Society" (Ph.D. diss., University of California, Berkeley, 1986), pp. 147–48.

[42] See Jacqueline Roubert, "L'adoption des enfants par des particuliers à Lyon sous l'Ancien Régime," *Société française d'histoire des hôpitaux* 36–37 (1978): 7-8.

foster parents, who broke into tears and comforted him: "Do not cry, you will come with us and we will never leave you again." At that moment, as Royer recounts, the foster parents named Pierre their heir by making him a donation of all of their property: "All will be for you," they promised.[43] In this theatrical tale, the wet-nursing family chose to adopt Pierre once they had lost their own children. Yet, their words and actions, as described by Prost de Royer, indicate that the couple had formed an emotional bond with Pierre during his initial stay with them.

MOTIVES FOR ADOPTION

Just as in the case of this foster family from Lyon, most of the families who adopted a child from the Parisian Couche were moved to do so because they had no children of their own.[44] In the three sample cases outlined all three sets of adoptive parents—Jehan Damiot and Marguerite Fleuryet, Marie Poussin, and Thomas Vaucombert and Suzanne Cousteau—were childless when they approached the administrators of the Couche and requested to adopt a child. Childlessness prompted many other households to adopt a young foundling from the Couche. We saw that when Jean Collin adopted Nicolle de l'Hostel Dieu from the Couche in 1604 he explained that the principal motive behind his decision to adopt was that "he had no children since the dissolution of his marriage" and, moreover, that "he did not want to die without an heir."[45] In the same year Philippe Perlot and Jehanne Tresorier adopted Martine Dupont, another foundling, stating that "at the present time they have no children born to them."[46] A year later, in 1606, Jacques du Rozay and Françoise La Teu, also without children of their own, adopted Geneviève Roger from the Couche "to be their child."[47]

While the birthrate in early modern France was much higher than today (attributable in large part to the absence of sophisticated birth-control methods), the chances of a couple remaining childless were still great due

[43] Prost de Royer, *Dictionnaire de jurisprudence et des arrêts*, vol. 3 (Lyon, 1783), p. 95.

[44] Both Paul Gonnet and Jacqueline Roubert found that the majority of households adopting orphans and foundlings in Lyon also were childless at the time of the adoption. See Gonnet, *L'adoption lyonnaise des orphelins légitimes (1536–1793)* (Paris, 1935) vol. 1, and Roubert, "L'adoption des enfants," p. 8. Roubert notes that in the seventeenth century it became more common for households with children to adopt another child, a change she attributes to a growing notion that the ultimate goal of the institution of adoption was for the good of the child.

[45] AN, MC, Et. XXIII, 161 (1604). This is one of the few cases encountered of a nonmarried man adopting a girl.

[46] AN, MC, Et. XXIII, 162.

[47] AN, MC, Et. XXIX, 158.

to extremely high rates of infant mortality. In fact, statistics for the seventeenth and eighteenth centuries reveal that mortality rates for infants in their first month was 150 to 180 per 1,000 births. Moreover, one child out of every four died before reaching the age of one year and only 500 out of every 1,000 would survive until the age of fifteen.[48] These demographic realities help to explain why many of the parents who adopted from the Couche noted in the contracts that they had "no surviving children of their own." In addition to the likelihood of infant death, sterility was a factor affecting a portion of the population, and remedies to combat infertility are found in numerous early modern midwives' and physicians' manuals.[49] To many contemporaries it made perfect sense that childless couples or individuals would turn to the avenue of "adoptive reproduction" to gain a child and an heir. The eighteenth-century jurist and director of the Aumône générale in Lyon, Prost de Royer, defended the institution of adoption by highlighting its child-giving capacities:

> Of all of the affections of the soul, that which unites the father, mother, and children is the most natural and durable . . . but what if these children die, or what if one was unable to have any in the first place, shouldn't one be able to compensate for this misfortune? Will one be condemned to live alone amongst indifferent citizens or avaricious kinsfolk?[50]

The Adopted Children

Unfortunately, for the most part the contracts remain silent regarding the adopted children themselves. The majority of the children were abandoned anonymously and the Couche did not begin to record formally the information about the children garnered from identifying tags that were left on them until 1639. Most of the contracts do, however, indicate the approximate age of the child at the time of the adoption. In the group of

---

[48] See the discussion in André Burguière, ed., *Histoire de la famille* (Paris, 1986), 2:18ff; René Pillorget *Nouvelle histoire de Paris: Les premiers Bourbons, 1594–1661* (Paris, 1988), 1:103; Michaël Flinn, *The European Demographic System* (Brighton, 1981).

[49] On sterility and remedies to combat it, see Louise Bourgeois, *Observations diverses sur la stérilité, perte de fruict, foecondité, accouchements et maladies de femmes, & enfants nouveaux naiz* (Rouen, 1626), and Angus McLaren, *Reproductive Rituals: The Perception of Fertility in England, 16th–19th Centuries* (London, 1984).

[50] "De toutes les affections de l'âme, celle qui unit le père, mère et les enfans est la plus naturelle et le plus durable . . . mais si ils meurent, ces enfans, ou si l'on n'en eut jamais, ne peut-on pas réparer ce malheur? Sera-t-on condamné à vivre seul au milieu des citoyens indifférents ou de collatéraux avides? Et après avoir embrassé toute la famille humaine, ce sentiment ne pourra-t-il pas se fixer sur quelque individu?" In Prost de Royer, *Dictionnaire de jurisprudence et des arrêts*, 3:94.

adoptions from 1588 to 1613 the age of adopted girls varied rather widely, ranging from six to twelve years old. The age of boys, four to eight years old, varied somewhat less. The contracts from this period also indicate that the married couples and individuals who approached the Couche to adopt a child were just as likely to take a young girl home with them as a young boy. The equal rates of adoption of children of both sexes from the Couche corresponds with the studies of Paul Gonnet and Jacqueline Roubert on adoption from the charity hospices in early modern Lyon, which also show no discrimination in the adoption of girls and boys (out of forty-two cases of adoption from the Aumône over the course of the sixteenth century, for example, Paul Gonnet records twenty adoptions of boys and twenty-two of girls).[51]

The decision to adopt a girl in early modern France, especially when she was named as a full or partial heir to the family property, is somewhat surprising considering that popular folklore and medical literature of the day were filled with advice on how to ensure the birth of a male child.[52] Moreover, the adoption of a girl could prove to be a more substantial financial commitment for a family inasmuch as the adoptive parents were bound to provide a daughter with a dowry upon her marriage. The pattern of adopting girls might be attributable to higher rates of abandonment of female infants in this period, which left the Couche with a greater number of girls available for adoption. This explanation is only partially satisfactory, however, considering that a leading motive for abandoning one's child, alongside poverty, was the desire to conceal the illegitimate birth of a child of either sex. It might also be that girls were preferred by some families because they did not present a permanent "threat" to the bloodline considering that a family's lineage was not normally perpetuated through daughters. In fact, the only significant difference regarding provisions made for adopted sons was the donation of the father's surname in order to conserve the family name for future generations. In at least in two cases boys from the Couche were awarded the father's surname when the contract was signed: Thomas Vaucombert gave his last name to Claude when he and his wife Suzanne Cousteau adopted him from the Couche in 1605, and Claude Fleury gave his surname to his adopted son Jean in 1647.[53]

[51] See Gonnet, *L'adoption lyonnaise*, 1:76.

[52] For some examples of popular talismans for procuring male children, see Madeleine Jeay, ed., *Les évangiles des quenouilles*, (Montreal, 1985). See also Pierre Darmon, *Le mythe de la procréation à l'âge baroque* (Paris, 1981). Darmon cites, for example, a thesis defended before the Medical Faculty of Paris in 1554 entitled "Si le sommeil favorise plutôt la conception des males? (Réponse affirmative)" (p. 6).

[53] AN, MC, Et. XXIX, 183 (24 October 1647). There is no evidence from the contracts that adopted daughters took on the family name of their adoptive father or mother, although

Whereas married couples adopted girls and boys at equal rates, widows, *filles majeures,* and married women who had regained control of their dotal properties, almost always adopted young girls as their heirs. We have already encountered Marie Poussin who had separated her lineal property from the marital community of property. Marie employed her legal latitude to make a *donation entre vifs* of all of her movable and immovable property to her adopted daughter Magdeleine de la rue Perpignan.[54] Widows also approached the governors of the Couche and requested to adopt one of the foundlings to raise "like their own children." We have also met the widow Vincente Hondeau, who adopted a fifteen-day-old girl from the Couche in 1610, whom she promised to baptize and raise.[55] In addition to widows, unmarried women who had reached their majority of twenty-five years, and who were known legally as *filles majeures,* went to the Couche to create families of their own through adoption. Marguerite d'Allu, a *fille majeure* in 1613 adopted an infant girl from a wet nurse hired by the Couche, promising to raise her "as if she were her own child."[56]

Charitable Motives

While adopting a child from the Couche served the practical function of offering an heir to a family (or a single parent) without progeny, charitable motives oriented toward the welfare of the child also compelled some families to foster and even formally to adopt one of the foundlings. A few of the contracts contain the traditional language of charity familiar from medieval arrangements of short-term fostering by which the adoptive parents pledge to care for a child for the "love" or "honor" of God. In 1588 Marie Filleyet adopted Claudine "as her child and as her principal heir," due to the "great affection" she held for Claudine and for the "honor of God."[57]

Legal scholars have traditionally drawn a distinction between true adop-

---

we should not rule out the possibility altogether (there is the precedent in early modern France for sons and daughters to adopt their mother's last name when they received letters of legitimation from the king).

[54] AN, MC, Et. XXIII, 157 (1599).

[55] AN, MC, Et. LXXIII, 173 (26 March 1610). Presenting an exception to this pattern, we have seen that Charlotte Chantellet adopted Pierre de la Rue Bourtibourg as her heir in 1589, most likely as a safeguard to continue the family line in the case of the death of her sickly son.

[56] AN, MC, Et. XIX, 380 (12 July 1613).

[57] AN, MC, Et. XXIII, 149 (24 October 1588). As noted earlier, Claudine was later adopted by Jehan Damiot and Marguerite Fleuryet.

tions as strategies of heirship and instances of destitute children fostered temporarily for the "love" or "honor" of God, in which case, it is assumed, ties of familial alliance were not forged and the child was not named as an heir.[58] We have seen that the phrase "for the love of God" (*ob amorem dei*) surfaced in the fifteenth-century fostering arrangements overseen by the Chapter of Notre-Dame. By the terms of these agreements children were placed in private homes throughout Paris, though they were not formally named as their families' heirs. The sixteenth-century cases of adoption indicate, however, that charitable and practical motives were not necessarily mutually exclusive, and that the contracts that employ the phrase "adopted for the honor of God" might also designate the child as the family's heir.

The elaboration of a case from 1589 involving Charlotte Chantellet, a widow from Bretigny who adopted Pierre de la Rue Bourtibourg, reveals an intriguing combination of practical and charitable motivations behind a family's decision to adopt a foundling.[59] The surprising element in this case is that Charlotte already had a biological son, Jehan Gardiez, by her deceased husband Claude Gardiez when she adopted Pierre. Why, we must ask, would Charlotte adopt a foundling and name him as her heir while her biological son was still living? Charlotte explains this action by recounting that just before her brother Pierre Chantellet died he charged her, as his sole heir, "to take a poor child to succeed him after her death," and that "part of his movable and immovable goods would be given to this poor child." Following her brother's wishes, Charlotte pledged that if both sons were to outlive her, the adopted son Pierre would split the inheritance with her biological son Jehan Gardiez. Another possible explanation for Charlotte's actions is that her biological son Jehan was infirm and thus unlikely to outlive her. Indeed, Charlotte makes clear that if her son were to die before her, Pierre would stand as the family's sole heir. In addition to suggesting the practical motivation of procuring a male heir to the family line, this intriguing case of adoption reveals the charitable motives that might compel an individual to adopt one of the "poor foundlings." We saw, for instance, that Charlotte's brother charged her with adopting a destitute child to inherit a portion of his property after his sister's death. Perhaps Pierre Gandellet's request had two aims: to name a healthy and secure male heir for the Gandellet line and, at the same time, to alter the course of a destitute child's life.

Charitable motives also played a role in several short-term fosterings of foundlings arranged by the Couche. Altruism seems to have inspired

---

[58] See Gonnet, *L'adoption lyonnaise*, 1:150–73, and François Olivier-Martin, *Histoire de la coutume de la prévôté et vicomté de Paris* (Paris, 1922), 1:151n. 1.

[59] AN, MC, Et. XXIII, 155 (1589).

Marin Loret, a sergeant in the bailiwick of St. Germain-des-Prés, and Jacqueline Sauval, his wife, to take in from the Couche a seven-year-old boy, named Jehan de Parne, in 1603. Marin and Jacqueline promised Jehan to instruct him "in the Catholic faith" and to provide an apprenticeship "so that he might become a virtuous man [*homme de bien*]."[60] This fostering case differs from the full-scale adoptions in several respects. For one, the word "adoption" does not appear in the contract, nor do the phrases indicating that Jehan would be cared for by Marin and Jacqueline "like their own child." In addition, there is no mention of Jehan being named an heir to the family patrimony. It might be that Marin and Jacqueline already had biological children, and thus an heir, when they brought Jehan into their home. Often it can only be surmised from the language of the contracts whether natal children were present at the time of the adoption. Because most of the contracts state explicitly that a couple (or a single woman) "has no living children of its own," or "no children born to them," it seems fair to conclude that when this condition is not mentioned, the couple did have a biological child. This seems reasonable inasmuch as most of our contracts were drawn up in one of two notarial offices and are fairly consistent in the language used. Why, then, if Marin and Jacqueline had other children, would they have taken Jehan from the Couche in the first place? The contract reveals their hope that in the future Jehan would have the chance of becoming a "good man" (*homme de bien*), a chance he might not have realized if he had remained at the foundling hospital. Although we cannot be certain about the motives for adopting Jehan, we should not discount the possibility of pious or charitable incentives in a case such as this.

In another short-term fostering case from 1607, Raphael Bonnart, a merchant of secondhand goods from Paris, signed a contract giving over Pierre Sève, an eight-year-old boy he had originally taken in from the Couche, to the care of a man named Hiérome Du Berle, a wine merchant also from Paris. Hiérome Du Berle promised to educate Pierre in the Roman Catholic faith, to furnish him with all of his necessities, and to apprentice him in the wine-selling trade.[61] In this instance we are able to consult a wider range of documents, which help to illuminate the motives behind Pierre's multiple pensionings.[62] Although we do not have the original

---

[60] AN, MC, Et. XXIII, 158 (1603).

[61] AN, MC, Et. XXIX, 159 (1607).

[62] In 1616 Raphaël Bonnart and his wife Claude Prudhomme made a mutual donation of their goods, which was signed in front of a notary. As the New Custom of Paris of 1580 stipulates, such a donation could only be made if the couple had no children who would otherwise inherit from them. The donation, accordingly, states that Raphaël Bonnart and Claude Prudhomme "Do not at present have any children." Thus, the couple might have originally wanted Pierre as an adopted son in their otherwise childless household.

contract of Pierre's placement by the Couche with Raphaël, Raphaël's last will and testament of 1616 suggests that charitable motives might have influenced his decision to take Pierre from the Couche. Raphaël's instructions for his funeral procession in his testament reveal a piety oriented particularly toward the destitute children of Paris. In his funeral procession, for instance, the children of the Trinité were instructed to carry a dozen torches around his coffin. The children of St. Esprit, the hospice of the Enfants Rouges, and the Charité were also asked to participate in the procession and all were to receive one solz tournois. In addition, Raphaël left money to the poor of the Hôtel-Dieu and to the Confraternity of Notre-Dame, both of which were connected in some way with the Couche and the care of the foundlings.

The Adoption of Labor?

While benevolent inclinations might have inspired some individuals such as Raphaël Bonnart to foster a destitute child from the Couche, some children may have been fostered primarily to serve as laborers. The Couche, in fact, was accused in the mid-seventeenth century by Vincent de Paul and others of selling some of its foundlings to beggars and other itinerants who treated them harshly and exploited them in order to evoke the pity of passersby. An eighteenth-century history of the establishment of the foundling hospital describes the children of the Couche at the mercy of avaricious and ruthless caretakers, "vile and mercenary souls," who "sell the young children to women beggars [*mendiantes*] who, in turn, use them as ploys to elicit alms from the public."[63] We have no way of knowing whether such "sales" of the foundlings actually occurred, although it should be kept in mind that reports of the wretched state of the Couche were often exaggerated in order to highlight the pious work undertaken on behalf of the foundlings by Vincent de Paul and the Ladies and Sisters of Charity after 1638.

In order to evaluate the relationship between adoption and labor, it is important to recall the spectrum of ways in which destitute abandoned and orphaned children were placed in households by various Parisian charity hospices. As we saw in the preceding chapter, the orphanages of St. Esprit, the Trinité, and the newly created municipal social welfare organization, the Great Bureau of the Poor, routinely pensioned out children as

---

[63] "Ces âmes viles et mercenaires vendoient ces jeunes enfans à des mendiantes qui s'en servoient pour exciter les charités du Public en le trompant." Anonymous, "Abrégé historique de l'établissement de l'hôpital des enfants trouvés," AN, Series S, 4931a, n.d. (most likely mid-eighteenth century).

servants and apprentices with families throughout the city. Unlike the adoptions from the Couche, which established lifelong ties of familial alliance, these service and apprenticeship arrangements entailed the child laboring in the household in exchange for the learning of a trade (and sometimes a small donation at the end of the term of service). In these instances the servants and apprentices were always taken in as adolescents and the foster family did not have the responsibility of raising the children from infancy to adulthood. The foster households thus received the benefit of the children's labor without having to commit to the long-term care of the child (in addition, the foster family often was paid by the charity hospice a fixed sum to cover the cost of the child's upkeep during the term of the service). The contracts from the Couche, on the other hand, state quite clearly that the adopting households were paid nothing for adopting a child; the adoptive parents routinely acknowledged in the contracts that "nothing was given to them, nor were they paid anything."[64] Rather, the adoptive families assumed complete parental responsibility for their adopted child, thereby releasing the administrators of the Couche and the canons of Notre-Dame from any future obligation.

The distinction between short-term fostering and permanent adoption does not exclude the possibility that the foundlings adopted as heirs from the Couche were expected to labor in their new households. As with biological children, adopted children would be expected to contribute labor to aid the household economy and we should not be surprised if this was indeed one motivating factor in the decision of childless households to adopt a child from the Couche. Yet, even so, we can safely place adoptions from the Couche in a separate category defined primarily by the desire for a child and an heir, and distinguished by the wide range of parental duties and responsibilities that accompanied the adoption. It seems fair to conclude that if a household did desire a child primarily as a source of labor, it would have opted to take in a servant or apprentice from one of the many charity hospices in the city that pensioned out children under these terms rather than to undertake a full-scale adoption from the Couche, with all of the attendant duties and obligations this entailed.

---

64 "Ilz leur soit baillé ny payé aucune chose." AN, MC, Et. XXIII, 152: adoption of Barbe Trouvez by Jehan la Borive and Laura Combaultz (20 May 1589). The only explicit case of payment by the Couche appears in the following pension of a young boy in 1599: "There was present in his person, Nicholas Four, a master cobbler living in the faubourgs of Paris in the parish of St. Laurent, who, has willingly recognized and confessed that for the past six months he has been paid by the Couche of the Poor Foundlings of the city of Paris to take in a young boy named Valenty. Du Four promises to feed, lodge, and care for him, gently, as is the custom, and in the future to teach him his trade so that he may earn his own living." AN, MC, Et. XXIII, 157 (22 November 1599).

The Foundlings as Heirs

What conclusions can be drawn regarding the legal status of the found-lings as heirs in the period 1588–1613 when the Couche was administered by the canons of the Chapter of Notre-Dame? In spite of the fact that Parisian customary law stated explicitly that "adopted children cannot inherit," we have seen that many of the contracts from the Couche explicitly name the children as heirs to the family property. Does this indicate that in the eyes of the law the children were considered full and legitimate heirs to the name and property of their adoptive parents? At the Aumône générale in early modern Lyon, Gonnet maintains that the adopted orphans did, in fact, take on the status of natural heirs, granting them the right to inherit *ab intestat* from the adoptive parent.[65] Gonnet hinges his argument on the language of the contracts, which describe the children's status in their adoptive families as "natural and legitimate, born in legal marriage." The adopted children inherited "naturally," Gonnet argues, because the act of adoption secured their status as "natural and legitimate" members of the family. Gonnet cites one case of adoption in particular from 1583 to substantiate his contention that the Lyonnais orphans succeeded as natural heirs. In this case a young boy named Guillaume, an orphan adopted from the Hôtel-Dieu in Lyon, was poised to inherit all of his adoptive family's property as a "natural and legitimate son." The relevant section of the contract reads:

> The said couple, considering that they have no children from their marriage, have adopted and taken Guillaume as their adopted son, wishing and consenting that, in the case they die without legitimate heirs of the body, Guillaume, their adopted son, will inherit all of their movable and immovable property . . . as if he were their natural and legitimate (son), born to them in legal marriage.[66]

Can we conclude for the adoptions from the Parisian Couche, as Gonnet has done for Lyon, that "the adopted child in the middle of the sixteenth century succeeded his parents, not only in the manner of a legitimate child, but exactly like a legitimate child?"[67] It is tempting to concur with Gonnet inasmuch as similar phrases appear in the Parisian contracts indicating that the adoptive family intended to leave the adopted child "their property as they would do for their own legitimate child"[68] or

---

[65] "Le fils adoptif succède ab-intestat, à Lyon, au XVIe siècle, à son père adoptif." Gonnet, *L'adoption lyonnaise*, 1:101.

[66] Ibid., 1:95 (27 August 1583 at the Bureau de l'Hôtel-Dieu du Pont du Rosne).

[67] Ibid., 1:97.

[68] AN, MC, Et. XXIX, 157 (12 December 1605).

as if the child were the parents' "own natural and legitimate child"[69] or as if the child were the family's "own child born from them in legal marriage."[70] Can we extrapolate from this language of legitimation, however, and conclude that the adopted foundlings in early modern Paris were accorded the status of "natural" heirs, complete with the right to succeed *ab intestat*? Although Gonnet concludes that such privileges were accorded to the adopted children in Lyon, the chances are less likely that such rights would have been recognized officially in the Paris region. Whereas the administrators of the Lyonnais Aumône could draw on the legacy of Roman law, which accorded full inheritance rights to adopted children, the Parisian notaries and the governors of the Couche were compelled to operate within customary law traditions, which had clearly rejected the Roman model of adoption. As we have seen, it was precisely because they could not rely on the ability of the adopted foundlings to inherit *ab intestat* that the Parisian notaries turned to the *donation entre vifs* in order to secure an inheritance for the children. Conversely, because the civil law of Lyon allowed adopted children to inherit through a testament or even, it appears, through *intestate* succession, the contracts of adoption overseen by the Aumône générale in sixteenth- and seventeenth-century Lyon did not employ the *donation entre vifs*. From a strictly legal standpoint, then, we cannot conclude that the adoptions from the Parisian Couche created legitimate ties of filiation that granted full inheritance privileges to the adopted children. From the perspective of the social and cultural history of family life, however, we can conclude that the *donation* provided adoptive parents with an alternative means to forge de facto ties of filiation as well as an alternative—and legal—avenue through which to transmit property to their adopted children.

ADOPTIONS IN THE LATE SEVENTEENTH CENTURY

The Hôpital des Enfants Trouvés and the Hôtel-Dieu

Following a gap in the evidence of adoption after 1613, further notarized contracts from the Couche surface after 1645 when the hospice was reorganized under Vincent de Paul and moved to new quarters in the faubourg St. Denis. It is important to note that these midcentury adoptions were transacted in a period in which the Couche was receiving a steadily increasing number of abandoned children. St. Vincent estimated that the Couche had received as many as 1,200 infants between 1640 and 1643.[71]

---

69 AN, MC, Et. XXIII, 157 (1599).
70 AN, MC, Et. XXIII, 162 (1605).
71 See the figures cited in Dupoux, *Sur les pas de Monsieur Vincent*, p. 34n.1.

Once rescued, the infant foundlings were sent to be wet-nursed in the countryside where they often remained until the age of twelve, at which time they returned to Paris to be provided for an apprenticeship (boys began their apprenticeship at age twelve, whereas the girls waited until age fifteen).[72] The practice of placing the children as apprentices does not fall under the rubric of "adoption" inasmuch as the ties between the host family and the foundling were severed once the apprenticeship was over. I located two notarized contracts of adoption that suggest that, alongside the short-term apprenticeships, the foundling hospice continued to place some of the children in permanent adoption arrangements similar to those overseen earlier by the Couche at St. Landry. One contract of adoption from this period recounts that on 30 December 1646 Guy Roger and his wife Denise Regaud, who lived at the place des Halles in the parish of St. Eustache, went to the hospice at St. Denis and took home with them a six-year-old foundling named Jacqueline. Guy and Denise promised the Ladies of Charity who oversaw the adoption to raise Jacqueline in their home "as if she were their own child" in the Roman Catholic faith and to teach her a trade when she matured. The couple also gave Jacqueline a donation of sixty livres worth of their property. Additionally, the couple promised the governesses of the hospice to report regularly on Jacqueline's progress and condition.[73] In 1647 Claude Fleury, a "bourgeois" from Bourbonnais adopted a six-year-old foundling named Jean, to whom Claude gave his surname of Fleury. Claude recounted that he had adopted Jean out of a "pure and free charity and without any animosity toward his kin and friends," promising to Jean to feed him, to care for him, and to raise him in his home "like his own child." Claude also pledged to raise Jean in the Roman Catholic religion, to teach him to read and write, and to apprentice him in a trade to enable him to earn his own living in the future. Claude also made a donation to Jean [Fleury] of sixty livres worth of his property, which was accepted for Jean by sister Mathurine Sican, the governess of the hospice and one of the Sisters of Charity.[74]

The endurance of formal adoption at the foundling hospice in the years after its transferral to St. Denis can be interpreted as a logical outgrowth of the philosophy of poor relief espoused by St. Vincent, who frequently articulated the hospice's mission to the foundlings in the metaphorical language of adoption. For instance, pleading in the 1640s with the Ladies of Charity not to abandon their work with the foundlings, St. Vincent proclaimed that "providence has rendered you the adoptive mothers of these

---

[72] See Danielle LaPlaige, *Sans famille à Paris: Orphelins et enfants abandonnés dans la Seine au XIXe siècle* (Paris, 1989).

[73] This case is found in Jean Sandrin, *Enfants trouvés, enfants ouvriers: XVIIe–XIXe siècle* (Paris, 1982), p. 61.

[74] AN, MC, Et. XXIX, 183 (1647).

infants," noting further that "compassion and charity led you to adopt these children for your own children."[75] According to St. Vincent one of the central goals of the hospice was to offer the abandoned children of Paris the chance for an improved life. If properly assisted, St. Vincent maintained, the foundlings might grow up to be influential members of society:

> Perhaps among them are future great figures and saints. Remus and Romulus, the founders of Rome, were foundlings nourished by a she-wolf. According to St. Paul, Melchizedek had neither father nor mother and was therefore a foundling; John the Baptist was like a foundling in the desert. Finally, Moses was an abandoned child found by the sister of the Pharaoh.[76]

For foundlings such as Jacqueline and Jean Fleury, the placement in new families through adoption might have offered that "second chance" hoped for by St. Vincent.

Although the two cases of adoption from 1646 and 1647 offer only fragmentary evidence of adoption practices at the Couche in the St. Denis period, we are able to supplement our look at adoption in the second half of the seventeenth century by turning to the registers of an auxiliary order associated with St. Vincent de Paul, the Ladies of Charity of the Hôtel-Dieu. Records of the Hôtel-Dieu beginning in 1656 show that the Ladies of Charity and the governors of the Hôtel-Dieu arranged for both orphans and foundlings to be adopted by Parisian families who had no children of their own.[77] Just as in the earlier adoptions from the Couche at the Port St. Landry and at St. Denis, these arrangements ranged in scope from short-term charitable pensionings with a fixed termination date (usually after the child's apprenticeship) to more comprehensive adoptions in which lifelong ties of familial alliance were forged and in which the child was promised some form of inheritance.

The central features of the adoptions from the Hôtel-Dieu are similar to the adoptions from the Couche: childless couples and individuals who, inspired by a combination of practical and charitable motives, opted to take a destitute child into their home to raise "like their own child." Such a combination of factors led a married couple who had no children of their own, Noel Sontif, a master carpenter, and his wife Marie Ronsel, to adopt in 1675 a two-year-old boy who had been abandoned only hours before the adoption at the Hôtel-Dieu. The couple described the young boy to the notary as having "blond hair and dressed in a little grey dress, and,

---

[75] Dupoux, *Sur les pas de Monsieur Vincent*, p. 35.

[76] Cited in Pillorget, *Nouvelle histoire de Paris: Les premiers Bourbons*, p. 522.

[77] AP, Fonds de l'Hôtel-Dieu, liasse 877, "Titres des enfants nés à l'Hôtel-Dieu et confiés à des particuliers et aux Dames de la Charité des enfans trouvés" (42 pièces).

when asked, was unable to tell them his name." Noel and Marie explained that they had adopted the young boy "out of charity and due to the desire to have a child since they had none of their own."[78] Charity seems also to have encouraged Esmond de Gard, a merchant and "bourgeois" of Paris from the parish of St. Jacques de la Boucherie, to adopt a one-month-old infant girl, named Margueritte Barbaroux, who had been abandoned by her mother at the Hôtel-Dieu, in 1665. The contract relates that, "seized by charity," Esmond had agreed with the governors of the Hôtel-Dieu to aid a poor woman named Barbe (whose surname was omitted), who had given birth at the Hôtel-Dieu and then subsequently abandoned the infant at the home of François Villaut, a lawyer living on the rue des Massons. Having had no luck in the search for clues to the identity of the child's father (whose surname would be Barbaroux), the commissioners of the Châtelet had the infant taken to the Couche. It was then that Esmond stepped in and pledged to discharge the natal mother, Barbe, of all responsibility for her child and to raise Margueritte himself. As his first parental obligation, Esmond sent Margueritte to a wet nurse, Marie du Boiret, whom he agreed to pay eight livres per month. Esmond promised further to raise Margueritte once she left the wet nurse "for the rest of her days," including arranging to apprentice her, to instruct her in the Roman Catholic faith, and to provide her with all things "as a father would do." Although Esmond discharged Barbe entirely for Margueritte's care, he promised to provide her with news from "month to month" regarding Margueritte's condition.[79]

In several instances the adopted orphans from the Hôtel-Dieu were given donations from the family property to help support them after the parents' death. In 1667 a married couple whom we have already met, Jean Barbereau, a valet de chambre, and his wife Anne Barbereau from the l'isle d'Adam in Picardy, adopted an orphan from the Hôtel-Dieu named Catherine Cointel, whom they had first seen at the home of the infant's wet nurse in their town. In addition to raising her from infancy, the couple promised Catherine a future inheritance.[80] Anne Barbereau's testament which was drawn up in 1671 fulfilled this promise by donating to Catherine all of her movable property in addition to all of the wine in the basement, some wheat from a mill at Terville, some flour, and all the vegetables found in the attic. Anne provided further that, when she died, all of this property would be put into the hands of her husband, whom she charged with raising Catherine. When Anne died in 1672 Jean Barbereau approached the governors of the Hôtel-Dieu with his wife's will and ar-

[78] AP, Fonds de l'Hôtel-Dieu, liasse 877 (7 April 1675).

[79] AP, Fonds de l'Hôtel-Dieu, liasse 877 (16 August 1665).

[80] AP, Fonds de l'Hôtel-Dieu, liasse 877 (10 December 1669).

ranged to convert the value of the perishable property willed to Catherine into the sum of 400 livres, which would be given to her when she was old enough.[81] A comparable arrangement was made on 28 August 1677 when a widow, Margueritte Le Febvre from the parish of St. Gervais, adopted a newborn girl named Marie Magdeleine du Val, whose mother had died in childbirth only a few weeks earlier. The infant's father, Jehan du Val, a day worker who had relinquished all claims on his daughter, testified that Marie had been baptized in the parish of St. Sauveur on 10 August. Margueritte promised to feed, care for, and raise Marie in the Roman Catholic faith at her own expense. Margueritte also made an irrevocable donation of "a portion of her property" to Marie, which was accepted for the infant girl by Fabien Perrault, the director of the orphans at the Hôtel-Dieu.[82] Similarly, Jean Lebé and Marie Boquet from the parish of St. Paul made a donation of property to a two-year-old orphan named Nicolle Louise Desmarestre whom they adopted in July 1670. The couple promised to raise Nicolle "as their own child," a promise which they sealed by making her an irrevocable *donation entre vifs* of 1,000 livres worth of all of their property "due to the good friendship that they feel for Nicolle Louise." The couple provided further that, if one or both of the parents died before Nicolle reached her majority, the money would be put in the hands of the governors of the Hôtel-Dieu to be transferred to her at the appropriate moment (when Marie Boquet died, 500 livres were transferred to the governors of the Hôtel-Dieu to fulfill the terms of the original adoption contract).[83]

Not all of the arrangements placing the orphans from the Hôtel-Dieu in private homes were binding "for life." Some children were taken in from the Hôtel-Dieu by charitable individuals to raise until their majority. In a case from 1656, a Monsieur Pinard, an attorney in the Grand Conseil who lived in the parish of St. Germain l'Auxerrois, approached the governors of the Hôtel-Dieu stating that he "wished to have one of the infant male children under their care." The governors agreed to give Pinard a three-month-old-boy named Jean to adopt (whom Pinard took directly to a wet nurse he had selected). Pinard, "moved by charity," pledged to raise the young Jean "in the fear of God," instruct him in the Roman Catholic religion, and teach him a trade when he came of age. The governors of the Hôtel-Dieu provided Pinard with 400 livres tournois to be used for Jean's apprenticeship (at which time Pinard and his heirs were also released of all responsibility for the boy). We know from other records at the Hôtel-Dieu that the infant Jean was the illegitimate son of Marye Porlier, an unmar-

---

[81] AP, Fonds de l'Hôtel-Dieu, liasse 877 (30 April 1672).
[82] AP, Fonds de l'Hôtel-Dieu, liasse 877 (28 August 1674).
[83] AP, Fonds de l'Hôtel-Dieu, liasse 877 (10 August 1677).

ried minor, who had given birth to him at the Hôtel-Dieu. Shortly after the birth, Marye's mother, Marye Marschand, returned to the Hôtel-Dieu to abandon the infant boy because, as she later explained, "neither she nor her daughter had any property or any means of subsistence."[84] At the time of the adoption, both women were prisoners of the Chapter of Notre-Dame (presumably for having abandoned Jean at the Hôtel-Dieu), and it was here that the governors of the Hôtel-Dieu went to secure their permission to give Jean in adoption to a "pious and charitable person"—who turned out to be M. Pinard—to raise until he reached his majority.

Charitable motives seem to have compelled Jacques Rousseau, a merchant of braids and trimmings from the faubourg St. Marcel, and his wife Margueritte Petit to take into their home a ten-and-a-half-year-old boy who was stricken with an illness and whose chances of survival, they were told, would increase dramatically if he were removed from the hospital. The couple had first seen the boy while on a visit to the Hôtel-Dieu, and speaking with him had learned that he was originally from Seve in Picardy and that he had been baptized as Jean Perrier, the son of Edme Perrier. Jean declared that he did not know his mother's name because he was too young when she died. The contract recounts that this encounter so moved Jacques and Margueritte that they decided to ask for the child to take home and raise "as their own child." The couple signed a notarized agreement with Fabien Perreau, the master of the Hôtel-Dieu, promising to raise Jean in the "fear of God," to educate him, care for him and feed him in sickness and in health, and to give him "any necessary medications." In addition Jacques pledged to teach him a trade when the boy was old enough "as if he were his child."[85]

The Foundling Hospice after 1670

The records of the foundling hospice disclose that adoptions continued to be practiced from the houses at St. Denis in the closing decades of the seventeenth century. Although the foundling hospice was subsumed under the administration of the Hôpital général in 1670, it remained for a few years in the houses in the faubourg St. Denis before being moved to new quarters comprised of the "Maison de la Couche" on the rue Neuve-Notre-Dame, where the infants were kept, and at the "Maison de St. Antoine," which housed the older children. The deliberations of the administrators of the Hôpital des Enfants Trouvés, which commence in 1670, demonstrate that families from the city of Paris and its outlying regions continued

---

[84] AP, Fonds de l'Hôtel-Dieu, liasse 877 (6 September 1656).
[85] AP, Fonds de l'Hôtel-Dieu, liasse 877 (7 October 1667).

to approach the administrators of the hospice to request to adopt one of the foundlings to "raise like their own child."[86] Even after the hospice became dependent on the Hôpital général and evolved officially into a secular institution run by the Crown, the daily work at the hospice continued to be undertaken by the Ladies and Sisters of Charity. We can speculate, in fact, that the sisters, trained in St. Vincent's philosophy of poor relief, were influential in the hospice's decision to continue to employ formal adoption to integrate many of the abandoned children into Parisian society.

Beginning in 1670 the foundling hospice registered an abbreviated entry for each child placed with an adoptive family. A typical entry from 21 November 1670 notes that "M. Le Febvre, a surgeon living on the rue St. Antoine came to ask for Pierre Loysel, one of the *pauvres enfants trouvés*, who was given to him under the customary obligations, which were notarized." Another entry from 16 January 1671 recounts that "Marie Hélène, Jehanne le Pauvre, and Marie Magdeleine were given to three women who asked for them, all of whom were deemed honorable women by the governors, and all of whom made the customary obligations in front of the notary."[87] While such entries offer limited information regarding the specific features of adoption in this era, in a few instances we are able to gain a more complete picture by consulting the original contracts located in the notarial registers.[88]

The notarial evidence reveals that the central features of the adoptions from this period are similar to the earlier adoptions from the Couche in its Port St. Landry and St. Denis days. As in the earlier periods, the contracts demonstrate that it was primarily childless married couples who adopted from the foundling hospice. For instance, on 10 October 1670 Jean Le Gendre, a launderer, and his wife Marie Mynette from the parish of St. Nicholas du Champs arranged with Jeanne Cloiset, one of the Ladies of Charity, to adopt a six-year-old foundling named Anne du Chemin. The couple, who had no children of their own, promised to feed, house, and care for Anne, to instruct her in the Roman Catholic faith and to teach her a trade all "as if she were their own child" (*comme si elle était leur propre enfant*). The couple recounted to the notary that they decided to adopt Anne "out of the friendship [*l'amitié*] they felt toward her."[89] On the

---

[86] The registers of the deliberations of the administrators of the Hôpital des Enfants Trouvés, which begin in 1670, are preserved in AP, Fonds de l'Hôpital des Enfants Trouvés, liasse 9.

[87] The records of the hospice recorded a total of thirteen adoptions of children for 1670 and 1671.

[88] The adoptions from 1670 and 1671 were all drawn up by the notary Louis Conteillier (AN, MC, Et. LXIX, 63), who devised a standard contract covering the care to be given the children.

[89] AN, MC, Et. LXIX, 63 (10 October 1670). For other cases of "prises d'enfans" in this

same day in 1670 Henry Gellain, a gardener and a florist to the queen, went with his wife Barbe du Bois to the hospice in order to adopt an eight-year-old girl named Louise Masson, which was approved by Nicolle Haran, a Sister of Charity and the reigning governess of the hospice. They explained that "since they do not have any children of their own," they pledged to feed, lodge, and raise Louise "in the Roman Catholic" faith and, later, to apprentice her in a trade "as they would for their own child." Henry and Barbe recounted that they adopted Louise "for their own satisfaction and due to the friendship they had developed for her."[90] Again in 1670 another childless couple, Nicholas Duval, a master carpenter in Paris, and his wife Françoise Robillard adopted a three-year-old boy named Paul Cézard from the hospice. The couple recounted that they had originally taken Paul home with them after a visit they had made to the foundling hospice the previous Sunday and were now returning to formalize the arrangement. Nicholas and Françoise promised to raise Paul as a Roman Catholic and to apprentice him in trade at the appropriate age "as they would do for their own child." This last contract, like many others from this period, highlights the emotional ties that often formed during a child's initial stay with a foster family, and which, in turn, served as a motive for the parents to formalize the adoption.[91]

In addition to childless married couples and widows, unmarried women also arranged to adopt children from the foundling hospice at St. Denis. Thus in 1670 Margueritte Henry, a *fille majeure*, adopted a five-month-old girl named Claude Laneuve from the foundling hospice. Margueritte promised to feed, lodge, and maintain Claude, to instruct her in the Roman Catholic faith and teach her a trade "as she would for her own child."[92] I came across only one case in this period of an unmarried woman adopting a son: in 1670 Nicolle Roze, the widow of François Le Clerc, a merchant draper, who had no children of her own, adopted a five-year-old boy, Philippe de Lestre, from the Enfants Trouvés. Nicolle made the customary pledges to care for him, house him, maintain him, instruct him in the Roman Catholic faith, teach him a trade, and to do all this "as she would for her own child."[93]

Interestingly, these late seventeenth-century contracts do not employ the word "adoption." Perhaps by the end of the seventeenth century the rejection of adoption by the revised Custom of Paris of 1580 had begun to

---

notarial register, see Et. LXIX, 63 (2 October 1670), (10 October 1670: two cases), and (17 October 1670).

[90] AN, MC, Et. LXIX, 63 (10 October 1670).

[91] AN, MC, Et. LXIX, 63 (19 December 1670).

[92] AN, MC, Et. LXIX, 63 (17 October 1670).

[93] AN, MC, Et. LXIX, 63 (10 October 1670).

influence notarial practices to a greater extent than had been the case with the earlier adoptions drafted by notaries connected with the Couche. Whatever the cause, these contracts also fail to make explicit inheritance provisions for the adoptive children. As suggested earlier, however, the absence of an inheritance clause does not preclude the possibility that these children did ultimately receive property from their adoptive parents. In the end, although the structure of these late seventeenth-century contracts diverges from the form we have seen thus far, the goal of the notarized contracts remained constant: providing families interested in adoption with an alternative avenue to circumvent the prohibitions of the customary law in order to forge de facto ties of filiation.

The enduring appeal of adoption as a means of placing the foundlings with adoptive households stemmed in large part from the vast numbers of abandoned children under the hospice's care at the close of the seventeenth century. The registers of the hospice reveal, for instance, that in May 1671 the hospice had 1,087 foundlings under its care and that 423 infants had been brought to the hospice in 1670 alone. In addition to increasing rates of abandonment, frighteningly high mortality rates suffered by children kept inside the hospice also compelled the administrators to place the children as quickly as possible in private homes. Out of the 1,087 foundlings under the care of the hospice in 1671, 302 of the children were placed with wet nurses, and, out of the 120 children who were retained in the hospice, 118 died.[94] The combination of these demographic pressures and high mortality rates certainly played a role in encouraging the hospice to continue to employ adoption to place some of the foundlings in the care of private families. Indeed, the hospice seems to have gone to great lengths in these years to remind the Parisian community of the existence of the foundlings. On 6 June 1674 the directors decided to "show the foundlings to the public by undertaking a procession," from the house in the faubourg St. Antoine to the Cathedral of Notre-Dame, where the children "said prayers for the safekeeping of the king and the prosperity of his armies." According to the records of the hospital, 140 "of the fittest" children took place in the procession.[95]

CONCLUSIONS

Although this study has not undertaken a quest for archival evidence of adoption in eighteenth-century Paris, the records of the foundling hospice

[94] AP, Fonds de L'Hôpital des enfants trouvés, liasse 9, p. 10v.

[95] See H. Bordier and L. Brièle, *Les Archives Hospitalières de Paris, enfants-trouvés: Délibérations de l'Hôpital du 17e: Extraits* (Paris, 1877), p. 134 (6 June 1674).

suggest that the adoption practices characteristic of the sixteenth and seventeenth centuries continued to be employed.[96] According to one eighteenth-century witness, many of the girls from the foundling hospice were given over to the care of charitable families who promised to raise them and care for them.[97] A register of the Hôpital général from 1761 also records that foundlings of both sexes were routinely given to private households at the age of six when they returned from the care of the wet nurses.[98] The historian Léon Lallemand suggests that the practice of placing the children with foster families in the countryside was practiced frequently enough in the eighteenth century that the foundling hospice in Paris ended up ministering only to the newborn foundlings. Lallemand reports that the directors of the hospice made a conscious decision to leave the infant foundlings with their wet nurses beyond the age five or six so that closer emotional bonds might form and induce the wet-nursing families to keep the children permanently.[99] Supporting Lallemand's claim, a report from the Parisian "Committee on Poverty" in 1790 authored by M. Rochefoucauld-Liancourt noted that: "Almost all of the children . . . taken in by wet-nursing families are subsequently kept with these families, who treat them like their own children, until the children are married."[100]

Previous studies of poor relief in sixteenth- and seventeenth-century Paris have made no mention of the system of adoption employed by the Couche and by the Hôtel-Dieu to aid in the care of the multitude of abandoned and orphaned children consigned to their care in early modern Paris.[101] In fact, very little has been written about the Couche at all save for the era of St. Vincent de Paul. Albert Dupoux's classic study of the Couche, *Sur les pas de Monsieur Vincent*, for instance, laments the dearth of information on the Couche between 1570 and St. Vincent's reorganization of the hospice in the 1640s. This gap in the literature is unfortunate considering that the placement of abandoned and orphaned children into

---

[96] We know, for example, that formal adoptions from the Aumône générale in Lyon persisted into the eighteenth century. See Gonnet, *L'adoption lyonnaise*, 2:161–233.

[97] "Les filles qui sont aud. hôpital sont pour la plus grande partie données à des personnes charitables qui les demandent pour les élever et en prendre soin, et lors que ces personnes s'en chargent, elles font un acte de soumission devant notaires," in BN, Ms. fr. Collection Joly de Fleury, N. 1236, p. 46v (eighteenth century).

[98] *Extrait de registre des déliberations du Bureau de l'Hôpital général du . . . janvier 1761,* AP, Fonds de L'Hôp. gén., liasse 3, art. 3, p. 7.

[99] Léon Lallemand, *Histoire des enfants abandonnés et délaissés* (Paris, 1885), p. 65.

[100] Lallemand, *Histoire des enfants abandonnés*, pp. 65–66.

[101] Marcel Fosseyeux does not offer an in-depth examination of the workings of the Couche in his otherwise valuable "L'assistance parisienne au milieu du XVIe siècle," in *Mémoires de la société d'histoire de Paris et de l'Ile de France* 43 (1916): 83–128. In *Les orphelins et les enfants trouvés à Paris à la fin du moyen-âge*, Mémoire maîtrise lettres (Paris, 1967), Paule Bavoux also does not mention the adoptions from the Couche.

private households in the city and outlying regions of Paris formed a notable part of the poor relief administered by both the Couche and the Hôtel-Dieu.

The evidence of adoption reveals that Parisian charity hospices did not operate on a static model of poor relief; while some of the destitute children surely lived out their lives in the institutional setting of the hospices, many other children, Claudine des Petitz Champs, Magdeleine de la rue Perpignan, and Claude Vaucombert among them, left the hospices at an early age to be adopted into private households. Although traditional medieval fostering arrangements were typically short-term, the formal adoption arrangements made by the Couche and the Hôtel-Dieu beginning in the mid-sixteenth century established lifelong ties of familial alliance between the adoptive parents and the adopted children. Similar to the two-household adoptions, the married couples and individual parents who went to the Couche had, for a variety of reasons, turned to adoption as an alternative pathway to parenthood. The decision to adopt a foundling from the Couche rested on a combination of factors: the wish to raise a child to consider one's own, the desire to pass on one's worldly goods to a child of one's choice, the need to increase the number of individuals working in the household, and the securing of a caretaker in one's old age. In return, the adopted foundlings received numerous benefits from the adoptions arranged for them by the Couche: a new set of parents who offered them basic care, an apprenticeship, a dowry, an inheritance, and the opportunity to forge a new life outside of the institutional confines of the foundling hospice.

The revised portrait of the operation of the Parisian charity hospices suggests some modifications in our depiction of the fate of abandoned children in the early modern period. For instance, John Boswell, in his study of abandonment practices in western Europe from antiquity to the Renaissance, has underscored a distinction between an older, noninstitutionalized model of abandonment and adoption by which foundlings were left in public places and subsequently taken in on an informal basis by charitable individuals, and a newer model represented by the foundling homes that were established throughout Europe in the fourteenth century. Boswell suggests that the institutionalization of abandonment and adoption served to sever the—now more stigmatized—infants from the "kindness of strangers," which had earlier prompted community members to foster them. Boswell contends that foundling homes created "classless, familyless, unconnected adolescents with no claim on the support of any persons or groups in the community."[102]

---

[102] See John Boswell, *The Kindness of Strangers: The Abandonment of Children in Western Europe from Late Antiquity to the Renaissance* (New York, 1988), p. 421.

Although the foundling homes altered earlier models of abandonment and adoption, the evidence of adoption from the Couche and Hôtel-Dieu in the early modern period suggests that, at least in Paris, communal involvement in the care of foundlings and orphans continued to form an integral part of the city's care of its destitute children. Thus, by actively encouraging the integration of many of the orphaned and abandoned children into Parisian society, charity hospices such as the Couche and the Hôtel-Dieu in Paris (like the Aumône générale in Lyon) paint an alternative portrait of early modern poor relief from the image of the "great confinement of the poor."[103] Rather, it appears that a more fluid system of poor relief endured into at least the late seventeenth century; this system persisted in large measure because adoption offered a solution to the dilemma of rapidly growing numbers of orphaned and abandoned children assigned to the care of the city's charity hospices.

In addition to expanding our understanding of early modern poor relief, the case studies of adoption offer an interesting new perspective on family life in early modern Paris. Despite the rejection of adoption by customary law and by the noble classes, our evidence has demonstrated the continued appeal of adoption to laboring, artisan, and merchant families, the majority of whom, as we have seen, had no biological children of their own. In its broadest terms, the evidence of adoption from the Couche and the Hôtel-Dieu brings to light the existence of a sector of Parisian society that did not subscribe to the conviction held by the jurists of the day that adoption ran "contrary to Nature." Rather, adoption afforded these childless couples and individuals the opportunity to "repair Nature," as contemporaries might have commented, and to forge alternative domestic structures that ensured the continuity of the family line into the next generation.

---

[103] See Michel Foucault, *Madness and Civilization: A History of Insanity in the Age of Reason*, trans. Richard Howard (New York, 1965), chap. 2: "The Great Confinement."

Revolutionary Visions of Blood Ties
and Adoptive Ties

The National Assembly decrees that its legislative
committee will include in its general plan civil
laws on adoption.
(*J. B. Rougier-Labergerie, January 1792*)[1]

THE ACCEPTANCE of adoption by French civil law in the aftermath of the
Revolution stands in marked contrast to the prevailing attitude toward
adoption characteristic of the two preceding centuries, when, as we have
seen, adoption was deemed "unnatural" and was rejected by civil law.
Amid the egalitarian fervor of revolutionary France, however, the en-
trenched prejudice against adoption receded and the institution took on a
new role as an avenue to achieving the social and political aims of the
newly founded republic. Rather than fearing adoption as a menace to society, revolutionary legislators now lauded adoption as an expedient means
to break down class barriers and to redistribute wealth among the citi-
zenry. Thus Cambacérès, introducing one of three projects of adoption for
the Civil Code to the Convention in 1793, proclaimed it: "An admirable
institution . . . and one that is naturally linked to the constitution of a
republic inasmuch as it fosters, without producing a crisis, the division of
great fortunes!"[2] The Jacobin Oudot went so far as to proclaim adoption a
"sacred duty, indispensable for every childless citizen," proposing that by
the age of thirty every male citizen had to marry or to adopt a child.[3]

---

[1] Decree of 18 January 1792. Rougier-Labergerie was the deputy to the legislative committee from the Yonne. Cited in Françoise Fortunet, "Le rétablissement du principe de
l'adoption: Une entrée par effraction?" in Irène Théry and Christian Biet, eds., *La famille, la
loi et l'état, de la Révolution au Code civil* (Paris, 1989), p. 196.

[2] In P. A. Fenet, *Recueil complet des travaux préparatoires du Code civil*, 15 vols. (1827;
repr., Osnabrück, 1968), 1:7. Cambacérès was a jurist from an old *noblesse de robe* family from
Montpellier. The potential for adoption to mix social classes was also claimed by Bernardin
de Saint-Pierre in his *Voeux d'un solitaire* (Paris, 1789), where he calls upon the French
nobility to emulate the Roman patrician families who adopted plebeians.

[3] From a speech presented to the Legislative Assembly (25 June 1792) and cited in Marcel Garaud and Romauld Szramkiewicz, *La Révolution française et la famille* (Paris, 1978),
p. 96. Oudot was the deputy to the convention from the Côte d'Or.

In the immediate aftermath of the Revolution the merits of adoption were proclaimed not only in the legislative sphere but also through popular ceremonies and in the popular press. Children such as the orphaned daughter of the assassinated revolutionary hero Lepeletier were adopted "in the name of the nation" to be "raised as good citizens."[4] Such adoptions "by the nation" continued to be practiced under the empire and in the later period for orphans whose parents died in the revolutions of 1848 and 1870. Subsequently, a decree of 27 July 1917 carried on the tradition by which the state adopted war orphans as pupils of the nation. In addition to state-sponsored adoptions, the revolutionary enthusiasm for adoption inspired myriad festivals, which were held throughout the country to honor individual families who adopted children.[5] Popular theater followed suit with the production of patriotic plays celebrating the new role of adoption in family life. In one play, *La nourrice républicaine ou les plaisirs de l'adoption*, a local mayor officiating at the adoption of a young orphan, remarks "what a difference between the rituals of the old regime, and those of the new!" At the end of the play the chorus sings the refrain: "Long live the Republic and the law of adoption!"[6]

Prior to the abolition of the monarchy, adoption was even proposed by some as a means to fashion a more "egalitarian" royal family. A treatise written in 1790 by Madame de Brulart, the ex-governess of the Dauphin, entitled *Discours sur l'éducation de M. le Dauphin et sur l'adoption*, reveals that some early revolutionaries believed that adoption could bring about such changes. Madame de Brulart linked the practice of adoption to a republican social order in which lineage no longer determined the social hierarchy:

> The pride inspired by social rank and birth could present the only logical opposition to adoption; but how can it be feared in this memorable epoch, where man, now complete with his natural rights and new-found dignity, sees all around him as his equal.[7]

Envisioning a link between the institution of adoption and the public's right to oversee the education of its future leaders, Mme de Brulart recom-

---

[4] Decree of 25 January 1793. Her adoption caused debates over matters of "paternal authority" and inheritance. See the "Réponse à l'opinion du représentant du peuple B. Laujacq dans l'affaire de la mineure Lepeletier" (Paris, n.d.). Adoptions "by the nation" were ushered in by a decree of 28 June 1793: tit. 1, sec. 2, art. 1, which reads that, "la Nation se charge de l'éducation physique et morale des enfants connus sous le nom d'enfants abandonnés." On the "national adoptions" see Garaud and Szramkiewicz, *La Révolution française et la famille*.

[5] See James F. Traer, *Marriage and the Family in Eighteenth-Century France* (Ithaca, N.Y., 1980), p. 153.

[6] C. Piis, *La nourrice républicaine ou les plaisirs de l'adoption: Comédie en un acte mêlée de Vaudevilles* (Paris, Year II [1793]): (scène 10, p. 24); (scène 13, p. 31).

[7] *Discours sur l'éducation de M. le Dauphin et sur l'adoption, par Mme. de Brulart, ci-devant Mme. de Sillery gouvernante des enfans de la maison d'Orléans* (Paris, 1790), p. 72.

mended further that the prince be fostered by the people of the country-side in order to infuse him with democratic ideals.[8] In this regard, the author proposed a cross-class project of adoption which she claimed would "destroy all prejudice":

> Those among the old nobility who cherish the New Constitution, if they wish to adopt children, let them do so without regard for social class. A citizen holding a one-time illustrious name could then give it to the son of an artisan or merchant.[9]

THE FAMILY, CIVIL LAW, AND SOCIAL CHANGE

In many respects the family stood at the center of plans to restructure French society according to the revolutionary tenets of "liberty, equality, and fraternity."[10] As Lynn Hunt has suggested, the republicans "found themselves advocating radical changes in family law and opening up fundamental questions about family arrangements as a consequence of their desire to break with the monarchical and aristocratic past."[11] In order to transform the nature of the familial sphere to accord with the new revolutionary vision of society, the legislators had first to dismantle the foundations of the old regime "system of succession."[12] Beginning in 1790, a wave of legislation on inheritance was passed that aimed at dispersing family fortunes (especially those of the nobility) and promoting equality of inheritance within families across the social spectrum.[13] In order to orient the rules of inheritance away from a focus on individual family lineages,

[8] Ibid., pp. 24–25.

[9] Ibid., p. 66.

[10] On the relationship between law and society, see J. Commaille, "Ordre familial, ordre social, ordre légal: Éléments d'une sociologie politique de la famille," *L'année sociologique* 37 (1987): 265–90; Garaud and Szramkiewecz, *La Révolution française et la famille*; C. J. Greenhouse, "Courting Difference: Issues of Interpretation and Comparison in the Study of Legal Ideologies," *Law and Society* 22, no. 4 (1988): 687–707. For eighteenth-century France in particular, see *La Révolution et l'ordre juridique privé, rationalité ou scandale? Actes du colloque d'Orléans*, 2 vols. (Paris, 1988).

[11] Lynn Hunt, *The Family Romance of the French Revolution* (Berkeley, Calif., 1992), p. 151. Hunt argues that the domestic realm was so central to the revolutionary reordering of society because "the French had a kind of collective political consciousness that was structured by narratives of family relations" (p. xiii).

[12] On the legislative changes dealing with family law, see also Margaret Darrow, *Revolution in the House: Family, Class and Inheritance in Southern France, 1775–1825* (Princeton, N.J., 1989).

[13] The laws of 17 nivôse an II [1793] marked the culmination of the revolutionary dismantling of old regime customary laws, announcing that "toutes lois, coutumes, usages et statuts relatifs à la transmission des biens sont également abolis" (art. 61). For a review of the major legislative innovations, see Jacques Poumarède, "La législation successorale de la Révolution entre idéologie et la pratique," in Théry and Biet, *La famille, la loi, l'état*, pp. 167–82.

the category of the lineage property (the *propres*)[14] was rejected as was the *retrait lignager*, the right of extended kin to claim family property before it was donated outside of the kin group.[15] The testament, condemned as an instrument that favored one child above the others, was outlawed. Similarly, male primogeniture was abolished in the many places in France where it still existed. Additionally, the strict equality of all heirs was proclaimed, the "substitution" of a future heir was eliminated, and illegitimate children were accorded full inheritance rights.[16] Finally, as we have seen, a call was heard from various quarters of French society for the institution of comprehensive adoption laws. One group calling for the enactment of adoption laws was the "Parisian Society for Equality within Families" (La Société de Paris des Amis de l'Union et de l'Egalité dans les Familles). In 1791 the president of the society, Lanthenas, sent a letter to the Constituent Assembly, which was signed by citizens from all over the country and which demanded that adoption be made available to all those without progeny.[17]

In their desire to reshape the family sphere, the revolutionary laws on inheritance, including the project for adoption, were guided by an ideology intent upon enforcing the antihierarchical principle of equal inheritance, which challenged the "despotism of fathers,"[18] much in the same way that the Revolution itself had overturned the "despotism of the king." In this context, the various projects for instituting and regulating adoption laws went beyond the issue of giving a child to a new family—they formed part of the broader political debate over the fundamental structures of postrevolutionary French society. One of the first comprehensive projects for adoption, proposed by Berlier in 1793, envisioned adoption both as a means to mix social classes and as a charitable measure oriented toward the welfare of children.[19] Berlier proposed that adoption be available to all

[14] The propres consisted of the real property (the immovables or immeubles) that an individual received from members of the lineage. A portion of the *propres* (for the Custom of Paris the amount was four-fifths) was reserved for the lineage and could not freely be alienated away from the lineal line. See François Olivier-Martin, *Histoire de la coutume de la prévôté et vicomté de Paris* (Paris, 1922), 2:316–17.

[15] By the terms of the *retrait lignager*, collateral kin held first rights to buy back alienated family properties (the *propres*). On these laws for the Paris region, see Olivier-Martin, *Histoire de la coutume*, 2:320–43.

[16] See Florence Bellivier, "Des droits pour les bâtards, l'enfant naturel dans les débats révolutionnaires," in Théry and Biet, *La famille, la loi, l'état*, pp. 122–44.

[17] See Garaud and Szramkiewicz, *La Révolution française et la famille*, p. 95.

[18] The "despotism of fathers" was seen to reside primarily in the *puissance paternelle*, which was rejected by the revolutionary legislators.

[19] See also Oudot, "Essai sur les principes de la législation des mariages privés et solonels, du divorce et de l'adoption qui peuvent être déclarés à la suite de l'Acte constitutionnel," which notes that "Ceux à qui la nature a refusé des enfants sont malheureux sans doute, et dignes de sollicitude du législateur; mais c'est moins pour les consoler, que pour venir au secours des enfants qui ont perdus leurs protecteurs naturels et pour les suppléer, que l'adop-

men over the age of majority, even in the case that they already had biological children. Berlier asked further that adopted children be allowed to inherit equally alongside biological children.[20] Cambacérès followed many of Berlier's suggestions in the project for adoption he presented to the Convention in August of 1793, although his proposals focused more on the goal of leveling the existing social hierarchy than on the charitable ends of adoption.[21]

In spite of the enthusiastic embrace of adoption by the early legislators, the initial revolutionary projects for adoption were never formally promulgated.[22] Even the first drafts of the Civil Code drawn up under Napoleon neglected to include a section on adoption. Although the drafts of the Code submitted by Cambacérès in August 1793 did contain a section on adoption, the revolutionary legislators failed to pass a general law of adoption in 1793 or 1794, anticipating that it would be included in the future Civil Code.[23] Strong pressure from the public in support of adoption pushed the legislators to proceed. Appellate courts in cities such as Paris, Lyon, and Nancy, which had originally been consulted about the proposals for adoption legislation, protested its exclusion from the first drafts of the Code. The historian Marcel Garaud notes that "the Parisian courts were particularly surprised by the exclusion of adoption laws, considering that adoption had been recommended to the legislators by many influential people, and that many citizens, not to mention the republic itself, had already adopted children."[24] Despite the popular support for adoption, in the end it was principally Napoleon's own dynastic concerns and his hopes to adopt a successor that ensured the inclusion of adoption in the Code.[25]

Indeed, the later framers of the Code recoiled from the radical social and political programs articulated by the early revolutionary legislators. Thus, in 1803, Berlier, nominated by Napoleon to present the project of adop-

---

tion doit être instituée." Presented at the convention in the name of the Legislative Committee, 4 June 1793.

[20] In addition, Berlier recommended that the adopted child cut all legal ties with the natal family. See "De l'adoption: Idées offertes à la méditation de ses collègues" (Paris, 1793), chap. 8.

[21] See Garaud and Szramkiewicz, *La Révolution française et la famille*.

[22] The decree of the Legislative Assembly of 18 January 1792 cited at the outset had reestablished adoption in principle, but had failed to organize it in practice.

[23] See Fenet, *Recueil complet*, 1:29–30, 110–11.

[24] "Celui de Paris, notamment, s'en étonnait. Il faisait observer que l'adoption avait été louée et recommandée aux législateurs par un grand nombre de personnes auxquelles on ne pouvait 'contester des lumières et de la sagesse,' que beaucoup de citoyens et la République, elle-même, avaient adopté." Cited in Garaud and Szramkiewicz, *La Révolution française et la famille*, p. 102, taken from the *Conférence des tribunaux d'appel sur le projet de Code Civil* (Paris, Thermidor, year IX [1800]).

[25] See Garaud and Szramkiewicz, *La Révolution française et la famille*, p. 101.

tion to the legislature, spoke more cautiously than he had in the 1790s about introducing a project for adoption:

> In pronouncing the name of an institution, which, until the time of the Revolution, held no place within our civil law, and which, even since that time, has not received any clear formulation, I ask that your attention be directed toward this institution with interest and perhaps even with the hesitation that necessarily accompanies any novelty in legislative matters.[26]

Although the legislators still envisioned a socially useful role for adoption as a consolation to childless households and as a charitable measure for children without families of their own, fears were expressed that easy access to adoption might render extinct the institution of marriage.[27] Even more worrisome to the framers of the Code, was the fear that adoption sanctioned the displacement of legitimate and biological heirs (fears that harken back to the sentiments of our sixteenth- and seventeenth-century jurists). In contrast to the initial revolutionary impulse to encourage adoption in order to redistribute wealth and to erase the distinction between "biological" and "fictive" family ties, the Code ultimately restricted the availability of adoption to childless couples over the age of fifty,[28] to infirm celibates, and, on the other side, to children over the age of twenty-five without families of their own. As the *procès-verbaux* of 1803 concluded, in this way adoption would refrain from causing any undue "mutations within families." Under the consulate, then, adoption's potential to fashion alternative family structures was shunned as postrevolutionary French society recoiled from the initial goal of restructuring the social and familial realms.

THE REVOLUTIONARY ADOPTION LAWS: CONTINUITY AND CHANGE

What were the precedents, both legal and social, for the initial enthusiasm toward adoption displayed by the legislators in the revolutionary era? Histories of the family have underscored the discontinuity between the revo-

---

[26] "En prononçant le nom d'une institution qui, jusqu'à la Révolution, n'avait point figuré parmi les actes de l'état civil des Français, et qui, même depuis cette époque, n'a reçu aucune organisation, je vois votre attention se diriger sur elle avec intérêt et peut-être même cette inquiétude qui environnent tout essai en matière de législation," *Procès-verbaux du conseil d'Etat contenant la discussion du projet de Code civil*, Séance du 21 Ventôse (Paris, 1803), p. 587.

[27] Fenet, *Recueil complet*, p. 591.

[28] Individuals were barred from adopting as "l'exception en faveur des époux est tracée par la nature des choses." *Procès-verbaux du conseil d'État contenant la discussion du project de Code civil* (Paris, 1803), p. 592.

lutionary model of the family and the norms of family life characteristic of the prerevolutionary era. In this light, the revolutionary projects for adoption are generally presented as the resuscitation of an institution lost to western Europe since the end of the Roman era. Indeed, in many respects the revolutionary stance on adoption did represent a dramatic break with the norms of prerevolutionary French society. Whereas revolutionary laws proclaimed equal inheritance for biological and adopted children, early modern customary law had explicitly denied adopted children inheritance rights. Additionally, whereas the revolutionary vision of the social order hailed adoption as a means of collapsing domestic boundaries, sixteenth- and seventeenth-century commentators had emphasized notions of individual family "stock" inherited through the blood. We have seen that for noble families, adopted children were deemed "biological interlopers" who threatened the "purity" of the family lineage. Noble status could not be contracted or bought, claimed members of the Second Estate, but could only be inherited through the blood. Conversely, the revolutionary projects for adoption aimed to dismantle the old social hierarchy. In this new cultural climate, the exchange of children between sets of parents and households was perceived as a way of diversifying and strengthening the social order. Hence, revolutionary texts such as Madame de Brulart's treatise on adoption called on the nobility to transcend concerns about pedigree and to adopt the children of "artisans and merchants."

Although the revolutionary embrace of adoption in many respects stands in dramatic contrast to the norms of family life in the prerevolutionary era, we can also point to certain intellectual, legal, and social trends that preceded and may have worked to shape the revolutionary legal reforms. In terms of legal precedents, the revolutionary rejection of the established customary law was facilitated by the emergence in the eighteenth century of a school of legal thought that deemed the customary laws on inheritance "unenlightened" and repressive.[29] The calls for legal reform by Enlightenment figures such as Rousseau and Voltaire set important precedents for the revolutionary restructuring of the inheritance system, including the rehabilitation of adoption laws.[30] Additionally, the revolutionary vision of adoption as a charitable institution oriented toward the

[29] Many aspects of customary laws on succession, such as the *droit d'aînesse*, had their critics in the sixteenth century as well: Dumoulin commenting on art. 13 of the Custom of Paris deemed it "exorbitant et contraire au droit commun," while Montaigne (*Essais*, 1:26, "De l'institution des enfans") remarked that laws favoring the eldest son "détrompent et relâchent la soudure fraternelle."

[30] For eighteenth-century intellectual antecedents, see Robert Villers, "Les premières lois successorales de la Révolution (1790–1792)," in *La Révolution et l'ordre juridique privé*, 1:335–43. For a discussion of the influence of Locke and Rousseau (particularly concerning a contractual equality within the family), see Giovanni Incorvati, "La 'force de législation' contre la 'force des choses'? Rousseau et le droit civil de la Révolution," in *La Révolution et l'ordre juridique privé*, 1:4–13.

welfare of destitute children had roots in the earlier period. Social reformers in the decades leading up to the Revolution had made repeated calls for the introduction of adoption laws to help solve the growing problem of destitute children cared for by the state.[31] In his *Dictionnaire universel* (1777), Robinet urged the promulgation of adoption laws as a means of placing orphaned and abandoned children with private families. Louis-Sébastien Mercier also viewed adoption as a solution for the plight of the growing numbers of destitute children filling the hospices of late eighteenth-century Paris: "The crowd of indigent grows daily, a law reestablishing adoption would certainly be one of the more useful laws that could be promulgated today in France."[32]

The revolutionary adoption projects also found a ready precedent in the tradition of notarized adoptions that we have traced in sixteenth- and seventeenth-century Paris. It is plausible, in fact, that this earlier model of adoption (with its alternative model of parenting grounded in "adoptive reproduction"), constituted the "popular roots" of the legal projects outlined by the revolutionary reformers. To be sure, the adoptive families we have met in the preceeding chapters would not have employed the same language as the revolutionary architects to explain the adoptions they undertook. For instance, although charity might have played a role, our families were certainly not motivated by the same revolutionary ideals of breaking down the social order. Nevertheless, the alternative model of the family forged through the adoption arrangements foreshadows in interesting ways the image of the domestic realm enshrined by the revolutionary legislators—primarily in its embrace of "fictive" ties of affiliation.

The new evidence of adoption practices in sixteenth- and seventeenth-century Paris opens up a unique window onto contemporary notions of parenthood and childhood among the laboring and artisan sectors of early modern Parisian society. The adoption contracts have brought to light a new model of parenting based on "adoptive reproduction," which existed alongside, and in many respects mirrored, the norm of biological reproduction. By way of conclusion we can propose that this model of parenting and of family life was ultimately accepted by the upper classes of French society, commencing with the wave of judicial reform inspired by the Revolution and culminating in the incorporation of adoption into the nineteenth- and twentieth-century legal codes.

[31] There was also a legal precedent set by the Prussian Code of Frederic II (1751), which was translated into French in 1753, and which contained a section regulating the institution of adoption.

[32] Louis-Sébastien Mercier, *Tableau de Paris* (Paris, 1783), 7: chap. 577.

Transcriptions of Selected
Adoption Contracts

EIGHT notarial contracts—four private adoptions and four adoptions arranged by the Couche—have been transcribed in order to give the reader a better sense of the nature of early modern adoption. I have chosen to transcribe cases that were not outlined in detail in the preceding chapters. In addition, I have retained the sixteenth-century spelling, punctuation (or lack of it), and the abbreviations employed by the notaries, although I have added accents in some instances. Indecipherable portions of the contracts are marked by an ellipsis.

PRIVATE ADOPTIONS

Adoption of Jacqueline Forestier AN, MC, Et. XXIII, 105 (14 April 1603)

"Pardevant les notaires et gardenottes du roy etc. . . . les soubzsignez furent présents en ses personnes Jehan Forestier maitre souvetier à Paris et demeurant rue neufve notre dame paroisse sainct christofe et nicolle ricard sa femme aujourdhuy auctorise par luy pour le suyvant. Lesdictz confessent de leur bonne grez que Jacqueline Forestier leur fille aagée de onze ans ou environ l'avoir . . . mis et délaissée de maintenant jusques à toujours et que lad. Jacqueline sera aage de mariage et quelle ait attainct l'aage de vingt ans . . . a hon. femme Marguerite Choquet femme de seu Geoffroy Dugue vivans maitre fondeur à Paris. Lad. veuve dem. a Paris rue de la barrilloy pss. st. bartholomew a accepté et accepte ladite Jacqueline Forestier comme sa fille adoptive et qu'elle adopte comme sa fille propre et naturelle et à laquelle elle promis et promest et oblige lad. à prendre son estat . . . les nouveau habitz, vestue et linge comme si elle estoit sa propre fille naturelle; et l'instruire en l'amour et craincte de dieu en la religion catholique, aussy tout en santé et malady; et luy fournyr tous quelle en besoin pour l'estat de mariage; et elle promest aussi à Jacqueline Forestier sa fille adoptive tous partie de ses biens tant meubles que immeubles que luy appartienderont.

Adoption of Thiomette de la Salle, AN, MC, Et. III, 476
(5 March 1605)

Marie Sauron femme sepparée de biens comme elle a dict de Jacques Gaugin son mary demeurant aux faulxbourgs St. Germain pres la croix rouge confesse avoir prins et retenu du tout a tousjours de Jehanne Choutiante veufve de seu Claude de la Salle . . . lad. demourant au Cimtière St. Jehan, Thiomette de la Salle fille dud. deffunt de la Salle et de lad. Choutiante et fillioulle de ladite Sauron. Ladite fille aagée de trois mois ou environ, laquelle petite fille lad. Sauron promest nourrir, ailliment, loger et la garder sain et malade et entretenir de tous ses habitz et la faire instruire et apprendre à gaigner sa vie en tous qu'elle aura attainct l'aage de cappacité; aussi elle promest la faire pourvoir pour mariage au mieulx qui luy sera possible (margin: retenu a ses fraiz et despense). Et a ceste huy luy a donné et donne par donnation irrevocable (margin: faicte entre vifs) sans la pouvoir revoquer ny rappelle en quelque sorte et manière que sa soit . . . de ses biens meubles que immeubles en luy comptent et que appartiendra tant pour le présent que pour ladvenir en quelques lieux . . . sitost que la decedz advenu de lad. Sauron. Cestz promesses et don faicts tout et cause que lad. Jehanne Choutiante ne vient mourir ainsy quelle a dict et comme lad. Sauron a aussy recognue pour nourrir alimenter lad. Thiomette de la Salle que en considération de la bonne amitié que lad. Sauron porte a lad. Thiomette de la Salle sa fillioulle et que tel est son plaisir et volonté de faire.

Adoption of Marguerite Denys AN, MC, Et. XC, 1 (1618)

Pardevant les nottaires et gardenottes du roy etc. . . . furent présents en leurs personnes Pierre Chevreu maitre cordonnier dem. en faulxbourgs St. Jacques et Claude Ducloz sa femme de luy auctorisee pour ce qui transpire; lesquelz sont addressés a la personne de Jehanne Faverolle veufve de sue Francois Denys vivant gaigne denier dem. es faulxbourgs St. Marcel estans en l'estude dud. notaire de Croyes . . . à laquelle ils remarquent dict et dèclarent quilz portent une particulier affection a Marguerite Denys fille dud. deffunt Denys et ladite Faverolle et duquoy ilz ont demandé a lad. Faverolle de voulloir bailler et del laisser lad. Marguerite Denys en vivre avec eulx jusques au qu'elle eest attainct l'age d'estre procurer par le mariage ou aultrement . . . jusques duquel temps lesdits Chevereux et sa femme promettent lung pour lautre et pour tous sans division ni distraction de loger nourrir et entretenir lad. Marguerite Denys de tous ses habitz linge chausseurs et de ses nécessitez que luy convien dront . . . tant en santé que malady; mesme la faire instruire en la Relligion catholique apostolique et Roumayne; Ilz ont promis et promettent lung pour lautre luy bailler la somme de [blank] deniers . . . Ladite Faverolle baille et mis es mains lad. Marguerite Denys a présent aagee de six ans ou environ de son voulloir et présentement audit. Chevereux et sa femme qui ont icelle pris et retenu avec eulx de la traicter doulcement et honnestement . . . laquelle Marguerite Denys a promis et promest servir lesdits Chev. et sa femme en toutes choses licites et honnestes.

Adoption of Anne le Tas, AN, MC, Et. XLII, 85 (12 June 1634)

Pardevant les nottaires et gardenottes du roy etc. . . . furent présents en leurs personnes Julien Vivier marchand de chevaulx dem. en faulxbourgs St. Honoré paroisse St. Germain et Charlotte le Tas sa femme de luy suffissament auctorisé pour ce qui ensuyt . . . Lesquelz mariez considérans quilz nont aulcuns denfants et que pour charité et amour confessent que ils ont adopté une fille pour la traiter comme leur fille. Ayans trouvé que Pierre le Tas gaigne denier frère de ladite Charlotte le Tas est décedé et qui ne laisse aulcuns biens pour ladvenir à Magdelaine Papelart à présent sa veufve et à Anne le Tas leur fille de présent aagée de six ans et duquoy lad. veufve estans en la grande nécessité quelle est contraincte de se mettre à cette conduite . . . Lesdictz. Vivier et sa femme qui de la bon gré et volonté ont recognue et confessé avoir adopter et choisy lad. Anne le Tas en leur charge comme leur propre enfant. Et laquelle Papelart sa mere à présent a baillé volontairement lad. Anne le Tas sa fille au ledits Vivier et sa femme qui l'ont prise et retenue comme leur fille adoptive; et promis de instruire ladite Anne le Tas en bonnes moeurs selon la saincte religion catholique appostolique et Romaine; la nourrir comme leur propre fille et la pourvoir par mariage lors quelle ait attainct aage de Raison au mieulx quilz pouroit selon leur condition, mesme en cas que led. Vivier et sa femme nayans aulcuns enfants de leur procurez d'eux deux voullu et intendu que lad. Anne le Tas quilz deux font don a présent . . . de tous et chacun de leurs biens tant meubles que immeubles . . . touttefoys leurs Testaments accomplys et leur dettes payer, et tout ainsy que si estoit leur propre fille à la charge que lad. Anne le Tas scra tenue obeyr audit Vivier et sa femme comme à ses propres père et mère en toutes choses licittes et honnestes. Declarait lad. veufve le Tas quelle ne veulx cy apres retient ny faire distraire lad. Anne le Tas sa fille hors la compaignie des. Vivier et sa femme et ou elle faire le contraire elle sera tenue et promest leur rendre et payer les frais quilz auroient frayé tant a la nourriture et habillementz fourny dicelle Anne le Tas tant en santé que maladie jusques au jour de labsens et du partie d'icelle Anne le Tas . . . les partys ont voulu et consenty car present estoit insinué au Greffe des Insinuations dud. Chastelet et partout ailleurs.

ADOPTIONS FROM THE COUCHE AND THE HOTEL-DIEU

Adoption of Pierre de Bourges-St.-Jacques, AN, MC, Et. XXIII, 158 (11 October 1601)

Pardevant les nottaires et gardenottes du roy etc. . . . furent présents en leurs personnes Noël Hoffeau charretier dem. a pres. de la porte St. Martin, Pss. St Nicholas des Champs et Nicolle Housset sa femme de luy auctorisé pour faire et passer avec luy en tout qui ensuyt. Desquelz de leur bonne et libre vollontez ont recognue et confessé avoir prins en la Couche des pauvres enffans trouvez de ceste ville de Paris, Pierre de Bourges-St-Jacques, l'ung des enffants trouvez (margin: quilz avoient en nourrice depuis trois ans). Et quel enffan led. Hoffeau et sa femme ont volontairement adopté et adoptent a sienne enffan, promis et promettent icelluy nourrir et endoctriner et faire endoctriner en la foy et religion Catholique aposotolique et Romaine et luy faire apprendre mestier pour gaigner sa vye à l'advenir quand icelluy soit a venu en aage de luy delaisse leur d'eux leurs biens meubles comme si estoit leur enffan legitime—auquel enffan absent cy acceptz soubzsignez M. Jacques Dieu, commissaire des haults justiciers ecclesiastiques en ceste ville de Paris—du fait quilz navions aulcunes enffans venans de ce mariage ils font don et cession irrévocable de tous leurs biens meubles.

Adoption of Nicolle de l'Hostel Dieu, AN, MC, Et. XXIII, 161 (1604)

Pardevant les nottaires et gardenottes du roy etc. . . . fut présents en sa personne Jehan Collin barbier et tisserand en etames demourans a Beavaisis estans de present en ceste ville de Paris. Il confesse d'avoir prins à la Couche des pauvres enfans trouvez de ceste ville de Paris Nicolle de l'Hostel Dieu l'un d'iceleux enfans trouvez et que nourrist Charlotte Feullet veufve de Bernard Guillet demourant a Tiremont. Laquelle enfant icelluy Collin ont vollontairement adopté et adopt pour son enfant, promet nourrir, entretenir, instruire, endoctriner et faire endoctriner en la foy et religion Catholique apostolique et Romaine et luy apprendre un mestier pour gaigner sa vie, et luy delaisse apres son dedcez ses biens meubles à quil aura au temps de son dedcez comme si estoit son enfant légitime—et quel enfant absent accept Jacques Dieu commissaire des haultz justiciers ècclésiastiques de ceste ville de Paris—du fait quil n'avoit aulcunes enfans lors de la dissolution de son marriage Jehan fait don et cession et estoit irrevocable en voire faire quil ne veult pas mourrir sans hoirs de son corps a Nicolle de l'Hostel Dieu de tous ses bien meubles comme si estoit sa fille légitime.

Adoption of Martine Dupont AN, MC, Et. XXIII, 162
(17 March 1605)

Pardevant les nottaires et gardenottes du roy furent présents en ses personnes Phillipe Perlot marchand frippier bourgeois dem. rue St. Jacques de la boucherie et Jehanne Trésorier sa femme de luy auctorise pour faire et passer ce qui ensuyt. Desquelz de leur bonne foy et libre vollontez prins a la Cousche des pauvres enffans trouvez en ceste ville de Paris, Martine Dupont l'ung desd. pauvres enffans trouvez. Laquelle Martine Dupont led. Perlot et sa femme adopter et adoptent pour leur enffans d'aveulz quilz nont quant a présent aulcun enffan procurez d'eulx. Et lequel enffant ils ont promis et promettent . . . devant Simon Quai, surgeon, and Bernarde Society, maistresse de la couche des pauvres enffans trouvez . . . de luy fournir son vie de boire et manger, ses allimentez corporelz, luy faire instruire en la relligion catholique apostolique et Romaine, et luy faire apprendre mestier quant elle sera venue en aage, et de la pouvoir par mariage, et silz nont enffans procurez d'eulx en loyal mariage ils luy ont donné et donnent par donation entre vifs tous et chascun de leurs biens meubles que immeubles comme si elle estoit son enffan légitime.

Adoption of Jean Fleury, AN, MC, Et. XXIX, 183 (24 October 1647)

Pardevenat les nottaires gardenottes du roy au Chastelet de Paris soubzsignez fut présent M. Claude Fleury bourgeois et habitans de Souvigny en Bourbonnois, lequel de son bon gré et bonne volonté sans force ny contrainct a confessé avoit pris et retiré de l'hospital des Enfans Trouvez de la ville et faulxbourgs de Paris, Jean [Fleury] l'un desditz enfans trouvés âgé de six ans ou environ et par d'une pure et libre charitté et sans aucune animosité de ses proches et amis que laquelle ledit Fleury aux renonciations accoustumés promet et oblige tout ce que led. Jean . . . à nourrir et entretenir et esleve en sa maison comme son propre enfan; Instruire et faire instruire en la Religion catholique apostolique et Romaine et luy faire apprendre à lire et escrire, et mesme luy faire apprendre un mestier pour gaigne sa vie. Et en cas que ledict Fleury soit surpris de la mort, donne et legue audit Jean [Fleury] la somme de soixante livres à prendre sur tous les biens dont il mourra vestu et saisy ce qui a esté accepté par soeur Mathurine Sican, l'une desdictzes soeurs dud. hostel dieu de charité des enfants trouvés.

Information on the Adoptive Parents and Adoptees

ALTHOUGH this book does not aim to offer a statistical analysis of adoption in sixteenth- and seventeenth-century Paris, some readers may find it useful to consult the numerical distribution of the following key features for the eighty-two adoption contracts penned between 1540 and 1690: marital status of the adoptive parents, sex and status of the adopted children, bonds of kinship, and donations of property.

PRIVATE ADOPTIONS

Out of a total of thirty-seven contracts (1545–1690), seventeen adoptions were undertaken by childless married couples. Twelve of these couples adopted girls (six kin and six non-kin), and four couples adopted boys (one kin and three non-kin). One couple contracted to adopt an unborn child whose sex was unknown.

Nine private adoptions were contracted by unmarried, widowed, and separated women. Eight women adopted girls (two kin and six non-kin), and one adopted a boy (from the same kin group).

Eleven private adoptions were arranged by men whose marital status cannot be determined. Six men adopted girls (one kin and five non-kin), and five adopted boys (two kin and three non-kin).

Of the privately adopted girls, ten were promised a donation of property by seven married couples and three unattached women. Six of these girls were related to their adoptive parents. Five adopted boys were promised donations of property (three by married couples and two by single men). One of these boys was related to his adoptive parents. The unborn child was also granted a donation of property.

ADOPTIONS FROM THE COUCHE AND THE HÔTEL-DIEU

Out of a total of forty-five cases (1540–1677), twenty adoptions were contracted by married couples, nineteen of whom were childless. Thirteen couples adopted girls (five orphans and eight foundlings), and seven adopted boys (three orphans and four foundlings). Seven girls (three orphans and four foundlings) were promised a donation of property; one male foundling was awarded a donation of property.

Fifteen adoptions (all foundlings) were contracted by unmarried, widowed, and separated women. Twelve women adopted girls, five of whom were promised a donation of property. Three women adopted boys, one of whom was promised a donation of property.

Ten adoptions were arranged by men whose marital status cannot be determined. Three men adopted girls (one orphan and two foundlings), and seven men adopted boys (one of whom was an orphan). Three girls (one orphan and two foundlings) and two male foundlings were promised donations of property.

DISTRIBUTIONS FOR THE ENTIRE BODY OF CONTRACTS

Out of the total of eighty-two contracts, thirty-seven adoptions (45%) were arranged by married couples; twenty-four (29%) by unmarried, widowed, and separated women; and twenty-one (26%) by men whose marital status remains unclear.

Overall, fifty-four girls (66%) and twenty-seven boys (33%) were adopted; the sex of one child is unknown. For comparative purposes, Jacqueline Roubert's study, which yielded ninety-three contracts of adoption from 1527 to 1713, reveals that fifty-two girls (56%) and forty-one boys (44%) were adopted.[1]

---

[1] See Jacqueline Roubert, "L'adoption des enfants par des particuliers à Lyon sous l'ancien régime," *Société française d'histoire des hôpitaux* 36–37 (1978): pp. 3–30.

Bibliography

Archival Sources

Archive Guides with Documents

Bordier, H., and L. Brièle. *Les Archives Hospitalières de Paris, enfants-trouvés: Délibérations de l'Hôpital du 17e: Extraits.* Paris, 1877.

Brièle, M. L., ed. *Inventaire sommaire des Archives hospitalières antérieures à 1790.* Vol. 3. Paris, 1869.

Campardon, E., and A. Teutey. *Inventaire des registres des insinuations du Châtelet de Paris, règnes de François Ier et de Henri II.* Paris, 1906.

Archives Nationales (AN), Paris

"Abrégé historique de l'établissement de l'Hôpital des Enfants Trouvés." AN, Series S, 4931a, n.d. [most likely mid-eighteenth century].

Délibérations de Chapitre de Notre-Dame. LL 105–232 (42), L590 (27).

Minutes du Parlement Criminel. X 2B, 60 (17 March 1570).

Minutier Central

  A. Notarial Registers cited for the Couche

    Et. XXXIII. 1539–49. Katherin Fardeau, rue St. Jacques.

    Et. XXIII. 1569–1608. Martin Jacques, rue des Marmousettes, Pss. de la Madeleine (la Cité).

    Et. XXIII. 1569–1608. Raoul Bontemps, rue des Canettes, Pss. Madeleine (la Cité).

    Et. XXIX. 1598–1624. François Chauvin, rue de la Vieille Draperie.

    Et. XXIX. 1637–66. Etienne Corrozet, rue de la Vieille Draperie.

    Et. LXXIII. 1585–1621. Mathieu Bontemps, rue St. André-des-Arts.

    Et. CII. Contains business contracts of the Chapter of Notre-Dame for the seventeenth century, some of which are relevant to the workings of the Couche.

    Et. LXIX (63). Louis Conteillier. Late seventeenth-century adoption contracts from the Hôpital des Enfants Trouvés at St. Denis.

  B. Notarial Registers for St. Esprit and the Grand Bureau des Pauvres

    Et. III, 476, 487. St. Esprit (sixteenth century).

    Et. XIX, 158, 170. Grand Bureau des Pauvres (sixteenth century).

  C. Notarial Registers for Two-Household Adoptions

    Et. XLIX, 90 (28 August 1549).

    Et. XXXIII, 35 (June 1550).

    Et. XXXIII, 35 (October 1550).

    Et. CXXII, 1365 (28 February 1554).

    Et. XXIII, 157 (9 December 1600).

    Et. XXIII, 158 (5 July 1601).

    Et. LXVII, 61 (1603).

Et. XXXIV, 12 (22 February 1603).

Et. XXIII, 105 (14 April 1603).

Et. III, 476 (5 March 1605).

Et. XVIII, 140 (3 December 1605).

Et. XXIII, 112 (6 July 1606).

Et. XVII, 144 (6 July 1606).

Et. XVII, 145 (31 August 1607).

Et. LXXII, 272 (26 October 1609).

Et. XXIX, 163 (7 November 1611).

Et. XIX, 380 (12 July 1613).

Et. XC, 1 (1618).

Et. CV, 343 (27 September 1621).

Et. CV, 529 (3 April 1624).

Et. CV, 345 (1627).

Et. XIII, 5 (15 May 1627).

Et. XXXIX, 59 (15 May 1627).

Et. XXXIX, 60 (28 May 1628).

Et. XXXIX, 59 (29 November 1629).

Et. CV, 381 (7 July 1631).

Et. XXIV, 340 (10 April 1634).

Et. XLII, 85 (12 June 1634).

Et. XXIX, 178 (5 April 1638).

Et. XIX, 424 (23 August 1642).

Et. XIX, 426 (2 May 1643).

Et. XIX, 437 (8 May 1648).

Et. XXIX, 183 (14 July 1646).

Et. LIII, 7 (27 June 1648).

Et. XIX, 439 (27 May 1649).

D. Notarial Registers for Private Foster Care Arrangements

Et. XXXIX, 12 (13 February 1602).

Et. XXIII, 160 (26 December 1608).

Et. II, 71 (21 December 1610).

Et. XXIX, 60 (23 May, 1628).

L553b (n. 29). "Information de Bureau Boucher sur la matière des enfants trouvez et exposez en ceste ville de Paris." (17 July 1501).

L553b (n. 35). "Inventaire de la production que mectent par divers bons nos seigneurs tenant le Parlement du Roy nostre sire en son Parlement à Paris les doyens et chappitre de l'église de Paris deffendeurs d'une part à l'encontre de monsieur le procureur général du Roy demandeur." (1519–36).

Registre des Insinuations, no. 1577 (15 January 1545).

Registres Capitulaires de Notre-Dame. Series LL 105–67; LL 295 (fols. 410–30: Special collection of extracts pertaining to the *pueri reperti*) (fifteenth through early sixteenth centuries).

Registres des enfants trouvez. Series Y 743 (seventeenth through eighteenth centuries).

Series F (enfants assistés, eighteenth and nineteenth centuries).

Series JJ (légitimations, naturalisations, sixteenth and seventeenth centuries).

Series K (légitimations, sixteenth century).

Series U (la Police). N. 11615. *Enfants trouvez* (sixteenth century).

Series Y (insinuations, tutelles, and curatelles). See Henri Stein, ed., *Répertoire numérique des Archives du Châtelet de Paris* (Paris, 1898); F. Olivier-Martin, ed., *Sentences civiles du Châtelet de Paris (1395–1505)* (Paris, 1914).

Titres Généalogiques. M 260. Dossier II. "Allègre (d')."

Archives de l'Assistance Publique (AP), Paris

Délibérations des Administrateurs de l'Hôpital des Enfants Trouvés (1670ff.) In Fonds de l'Hôpital des Enfants Trouvés (liasse 9).

Fonds de l'Hôtel-Dieu. "Titre des enfants nés à l'Hôtel-Dieu et confiés à des particuliers et aux Dames de la Charité des enfants trouvés." Liasse 877. 1656ff–.

Fonds des Enfants Rouges. "Information de Pierre Carrel sur le sort des enfants à l'Hôtel-Dieu." 1531.

Fonds de l'Hôpital général. "Extrait de registre des délibérations du Bureau de l'Hôpital général de Janvier 1761."

Bibliothèque Nationale (BN), Paris

Ms. "Anciens petits Fonds français." Collection Delamare, "Extraits des registres de Parlement," N. 21625, fols. 46ff. (exposition d'enfants, 1489–1776); N. 21802, fols. 368–414 (enfants trouvés et exposés, 1546–1722), fols. 282ff. (Bureau des Pauvres).

Ms. français. Clairambault, 771, fols. 113–23.

Ms. français. Collection Joly de Fleury. N. 1236: *Règlement concernant les enfants trouvés au Bureau de l'administration de l'Hôpital général* (7 January 1761).

Ms. français. N. 11778. St. Esprit. (Copy of a fourteenth-century manuscript.)

Printed Primary Sources

Albieges, Jacques d'. *Le grand coutumier de France.* Paris, 1514. *Arrests de la Cour, questions tant de droict que de coustume, prononcez en robbes rouges.* Paris, 1702.

Auger, Edmond. *Discours du saint sacrement de mariage.* Paris, 1572.

Automne, Bernard. *La conférence du droict français avec le droict romain.* Paris, 1610.

Bacquet, Jean. *Conférence des coustumes de France.* 2 vols. Paris, 1596.

———. *Les oeuvres.* Paris, 1688.

Bechet, C. *L'usance de Saintonge entre Mer et Charente.* Saintes, 1647.

Benedicti, Jean. *La somme des péchez et les remèdes d'iceux.* Lyon, 1545.

———. *La somme des péchez et les remèdes d'iceux.* Lyon, 1593.

Berlier. *De l'adoption: Idées offertes à la méditation de ses collègues.* Paris, 1793.

Beza, Theodore. *Tractatio de repudiis et divortiis.* Geneva, 1573.

Bignon. *Divers plaidoyers touchant la cause des gueux de Vernon.* Paris, 1665.

Bodin, Jean. *De la démonomanie des sorciers.* Reprint, Paris, 1979.

———. *Les six livres de la république.* Paris, 1583.

Boguet, Henri. *An Examen of Witches* (1603). Translated by E. A. Ashwin. New York, 1929.

Bordier, H., and L. Brièle. *Les Archives Hospitalières de Paris, enfants-trouvés: Délibérations de l'Hôpital de 17e: Extraits.* Paris, 1877.

Bouchel, Laurent. *La bibiliothèque ou trésor du droit français.* Paris, 1629.

———. *Decretorum ecclesiae gallicanae.* 8 vols. Paris, 1621.

Bourdot de Richebourg, Charles Antoine. *Nouveau coutumier général.* 4 vols. Paris, 1724.

Bourgeois, Louise. *Observations diverses sur la stérilité, perte de fruict, foecondité, accouchements et maladies des femmes, & enfants nouveaux naiz.* 1609. Edited by Françoise Olivier. Reprint, Paris, 1992.

Bouteillier, Jean. *La somme rurale ou le grand coustumier général de pratique civil et canon.* Paris, 1603.

Brillon, P. J. *Dictionnaire des arrests ou jurisprudence universelle des parlements de France.* 2 vols. Paris, 1711.

Brodeau, Julien. *Commentaire sur la coustume de la prévosté et vicomté de Paris.* Paris, 1658.

Bugnyon, Philibert. *Les loix abrogées . . . en toutes les cours du royaume de France.* Lyon, 1572.

Choppin, René. *Oeuvres complètes.* Paris, 1662.

Code du Roy Henri III, observations et annotations par L. Carondas le Caron. Paris, 1615.

Colas de Portmorant, Alex. *La famille chrestienne.* Paris, 1644.

Coquille, Guy. *Conférence des coustumes de France.* Paris, 1642.

———. *Les coustumes du pays et duché de Nivernois.* Paris, 1605.

Coras, Jean de. *Paraphrase sur l'édict des mariages clandestinement contractez par les enfans de famille, contre le gré et consentement de leur père et mère.* Paris, 1572.

———. *Résolution de droict, contenans cent questions de matières bénéficiales, civiles & criminelles.* Paris, 1610.

Cothereau, Philippes. *La théorique et pratique des notaires.* Paris, 1632.

Coyecque, Ernst, ed. *Recueil d'actes notariés relatifs à l'histoire de Paris au XVIe siècle.* 2 vols. Paris, 1905.

Des Maisons, M. F. *Nouveau recueil d'arrests et règlemens du Parlement de Paris.* Paris, 1667.

Des Roys, Pierre. *Traité des substitutions.* Lyon, 1644.

Dictionnaire de l'Académie françoise. Vol. 1, Paris, 1694.

Discours sur l'éducation de M. le Dauphin et sur l'adoption, par Mme. de Brulart, ci-devant Mme. de Sillery gouvernante des enfans de la maison d'Orléans. Paris, 1790.

"Documents inédits pour servir à l'histoire des usages et des moeurs aux XIVe et XV siècles." *Annuaire-bulletin de la société de l'histoire de France* 2 (1864): 80–115.

Du Fresne, Charles. *Glossarium an scriptores mediae et infirmae graectatis.* Lyons, 1688.

Du Fresne, Jean. *Journal des principales audiences du Parlement.* 2 vols. Paris, 1733.

Dumoulin, Charles. *Commentarii in parisienses totius Galiae supremi parlamenti consuetudines.* Paris, 1613.

———. *Commentarii in consuetudines parisienses.* Paris, 1576.

———. *Opera Omnia.* 4 vols. Paris, 1657.

———. *La coutume de Paris, conférée avec les autres coutumes de France.* Paris, 1666.

Espeisses, Antoine d'. *Les oeuvres.* Lyon, 1666.

Estienne, Robert. *Dictionnaire francoislatin, autrement dict les mots francois.* Paris, 1549.

Estienne Pasquier, lettres familières. Paris, 1974.

Félibien. *Histoire de la ville de Paris.* Paris, 1725.

Fenet, P. A. *Recueil complet des travaux préparatoires du Code civil.* 15 vols. 1827. Reprint, Osnabrück, 1968.

Ferrière, Claude de. *Corps et compilation de tous les commentaires anciens et modernes sur la coutume de Paris.* Paris, 1685.

———. *Dictionnaire de droit et pratique. . . .* 3d ed. Paris, 1749.

———. *Nouvelle traduction des Institutes de l'Empereur Justinien.* Vol. 1. Paris, 1770.

———. *La science parfaite des notaires.* Lyon, 1695.

Fortin, M. G. *La coustume de Paris conférée avec les autres coustumes de France.* Paris, 1666.

Fournel. *Traité de la séduction considérée dans l'ordre judiciare.* Paris, 1781.

Furetière, Antoine. *Dictionnaire universel.* 2 vols. Rotterdam, 1690. Reprint, Paris, 1978.

Glanville, Ranulf de. *De legibus et consuetudinibus regni Angliae.* Edited by George E. Woodbing. New Haven, 1932.

Grenier. *Traité des donations, des testamens et de toutes autres dispositions gratuites, suivant les principes du Code Napoléon.* Clermont-Ferrand, 1812.

Guessière, François Jamet de la. *Journal des principales audiences du Parlement, (1657–1666).* Vol. 2. Paris, 1678.

Guyot, M. *Répertoire universel et raisonné de jurisprudence civile, criminelle, canonique et bénéficiale.* Paris, 1784.

Helo, M. F. *La jurisprudence françoise conférée avec le droit romain, sur les Institutes de l'Empereur Justinien.* 2 vols. Paris, 1663.

Hotman, François. *Antitribonian ou discours d'un grand et renommé jurisconsulte de nostre temps sur l'estude des loix.* Paris, 1603. Reprinted in the series *Images et témoins de l'âge classique,* vol. 9. Paris, 1980.

Imbert, Jean. *Enchiridion ou recueil de droit écrit.* Paris, 1611.

Issali. *Les plaidoyez et harangues de M. le Maistre.* Paris, 1657.

Jacquet. *Abrégé du commentaire général de toutes les coustumes et des autres lois municipales en usage dans les différentes provinces du roiaume.* Paris, 1764.

Justinian's Institutes. Translated by Peter Birks and Grant McLeod. London, 1987.

Le Brun, Denis. *Traité des successions divisé en quatre livres.* 2 vol. Paris, 1776.

Le Caron, Louis. *Nouveau commentaire de L. Charondas le Caron . . . sur la coustume de la ville, prévosté, & vicomté de Paris.* Paris, 1613.

———. *Pandectes ou digestes du droit français.* Lyon, 1696.

———. *Responses et décisions du droict françois.* Paris, 1586.

Lescut, Nicolle de. *Commentaire des Institutes de Justinien.* Paris, 1543.

Li livres de jostice et de plet. Reprint, Paris, 1850.

Lobineau. *Histoire de Bretagne.* 2 vols. Paris, 1707. Reprint, Paris, 1973.

Lordelot, Benigne. *Plaidoyé contre un enfant supposé et déclaré un imposteur.* Paris, 1686.

Louet, Georges. *Recueil d'aucuns notables arrests donnez en la cour de Parlement de Paris.* Paris, 1633.

Loysel, Antoine. *Institutes coutumières.* Paris, 1846.

Marcilly, M. *Coutumes générales du bailliage de Troyes en Champagne.* Paris, 1768.

Marion, Simon. *Les plaidoyers de M. Simon Marion.* Paris, 1609.

Masuer. *La pratique judiciare.* Paris, 1606.

Mercier, Louis-Sébastien. *Tableau de Paris.* 12 vols. Paris, 1783.

Montaingne, Michel de. *Essais.* 3 vols. Paris, 1979.

———. *La police des pauvres à Paris.* In *Bulletin de la Société de l'histoire de Paris* (1888): 105.

Les notes de Maistre Chas. du Moulin sur les coutumes de France mises par matières. Paris, 1715.

Nouveau dictionnaire civil et canonique de droit et pratique. Par M. ***, avocat au Parlement. Paris, 1697.

Ordonnances des rois de France de la troisième race, recueillis par ordre chronologique. 21 vols. Paris, 1723–1849.

Ordonnances des rois de France: Règne de François Ier. 9 vols. Paris, 1902–89.

Les oeuvres de M. Claude Henrys. 2 vols. Paris, 1708.

Les oeuvres de M. François Grimaudet, Paris, 1664.

Les oeuvres de M. Simon d'Olive. Lyon, 1640.

Papon, Etienne. *Commentaire sur la loy si unquam C. de revocand. donat.* Lyon, 1616.

Papon, Jean. *Recueil d'arrests notables des cours souveraines de France.* Cologny, 1616.

———. *Les trois notaires.* 2 vols. Lyon, 1575.

Paré, Amboise. *Oeuvres complètes.* 2 vols. Paris, 1840.

Pasquier, Etienne. *L'interprétation des Institutes de Justinien.* Reprint, Paris, 1847.

———. *Des recherches de la France.* Paris, 1581.

Piis, C. *La nourrice républicaine ou les plaisirs de l'adoption: Comédie en un acte mêlée de Vaudevilles.* Paris, Year II [1793].

Plaidoyez de M. Jean Guy Basset. Grenoble, 1668.

Pommiers, Auroux de. *Coutumes générales et locales du pais duché de Bourbonnois.* Paris, 1732.

Pontas, Jean. *Dictionnaire de cas de conscience ou décisions des plus considérables et difficultes touchant la morale & la discipline ecclésiastique.* Paris, 1741.

Potier, Jacques. *Les coustumes du pays et duché de Bourbonnois.* Paris, 1754.

Prat, Pardoux de. *Théorique de l'art des notaires pour cognoistre la nature de tous les points de droit qui concernent l'estat, et office de notariat: nouvellement traduite de latin en francoys et succinctement adaptée aux ordonnances royaux.* Lyon, 1572.

Procès-verbaux du conseil d'Etat contenant la discussion du project de Code civil. Paris, 1803.

Prost de Royer. *Dictionnaire de jurisprudence et des arrêts.* Vol. 3, Lyon, 1783.

Recueil des plaidoyez et arrests notables. Paris, 1644.

"Réponse à l'opinion du représentant du peuple B. Laujacq dans l'affaire de la mineure Lepeletier." Paris, n.d.

Richard, Jean-Marie. *Traité des donations entre-vifs et testamentaires.* 2 vols. Paris, 1685.

Saint-Pierre, Bernardin de. *Voeux d'un solitaire.* Paris, 1789.

Serres, Claude. *Les institutions du droit françois suivant l'ordre de celles de Justinien.* Paris, 1753.

Servin, Loys. *Arrests notables et plaidoyez de M. Loys Servin.* Rouen, 1629.

Soëfe, Lucien. *Nouveau recueil de plusieurs questions notables . . . jugées par arrests d'audience de Parlement de Paris depuis 1640.* 2 vols. Paris, 1682.

Thaumassière, Gaspard Thaumas de. *Décisions sur les coustumes de Berry.* Bourges, 1667.

Tiraqueau, André. *De nobilitate et iure primogeniorum.* Paris, 1549.

———. *Opera Omnia du Andreae Tiraquelli.* 7 vols. Frankfurt-am-Main, 1597.

———. *Tractatus cessante causa cessat effectus, Le mort saisit le vif . . .* Lyon, 1559.

Tronçon, Jean. *Le droict françois et coustume de la prévosté et vicomté de Paris ou il est fait rapport du droict romain.* Paris, 1643.

Vigier, Jean. *Les coutumes du pais et duché d'Angoumois.* Angoulême, 1720.

Ville, M. J. C. de la. *Causes célèbres et intéressantes avec les jugemens qui les ont décidées.* Vol. 1. Paris, 1769.

Secondary Sources

Amyard, M. "Friends and Neighbors." In Roger Chartier, ed., *A History of Private Life,* vol. 3, *Passions of the Renaissance,* translated by Arthur Goldhammer, pp. 477–92. Cambridge, Mass., 1989.

Anderson, Michael. *Approaches to the History of the Western Family, 1500–1914.* London, 1980.

Annales de démographie historique. 1973. Special issue, "Enfant et sociétés."

Annales de démographie historique. 1983. Special issue, "Mères et nourrissons."

Annales de démographie historique. 1993. Special issue, "La mortalité dans le passé."

Ariès, Philippe. *Centuries of Childhood: A Social History of Family Life.* Translated by Robert Baldick. New York, 1962.

Ariès, Philippe, and Georges Duby, eds. *Histoire de la vie privée.* Vol. 2, *De l'Europe féodale à la Renaissance.* Paris, 1985.

———. *A History of Private Life.* 5 vols. Cambridge, Mass., 1987–91.

Aubenas, René. "L'adoption en Provence au moyen-âge (XIVe–XVIe siècles)." *Revue historique de droit français et étranger* 13 (1934): 700–726.

———. *Etude sur le notariat provençal au moyen-âge.* Aix, 1931.

Babelon, Jean-Pierre. *Nouvelle histoire de Paris. Paris au XVIe siècle.* Paris, 1986.

Barbarin, Renée. *La condition juridique du bâtard d'après la jurisprudence du Parlement de Paris du Concile de Trente à la Révolution française.* Mayenne, 1960.

Bartholet, Elizabeth. *Family Bonds: Adoption and the Politics of Parenting.* New York, 1993.

Basdevant, Jules. *Des rapports de l'église et de l'état dans la législation de mariage du Concile de Trente au Code civil.* Paris, 1900.

Bates, J. Douglas. *Gift Children: A Story of Race, Family, and Adoption in a Divided America.* New York, 1993.

Bavoux, Paule. *Les orphelins et les enfants trouvés à Paris à la fin du moyen-âge.* Mémoire maîtrise lettres, 1967.

Bayard, Françoise. "Naturalization in Lyon during the Ancien Régime." *French History* 4 (1990): 277–316.

Beaune, Henri. *Introduction à l'étude historique du droit coutumier français jusqu'à la rédaction officielle des coutumes.* Lyon, 1880.

Beckerman Davis, Barbara. "Poverty and Poor Relief in Toulouse, 1474–1560: The Response of a Conservative Society." Ph.D. diss., University of California, Berkeley, 1986.

Bell, Clair Haydn. "The Call of the Blood in Medieval German Epic." *Modern Language Notes* 37, no. 1 (1922): 17–26.

Bellivier, Florence. "Des droits pour les bâtards, l'enfant natural dans les débats révolutionnaires." In Irène Théry and Christian Biet, eds., *La famille, la loi, l'état de la Révolution au Code civil,* pp. 122–44. Paris, 1989.

Benedict, Phillip, ed. *Cities and Social Change in Early Modern France.* New York, 1989.

Benet, Mary. *The Politics of Adoption.* Boston, 1976.

Berriot-Salvadore, Evelyne. *Les femmes dans la société française de la Renaissance.* Geneva, 1990.

Berthelé, Joseph. "La vie intérieure d'un hospice du XIVe au XVIe siècle: L'hôpital du Saint-Esprit-en-Grève à Paris." *Revue de l'hôpital et l'aide sociale à Paris* 7 (1961): 81–93; 8 (1961): 225–35; 9 (1961): 375–83; 10 (1961): 537–41; 11 (1961): 687–703; 14 (1962): 221–29.

Berthet, Abbé. "Un réactif social: Le parrainage du XVIe siècle à la Révolution." *Annales: E.S.C.* 1 (1946): 43–50.

Bollenot, Gilles. "L'adoption au XIXe siècle: La Fortune de Gaspard de la comtesse de Ségur." *Revue historique* 271 (1984): 311–37.

Bordier, H. L., and Charles, Read. "Poursuites et condamnations à Paris pour hérésie de 1564 à 1572 d'après les Registres d'Ecrou de la Conciergerie du Palais." *Bulletin de la Société de l'histoire du Protestantisme français* 50 (1901): 573–641.

Bossy, John. *Christianity in the West, 1400–1700.* Oxford, 1985.

Boswell, John. "*Expositio* and *Oblatio*: The Abandonment of Children and the Ancient and Medieval Family." *American Historical Review* 89, no. 1 (1984): 10–33.

———. *The Kindness of Strangers: The Abandonment of Children in Western Europe from Late Antiquity to the Renaissance.* New York, 1988.

Bourdieu, Pierre. *Outline of a Theory of Practice.* Translated by Richard Nice. New York, 1977.

Boussault, Fernand. *L'assistance aux enfants abandonnés à Paris du XVIe au XVIIIe siècle.* Paris, 1937.

Brady, Ivan, ed. *Transactions in Kinship: Adoption and Fosterage in Oceania.* Honolulu, 1976.

Brindesi, Fausto. *La famiglia attica: Il matrimonio e l'adozione.* Florence, 1961.

Brissaud, Jean. *A History of French Private Law.* Translated by Rapelje Howell. Boston, 1912.

Burguière, André, ed. *Histoire de la famille* 2 vols. Paris, 1986.

Carroll, Vern, ed. *Adoption in Eastern Oceania.* Honolulu, 1970.

Casey, James. *The History of the Family.* Oxford, 1989.

Cavadini, John C. *The Last Christology of the West: Adoptionism in Spain and Gaul, 785–820.* Philadelphia, 1993.

Charpentier, Jehanne. *Le droit de l'enfance abandonné: Son évolution sous l'influence de la psychologie (1552–1791).* Paris, 1967.

Coleman, Emily R. "L'infanticide dans le haut moyen-âge." *Annales: E.S.C.* 29 (1974): 315–36.

Commaille, J. "Ordre familial, ordre social, ordre légal: Éléments d'une sociologie politique de la famille." *L'année sociologique* 37 (1987): 265–90.

Corbier, Mireille. "Constructing Kinship in Rome: Marriage and Divorce, Filiation and Adoption." In D. I. Kertzer and R. P. Saller, eds., *The Family in Italy from Antiquity to the Present*, 127–46. New Haven, 1991.

———. "Divorce and Adoption as Roman Familial Strategies." In Beryl Rawson, ed., *Marriage, Divorce, and Children in Ancient Rome*, 47–78. Oxford, 1991.

Courtemanche, Andrée. "Lutter contre la solitude: Adoption et affiliation à Manosque au XVe siècle." *Médiévales* 19 (fall 1990): 37–42.

Darmon, Pierre. *Le mythe de la procréation à l'âge baroque.* Paris, 1976.

Darrow, Margaret. *Revolution in the House: Family, Class and Inheritance in Southern France, 1775–1825.* Princeton, N.J., 1989.

———. *Structures et relations sociales à Paris au XVIIIe siècle.* Paris, 1961.

Davis, Natalie Z. "Ghosts, Kin and Progeny: Some Features of Family Life in Early Modern France." *Daedalus* 106, no. 2 (1977): 87–114.

———. *The Return of Martin Guerre.* Cambridge, Mass., 1983.

———. *Society and Culture in Early Modern France.* Stanford, Calif., 1975.

Delasselle, Claude. "Les enfants abandonnés à Paris au XVIIIe siècle." *Annales: E.S.C.* 30 (1975): 187–218.

Delumeau, Jean. *Rassurer et protéger: Le sentiment de sécurité dans l'Occident d'autrefois.* Paris, 1989.

Delumeau, Jean, and Daniel Roche. *Histoire des pères et da la paternité.* Paris, 1990.

Demars-Sion, Véronique. "Illégitimité et abandon des enfants: La position des provinces du Nord, 16e–18e siècles." *Revue du Nord* 65 (1983): 481–506.

Demos, John. *A Little Commonwealth: Family Life in Plymouth Colony.* New York, 1970.

Descimon, Robert. "Paris on the Eve of Saint Bartholomew: Taxation, Privilege, and Social Geography." In Phillip Benedict, ed., *Cities and Social Change in Early Modern France*, pp. 69–104. New York, 1989.

Desnoyers, M. J. "Les dépenses faites par la ville de Lille pour les enfants trouvés au XVe et au XVIe siècle." *Bulletin du comité de la langue, de l'histoire, et des arts de la France* 3 (1855–56): 444–80.

Devyer, André. *Le sang épuré: Les préjugés de race chez les gentilhommes français de l'ancien régime (1560–1720)*. Brussels, 1973.

Diefendorf, Barbara B. *Beneath the Cross: Catholics and Hugenots in Sixteenth-Century Paris*. Oxford, 1991.

———. *Paris City Councillors in the Sixteenth Century: The Politics of Patrimony*. Princeton, N.J., 1983.

———. "Widowhood and Remarriage in Sixteenth-Century Paris." *Journal of Family History* 7 (winter 1982): 379–95.

———. "Women and Property in Old Regime France: Theory and Practice in Dauphiné and Paris." In John Brewer and Susan Staves, eds., *Early Modern Conceptions of Property*, pp. 170–93. New York, 1995.

Dixon, Suzanne. *The Roman Family*. Baltimore, 1992.

Duby, Georges. *Medieval Marriage: Two Models from Twelfth-Century France*. Translated by Elborg Forster. Baltimore, 1978.

———. ed. *Histoire de la France urbaine*. 5 vols. Paris, 1980–85.

Dunn, Charles. *The Foundling and the Werewolf: A Literary-Historical Study of Guillaume de Palerne*. University of Toronto Studies and Texts, 8. Toronto, 1960.

Dupâquier, Jacques. *Histoire de la population française*. Vol. 1, *Des origines à la Renaissance*. Paris, 1988.

Duples-Agier, Henri. *Registres criminel du Châtelet de Paris du 6 sept. 1389 au 18 mai 1392*. 2 vols. Paris, 1861–64.

Dupoux, Albert. *Sur les pas de Monsieur Vincent: Trois cents ans d'histoire parisienne de l'enfance abandonnée*. Paris, 1958.

Eckhardt, K. A. *Studia Merovingica*. Bibliotheca Rerum Historicarum, 11. Aalen, 1975.

Engelmann, Jean. *Les testaments coutumiers au XV siècle*. Reprint, Geneva, 1975.

Estrin, Barbara L. *The Raven and the Lark: Lost Children in Literature of the English Renaissance*. London, 1985.

Fairchilds, Cissie. *Domestic Enemies: Servants and Their Masters in Old Regime France*. Baltimore, 1984.

Falletti, Louis. *Le retrait lignager en droit coutumier français*. Paris, 1923.

La famille, la loi, l'état de la Révolution au Code civil. Paris, 1989.

Familles et sociétés domestiques. Recherches économiques et sociales n.s., 2. Paris, 1982.

Farge, Arlette. *Fragile Lives: Violence, Power and Solidarity in Eighteenth-Century Paris*. Translated by Carol Shelton. Cambridge, Mass., 1993.

Farr, James R. *Hands of Honor: Artisans and the World in Dijon, 1550–1650*. Ithaca, N.Y., 1988.

Fildes, Valerie. *Wet-nursing: A History from Antiquity to the Present*. Oxford, 1988.

Filhol, René. *Le premier Président Christofle de Thou et la réformation des coutumes*. Paris, 1937.

Flandrin, Jean-Louis. "L'attitude à l'égard du petit enfant et les conduites sexuelles dans la civilisation occidentale." *Annales de démographie historique* (1973): 152–53.

———. *Families in Former Times: Kinship, Household and Sexuality.* Translated by Richard Southern. Cambridge, 1979.

Flinn, Michaël. *The European Demographic System.* Brighton, 1981.

Folktales of France. Edited by Geneviève Massignon. Translated by Jacqueline Hyland. Chicago, 1968.

Fortunet, Françoise. "Le rétablissement du principe de l'adoption: Une entrée par effraction?" In Iréne Théry and Christian Biet, eds., *La famille, la loi et l'état de la Révolution au Code civil*, pp. 196–203. Paris, 1989.

Fosseyeux, Marcel. "L'assistance parisienne au milieu du XVIe siècle." *Mémoires de la société d'histoire de Paris de l'Ile de France* 43 (1916): 83–128.

———. *L'Hôtel-Dieu de Paris au XVIIe et au XVIIIe siècle.* Paris, 1912.

———. "Les maisons d'apprentissage à Paris au XVIIe et XVIIIe siècles." *Bulletin de la société historique de Paris* 40 (1913): 36–56.

Foucault, Michel. *Madness and Civilization: A History of Insanity in the Age of Reason.* Translated by Richard Howard. New York, 1965.

Franklin, Albert. *Dictionnaire historique des arts, métiers, et professions exercés dans Paris depuis le treizième siècle.* Paris, 1906.

French Folktales from the Collection of Henri Pourrat. Translated by Royall Tyler. New York, 1989.

Friedmann, Abbé. *Paris, ses rues, ses paroisses du Moyen-Age à la Révolution: Origine et évolution des circonscriptions paroissiales.* Paris, 1959.

Fuchs, Rachel G. *Abandoned Children: Foundlings and Child Welfare in Nineteenth-Century France.* Albany, N.Y., 1984.

———. *Poor and Pregnant in Paris: Strategies for Survival in the Nineteenth Century.* New Brunswick, N.J., 1992.

Fukita, Sonoko. "L'abandon des enfants légitimes à Rennes à la fin du XVIIIe siècle." *Annales de démographie historique* (1983): 151–62.

Garaud, Marcel and Romauld Szramkiewicz. *La Révolution française et la famille.* Paris, 1978.

Garrioch, David. *Neighbourhood and Community in Paris, 1740–1790.* Cambridge, 1986.

Gaston, Jean. *La communauté des notaires de Bordeaux (1520–1791).* Toulouse, 1990.

Gaudemet, Jean. *Le droit privé romain.* Paris, 1974.

———. "Législation canonique et attitudes séculaires à l'égard du lien matrimonial au XVIIe siècle." *XVIIe siècle*, nos. 102–3(1974): 15–30.

Gavitt, Phillip. *Charity and Children in Renaissance Florence: The Ospedale degli Innocenti, 1436–1536.* Ann Arbor, Mich.,1990.

Gélis, Jacques. *History of Childbirth: Fertility, Pregnancy and Birth in Early Modern Europe.* Translated by Rosemary Morris. Boston, 1991.

Génestal, Robert. *Histoire de la légitimation des enfants naturels en droit canonique.* Paris, 1905.

———. *La tenure en bourgage: Étude sur la propriété foncière dans les villes normandes.* Paris, 1900.

Geremek, Bronislaw. *The Margins of Society in Late Medieval Paris.* Translated by Jean Birrell. Cambridge, 1987.

Gibson, Wendy. *Women in Seventeenth-Century France.* Basingstoke, 1989.

Giesey, Ralph E. "Models of Rulership in French Royal Ceremonial." In Sean Wilentz, ed., *Rites of Power: Symbolism, Ritual and Politics since the Middle Ages,* 41–64. Philadelphia, 1985.

———. "Rules of Inheritance and Strategies of Mobility in Pre-Revolutionary France" *American Historical Review* 82 (1977): 271–89.

Le Gnommon: Revue internationale d'histoire du notariat. Special issue, "Archives Notariales et Minutier Central Parisien," *Bulletin de Liaison* 18 (1980).

Gonnet, Paul. *L'adoption lyonnaise des orphelins légitimes (1536–1793).* 2 Vols. Paris, 1935.

Goody, Esther N. *Contexts of Kinship: An Essay in the Family Sociology of the Gonja of Northern Ghana.* Cambridge, 1973.

Goody, Jack. "Adoption in Cross-cultural Perspective." *Comparative Studies in History and Society* 11 (1969): 550–78.

———. *The Development of the Family and Marriage in Europe.* Cambridge, 1983.

Goody, Jack. *The Oriental, the Ancient and the Primitive.* Cambridge, 1990.

———. *Production and Reproduction: A Comparative Study of the Domestic Domain.* Cambridge, 1976.

Goody, Jack, Joan Thirsk, and E. P. Thompson, eds. *Family and Inheritance: Rural Society in Western Europe, 1200–1800.* Cambridge, 1976.

Gottlieb, Beatrice. "The Meaning of Clandestine Marriage." In Robert Wheaton and Tamera K. Hareven, eds., *Family and Sexuality in French History,* pp. 49–83. Philadelphia, 1980.

Greenhouse, C. J. "Courting Difference: Issues of Interpretation and Comparison in the Study of Legal Ideologies." *Law and Society* 22, no. 4 (1988): 687–707.

Gutton, Jean-Pierre. *Histoire de l'adoption en France.* Paris, 1993.

Haimes, Erica, and Noel Timms. *Adoption, Identity and Social Policy: The Search for Distant Relatives.* Brookfield, Vt., 1985.

Hanley, Sarah. "Engendering the State: Family Formation and State Building in Early Modern France." *French Historical Studies* 16, no. 1 (1989): 4–27.

———. *The Lit de Justice of the Kings of France.* Princeton, N.J., 1983.

Hanlon, Gregory, and Elsbeth Carruthers. "Wills, Inheritance and the Moral Order in 17th-Century Agenais." *Journal of Family History* 15, no. 2 (1990): 149–61.

Hardwick, Julie. "Widowhood and Patriarchy in Seventeenth-Century France." *Journal of Social History* 26 (fall 1992): 133–48.

Hareven, Tamara K. "The History of the Family and the Complexity of Social Change." *American Historical Review* 96, no. 1 (1991): 94–124.

Herlihy, David. "Family." *American Historical Review* 96, no. 1 (1991): 1–16.

———. *Medieval Households.* Cambridge, Mass., 1985.

Herrup, Cynthia B. *The Common Peace: Participation and the Criminal Law in Seventeenth-Century England.* Cambridge, 1987.

Hillaire, Jean. "Coutumes rédigées et gens du champs (Angoumois, Aunis, Saintonge)," *Revue historique de droit français et étranger* 4 (1987): 545–73.

Histoire, économie et société. 1987. Special issue, "L'enfant abandonné."

Hoksbergen, R.A.C., ed. *Adoption in Worldwide Perspective: A Review of Programs, Policies and Legislation in Fourteen Countries.* Berwyn, Ill., 1986.

Holmès, Catherine. *L'éloquence judiciare de 1620 à 1660, reflet des problèmes sociaux, religieux, et politiques de l'époque.* Paris, 1967.

Howell, Cicely. *Land, Family and Inheritance in Transition: Kinsworth Harcourt, 1280–1700.* Cambridge, 1983.

Hufton, Olwen. "Women, Work, and Family." In Arlette Farge and Natalie Z. Davis, eds., *A History of Women: Renaissance and Enlightenment Paradoxes,* pp. 15–45. Cambridge, Mass., 1994.

Hunecke, Volker. *Die Findelkinder von Mailand: Kindaussetzung und aussetzende Eltern vom 17. bis zum 19. Jahrhundert.* Stuttgart, 1987.

Hunt, David. *Parents and Children in History: The Psychology of Family Life in Early Modern France.* New York, 1970.

Hunt, Lynn. *The Family Romance of the French Revolution.* Berkeley, Calif., 1992.

Isambert, François-André. *Recueil général des anciennes lois depuis l'an 420 jusqu'à la Révolution de 1789.* 29 vols. Paris, 1821–33.

Jeay, Madeleine, ed. *Les évangiles des quenouilles.* Montreal, 1985.

Jeorger, Muriel. "Enfant-trouvé-enfant-objet." *Histoire, économie et société* 3 (1987): 373–86.

Johansson, S. Ryan. "Centuries of Childhood/Centuries of Parenting: Phillipe Ariès and the Modernization of Privileged Infancy." *Journal of Family History* 12, no. 4 (1987): 343–65.

Jouanna, Arlette. *L'idée de race en France au XVIe et au début du XVIIe siècles.* Montpellier, 1981.

Kelley, Donald R. *Foundations of Historical Scholarship: Language, Law and History in the French Renaissance.* New York, 1970.

Kent, Francis William. *Household and Lineage in Renaissance Florence.* Princeton, N.J., 1977.

Kertzer, D. I., and R. P. Saller, eds. *The Family in Italy from Antiquity to the Present.* New Haven, Conn., 1991.

Kettering, Sharon. "Friendship and Clientage in Early Modern France." *French History* 6, no. 2 (1992).

———. *Patrons, Brokers and Clients in Seventeenth-century France.* Oxford, 1986.

Klapisch-Zuber, Christiane. *Le maison et le nom: Stratégies et rituels dans l'Italie de la Renaissance.* Paris, 1990.

———. "Parents de sang, parents de lait: La mise en nourrice à Florence (1300–1530)." *Annales de démographie historique,* special issue, "Mères et nourrissons" (1983): 33–64.

———. "Parrains et Filleuls. Une approche comparée de la France, l'Angleterre, et l'Italie médiévales." *Medieval Prosopography* 6, no. 2 (1985): 51–77.

Klimrath, Henri. *Travaux sur l'histoire de droit français.* Paris, 1843.

Knibiehler, Yvonne. *Histoire des mères, du moyen-age à nos jours.* Montalba, 1980.

———. *Les pères aussi ont une histoire.* Paris, 1987.

Kurylowicz, Marek. *Die adoptio im klassichen romischen recht.* Studia Antiqua. Warsaw, 1981.

Labrousse-Riou, Catherine. *Droit de la famille: Les personnes.* Paris, 1984.

Lacey, W. K. "Patria Potestas." In Beryl Rawson, ed., *Marriage, Divorce, and Children in Ancient Rome,* pp. 121–44. Oxford, 1991.

Lallemand, Léon. *Un chapitre de l'histoire des enfants trouvés: La maison de la Couche à Paris (XVIIe–XVIIIe).* Paris, 1885.

———. *Histoire des enfants abandonnés et délaissés.* Paris, 1885.

Lapanouse, Jacques de. *Essai historique sur la protection des enfants orphelins au Moyen-age dans les pays coutumiers.* Paris, 1901.

LaPlaige, Danielle. *Sans famille à Paris: Orphelins et enfants abandonnés dans la Seine au XIXe siècle.* Paris, 1989.

Laslett, Peter. "Family, Kinship and Collectivity as Systems of Support in Pre-Industrial Europe: A Consideration of the 'Nuclear-Hardship' Hypothesis." *Continuity and Change* 3 (1988): 153–75.

———. *The World We Have Lost.* London, 1971.

Laws of the Salian and Ripuarian Franks. Translated by Theodore John Rivers. New York, 1986.

Lefebvre-Teillard, A. "L'enfant naturel dans l'ancien droit français." *Recueils de la société Jean Bodin.* Vol. 36, no. 2, (Brussels, 1976): 251–69.

Le Goff, Jacques. "Histoire médiévale et histoire du droit: Un dialogue difficile." In *Storia sociale e dimensione jiuridica,* pp. 23–63. Atti dell'incontro di studio, Florence, 26–27 April 1985. Milan, 1986.

Le Play, Frédéric. *L'organisation de la famille.* Paris, 1871.

Lepointe, Gabriel. *Droit romain et ancien droit français.* Paris, 1958.

———. *La famille dans l'ancien droit.* Paris, 1947.

Le Roy Ladurie, Emmanuel. "Family Structures and Inheritance Customs in Sixteenth-Century France." In Jack Goody, Joan Thirsk, and E. P. Thompson, eds. *Family and Inheritance: Rural Society in Western Europe, 1200–1800,* Cambridge, 1976.

Lévi-Strauss, Claude. *The Elementary Structures of Kinship.* Translated by James Harle Bell. Boston, 1969.

Levy, Marie-Françoise, ed. *L'enfant, la famille et la Révolution française.* Paris, 1990.

Loseth, E. *Le roman de Tristan, le roman de Palamède et la compilation de Rusticien de Pise.* Paris, 1891.

Lyall, Francis. "Legal Metaphors in the Epistles." *Tyndale Bulletin* 32 (1981): 79–95.

Lynch, Joseph. *Godparents and Kinship in Early Medieval Europe.* Princeton, N.J., 1986.

Maclean, Ian. *The Renaissance Notion of Woman: A Study in the Fortunes of Scholasticism and Medical Science in European Intellectual Life.* Cambridge, 1980.

Mahillon, Pierre. "Evolution historique de l'adoption depuis le droit romain." In *En hommage à Victor Gothot.* Liège, 1962.

Martin, David. *Die adoption im altbabylonischen recht.* Leipzig, 1927.

Mavrick, Elizabeth W. "Nature versus Nurture: Patterns and Trends in Seventeenth-Century French Child-Rearing." In Lloyd de Mause, ed., *The History of Childhood.* New York, 1974.

Maza, Sarah. *Servants and Masters in Eighteenth-Century France: The Uses of Loyalty.* Princeton, N.J., 1983.

McClaren, Angus. *Reproductive Rituals: The Perception of Fertility in England, from the Sixteenth Century to the Nineteenth Century.* London, 1984.

McCracken, Grant. "The Exchange of Children in Tudor England: An Anthropological Phenomenon in Historical Context." *Journal of Family History* 8 (winter 1983): 303–13.

McRoy, Ruth. *Openness in Adoption: New Practices, New Issues.* New York, 1988.

Metz, René. *La femme et l'enfant dans le droit canonique médiéval.* Reprint, London, 1985.

Michaud-Frejaville, Françoise. "Contrats d'apprentissage en Orléanais: Les enfants au travail (1380–1450)." In *L'enfant au Moyen-Age: Litterature et civilisation,* 61–72. Senefiance 9, Paris, 1980.

Moch, Leslie Page, and Rachel G. Fuchs. "Getting Along: Poor Women's Networks in Nineteenth-Century Paris." *French Historical Studies* 18 (spring 1993): 34–49.

Mollat, Michel. *Études sur l'histoire de la pauvreté: Le moyen-âge-XVIe siècle.* Paris, 1974.

Morland, J. "Marie le Jars de Gournay, la 'fille d'alliance' de Montaigne." *Bibliothèque de la Société des amis de Montaigne* 27 (1971): 45–54.

Mortari, Vincenzo Piano. *Diritto romano e diritto nazionale in Francia nel secolo XVI.* Milan, 1962.

Motley, Mark. *Becoming a French Aristocrat: The Education of the Court Nobility, 1580–1715.* Princeton, N.J., 1990.

Newall, Fiona. "Wet Nursing and Child Care in Aldenham, Hertfordshire, 1595–1726: Some Evidence on the Circumstances and Effects of Seventeenth-Century Child-Rearing Practices." In Valerie Fildes, ed., *Women as Mothers in Pre-Industrial England,* pp. 122–39. London, 1990.

Notaires, notariat et société sous l'ancien régime: Études réunies et présentées par Jean L. Lafont. Toulouse, 1990.

Olivier-Martin, François. *La coutume de Paris, trait d'union entre le droit romain et les législations modernes.* Paris, 1925.

———. *Histoire de la coutume de la prévôté et vicomté de Paris.* 2 vols. Paris, 1922.

Otis, Leah Lydia. *Prostitution in Medieval Society: The History of an Urban Institution in Languedoc.* Chicago, 1985.

Ourliac, Paul. "Histoire nouvelle et histoire du droit." *Revue historique de droit français et étranger* 3 (1992): 363–71.

Ourliac, Paul, and J.-L. Gazzaniga. *Histoire du droit privé français de l'An mil au Code civil.* Paris, 1985.

Ourliac, Paul, and J. de Malafosse. *Histoire du droit privé.* 3 vols. Paris, 1968.

Ozment, Steven. *When Fathers Ruled: Family Life in Reformation Europe.* Cambridge, Mass., 1983.

Paillot, Pierre. *La représentation successorale dans les coutumes du nord de la France: Contribution à l'étude du droit familial.* Paris, 1935.

Patlagean, Evelyene. "Christianisation et parentés rituelles: Le domaine de Byzance." *Annales: E.S.C.* 33 (1978): 625–36.

Pelikan, Jaroslav. *The Christian Tradition: A History of the Development of Doctrine.* Vol. 1, *The Emergence of the Catholic Tradition (100–600).* Chicago, 1971; Vol. 3, *The Growth of Medieval Theology.* Chicago, 1978.

Perraud, André. *Etude sur le testament d'après la coutume de Bretagne.* Rennes, 1921.

Phan, M. C. "Les déclarations de la grossesse en France (XVIe–XVIIIe): Essai institutionel." *Revue d'histoire moderne et contemporaine* 22 (1975): 61–88.

Pillorget, René. *Nouvelle histoire de Paris: Les premiers Bourbons, 1594–1661.* Paris, 1988.

———. *La tige et le rameau: Familles anglaises et françaises: 16e–18e siècles.* Paris, 1979.

Planiol, Marcel. *Histoire des institutions de la Bretagne.* 2 vols. Mayenne, 1981.

Poisson, Jean-Paul. *Notaires et société: Travaux d'histoire et de sociologie notariales.* 2 vols. Paris, 1985, 1990.

Pollock, Linda. *Forgotten Children: Parent-Child Relations from 1500–1900.* Cambridge, 1983.

Poumarède, Jacques. "La législation successorale de la Révolution entre idéologie et la pratique." In Irène Théry and Christian Biet, eds., *La famille, la loi, l'état de la Révolution au Code civil,* pp. 167–82. Paris, 1989.

Problèmes et méthodes d'analyse historique de l'activité notariale (XVe–XIXe siècles): Actes du colloque de Toulouse (15–16 septembre 1990). Toulouse, 1991.

Rawson, Beryl, ed. *The Family in Ancient Rome: New Perspectives.* London, 1986.

Razi, Zvi. "The Myth of the Immutable English Family." *Past and Present* 140 (August 1993): 3–44.

Révillout, E. "Contrats de mariage et d'adoption dans l'Egypte et dans la Chaldée." *Proceedings of the Society of Biblical Archeology* 9 (1887).

La Révolution et l'ordre juridique privé, rationalité ou scandale? Actes du colloque d'Orléans. 2 vols. Paris, 1988.

Roche, Daniel. *The People of Paris: An Essay in Popular Culture in the 18th Century.* Translated by Marie Evans. New York, 1987.

Rossell, William H. "New Testament Adoption: Graeco-Roman or Semitic?" *Journal of Biblical Literature* 71, no. 4 (1952): 233–34.

Roubert, Jacqueline. "L'adoption des enfants par des particuliers à Lyon sous l'ancien régime." *Société française d'histoire des hôpitaux* 36–37 (1978): 3–30.

Royer, Bernard. *L'enfant et la femme sous l'ancien régime: Précédé d'une étude sur la formation des noms de famille.* Paris, 1984.

Rubenstein, Lene. *Adoption in Fourth-Century Athens.* Copenhagen, 1993.

Sabean, David. "Aspects of Kinship Behaviour and Property in Rural Western Europe before 1800." In Jack Goody, Joan Thirsk, and E. P. Thompson, eds. *Family and Inheritance: Rural Society in Western Europe, 1200–1800* pp. 96–111. Cambridge, 1976.

Sabean, David, and Hans Medick, eds. *Interest and Emotion: Essays on the Study of the Family and Kinship.* Cambridge, 1984.

Sachdev, Paul. *Unlocking the Adoption Files.* Lexington, Mass., 1989.

Saller, Richard. "Roman Heirship Strategies in Principle and in Practice." In D. I. Kertzer and R. P. Saller, eds., *The Family in Italy from Antiquity to the Present,* pp. 26–49. New Haven, Conn., 1991.

Salvage-Gerest, Pascale. *L'adoption: Connaissance du droit.* Paris, 1992.

Sandri, Lucia. *L'Ospedale de S. Maria della Scala di S. Gimignano nel Quattrocento: Contributo alla storia dell'infanzia abbandonata.* Florence, 1982.

Sandrin, Jean. *Enfants trouvés, enfants ouvriers: XVIIe–XIXe siècle.* Paris, 1982.

Santaló, Leon Carlos Alvarez. *Marginación social y mentalidad en Andalucía Occidental: Expósitos en Sevilla (1613–1910).* Seville, 1980.

Schalk, Ellery. *From Valor to Pedigree: Ideas of Nobility in France in the Sixteenth and Seventeenth Centuries.* Princeton, N.J., 1986.

Schiff, Mario. *La fille d'alliance de Montaigne, Marie de Gournay.* Paris, 1910. Reprint, Geneva, 1978.

Schochet, Gordon J. *The Authoritarian Family and Political Attitudes in Seventeenth-Century England: Patriarchalism and Political Thought.* New York, 1975. Revised edition, New Brunswick, N.J., 1988.

Schultz, F. *Classical Roman Law.* Oxford, 1951.

Segalen, Martine. *Historical Anthropology of the Family.* Translated by J. C. Whitehouse and Sarah Matthews. Cambridge, 1986.

Semichon, Ernst. *Histoire des enfants abandonnés depuis l'antiquité jusqu'à nos jours.* Paris, 1886.

Shahar, Shulamith. *Childhood in the Middle Ages.* Translated by Chaya Galai. London, 1990.

———. *The Fourth Estate: A History of Women in the Middle Ages.* Translated by Chaya Galai. London, 1983.

Shell, Marc. *The End of Kinship: "Measure for Measure," Incest and the Ideal of Universal Siblinghood.* Stanford, Calif., 1988.

Shorter, Edward. *The Making of the Modern Family.* New York, 1975.

Silber, Kathleen. *Children of Open Adoption and Their Families.* San Antonio, Tex., 1990.

Simon, Rita J., and Howard Altstein, eds. *Transracial Adoptees and Their Families: A Study of Identity and Commitment.* New York, 1987.

Sneyd, Arthur. *A Relation, or rather a true account of the Island of England.* English translation. London, 1847.

Stone, Lawrence. *The Family, Sex and Marriage in England, 1500–1800.* London, 1977. Abridged paperback edition, New York, 1979.

———. "The Rise of the Nuclear Family in Early Modern England: The Patriarchal Stage." In Charles E. Rosenberg, ed., *The Family in History*, pp. 13–57. Philadelphia, 1975.

Stone, Lawrence, and Jeanne Fawtier Stone. *An Open Elite? England, 1540–1880.* Oxford, 1986.

Sumner Maine, Henry. *Ancient Law.* New York, 1873.

Sussman, George. *Selling Mother's Milk: The Wet-nursing Business in France.* Urbana, Ill., 1982.

Tardif, Adolphe. *Histoire des sources de droit français, origines romaines.* Paris, 1890.

Terme, J. F., and J. B. Monfalcon. *Histoire des enfants trouvés.* Paris, 1840.

Thompson, Stith. *Motif Index of Folk-Literature.* 6 vols. Bloomington, Ind. 1955–58.

Timbal, P. C. *Droit romain et ancien droit français.* Paris, 1960.

Traer, James, F. *Marriage and the Family in Eighteenth-Century France.* Ithaca, N.Y., 1980.

Trexler, Richard. "The Foundlings of Florence, 1395–1455." *History of Childhood Quarterly* 1 (1973): 259–84.

Trexler, Richard. "Infanticide in Florence: New Sources and First Results." *History of Childhood Quarterly* 1 (1973): 98–116.

Turlan, J. M. "Amis et amis charnels d'après les actes du Parlement au XIVe siècle." *Revue historique du droit français et étranger* 47 (1969): 645–98.

———. "Recherches sur le mariage dans la pratique coutumière (XIIe–XVIe)." *Revue historique de droit français et étranger* 35 (1957): 503–16.

United Nations, Department of Social Affairs. *Study on Adoption of Children: A Study on the Practices and Procedures Related to the Adoption of Children.* United Nations Document, ST/SOA/17. New York, 1953.

Vaissière, Pierre de. *Une famille les d'Alègre.* Paris, 1914.

Veyne, Paul. "The Roman Empire." In Paul Veyne, ed., *A History of Private Life,* vol. 1, *From Pagan Rome to Byzantium.* Translated by Arthur Goldhammer. Cambridge, 1987.

Viguerie, Jean de, and Evelyne Saive-Lever. "Essai pour une géographie socio-professionelle de Paris dans la première moitié du XVIIe siècle." *Revue d'histoire moderne et contemporaine* 20 (1973): 424–29.

Viollet, Paul. *Droit privé et sources. Histoire du droit civil français . . . 3 éd. du précis de l'histoire du droit français.* 2 vols. Paris, 1905.

———. *Histoire du droit civil français.* 3rd ed. Aalen, 1966.

Vogler, B., ed. *Les actes notariés, sources de l'histoire sociale XVIe–XIXe siècle.* Strasbourg, 1979.

Wall, Richard, and Peter Laslett, eds. *Family Forms in Historic Europe.* Cambridge, 1983.

Waltner, Ann. *Getting an Heir: Adoption and the Construction of Kinship in Late Imperial China.* Honolulu, 1990.

Wendel, François. *Le mariage à Strasbourg à l'époque de la Réforme, 1520–1692.* Strasbourg, 1928.

Wheaton, Robert, and Tamara K. Hareven, eds. *Family and Sexuality in French History.* Philadelphia, 1980.

Year Books of Edward II. Vol. 1, Edited by F. W. Maitland. London, 1904.

Yver, Jean. *Egalité des héritiers et exclusion des enfants dotés: Essai de géographie coutumière.* Paris, 1966.

Index

abandoned children: adoptions of, from the Couche, 124–47, 150–53; care for, provided at the Couche, 116–18, 120n.62, 146; display of, in the Cathedral of Notre-Dame, 117–18; illegitimate status of, 112–13; left at the Cathedral of Notre-Dame, 114–15; left at the Enfants-Dieu, 110; left at the Hôtel-Dieu, 108–9, 128, 150; left at St. Esprit, 108; local seigneur's responsibility for, 113; in medieval literary tales, 22, 115; placed in foster care by the Couche, 117–18; processions of, in Paris, 153; sale of, 142; sex of, 138; and stigma of illegitimacy, 107–8, 112, 113; surnames given to, 124n.1

abandonment of children: customs of, 102n.114, 119–20; as distinguished from infanticide, 115–16; and illegitimacy, 112–13; rates of, 118–20, 153

acquêts, 84; given to adopted children, 59, 131, 135

adopted children: ages of, 137–38; care given to, by adoptive parents, 11, 74–77, 128–31; civil status of, 99–101; filial obedience expected from, 77–78; as heirs, 81–85, 130–31; inheritance rights of, in customary law, 52–62; as laborers, 142–43; sex of, 138–39, 170–71

adoption: in ancient Egypt, 37; in ancient Greece, 37; in Babylonian law, 37; in Byzantium, 46; as a charitable measure, 86, 91, 146, 147–48, 160, 162, 163–64; Christian traditions of, 3, 6, 39–40, 41–47, 67; in the Civil Code, 7, 157, 161–62; in court cases, 20–25; definition of, 73; demise of, in early modern France, 3, 19–20; in early modern literary texts, 5, 22, 115nn.45 and 46; in early modern Lorraine, 57n.90; and fear of impostors, 24–25; in feudal law, 47–48; in Florence, 126n.5l; in the Hebrew Bible, 37; and impediments to marriage, 46–47; and intestate succession, 53, 61–62, 69; and laws of nature, 3, 156; as means to mix social classes, 24–25, 157,

158–59, 160; in medieval Brittany, 49–50; in medieval Italy, 48n.56; in medieval Spain, 48n.56; metaphorical uses of, 5–6; in modern Europe and the United States, 7n.18, 12–13; in modern France, 7; motivations for, 73–74, 79–81, 139–43, 163–64; and naturalization, 6, 58–59; nobility's attitudes toward, 4, 6, 78–79, 103, 158–59, 163; open nature of, in early modern France, 101–2; place of, in the history of civil law, 8, 13–14, 61; popular practice of, 60–62, 68–70, 72; prejudices against, in early modern France, 3–7, 12, 44–45, 157; in Roman law, 37–40; and royal succession, 158; and social construction of kinship ties, 12, 69–70; and social mobility, 24–25, 78–79, 132; survival of, in medieval Europe, 48–50, 69

adoption contracts: contents of, 11–12, 165–69

adoptionism, 42–43

adoptive families: and kin ties to adopted children, 170–71; marital status of, 170–71; residences of, 132–33; social status of, 78–79, 131–32

adrogation, 38, 86

affatomia, 40–41, 44n.38, 69

affiliation: ties of, 20, 24, 35, 45, 51n.68, 164

Alcuin, 43

Alègre (Allègre) family, 56–58, 60

apprenticeship: and child-rearing customs, 29–30; provided for adopted children, 71–72, 76, 125–26, 129, 165–69

Ariès, Philippe, 43n.35, 80n.36

Aubenas, René, 48, 50n.66

Aumône générale, Lyon: care of destitute children by, 9, 45, 107n.8, 110–11, 135–38, 144–45, 154n.96, 156; and inheritance rights of adopted children, 144–45

Bacquet (jurist), 59

Bavoux, Paule, 118n.56, 120n.64, 154n.101

Beckerman Davis, Barbara, 135

ABOUT THE AUTHOR

Kristin Elizabeth Gager is Assistant Professor of History
at the University of New Hampshire.